'FIRST CONTACTS' IN POLYNESIA

'FIRST CONTACTS' IN POLYNESIA

The Samoan Case (1722–1848)

Western Misunderstandings
about Sexuality and Divinity

Serge Tcherkézoff

Published by ANU E Press
The Australian National University
Canberra ACT 0200, Australia
Email: anuepress@anu.edu.au
This title is also available online at: http://epress.anu.edu.au/first_contacts_citation.html

National Library of Australia
Cataloguing-in-Publication entry

Author:	Tcherkezoff, Serge.
Title:	First contacts in Polynesia : the Samoan case (1722-1848) : western misunderstanding about sexuality and divinity / Serge Tcherkezoff.
Edition:	New ed.
ISBN:	9781921536014 (pbk.)
	9781921536021 (web)
Subjects:	Samoan Islands--Foreign relations--Europe.
	Europe--Foreign relations--Samoan Islands.
	Samoan Islands--History.
	Samoan Islands--Social life and customs.
Dewey Number:	327.961304

All rights reserved. No part of this publication may be reproduced, stored in a retrieval system or transmitted in any form or by any means, electronic, mechanical, photocopying or otherwise, without the prior permission of the publisher.

Cover: Moana Matthes, Bruce Harding, Emily Brissenden

Cover Illustrations:
Samoan fine mat: in possession of, and photographed by, Dr Patricia Wallace, MBCPS.
'Cook had taken great pains to make friends with the natives'; John Lang, *The Story of Captain Cook* (London & Edinburgh, TC & EC Jack, n.d.), opp. p.27. [The Children's Heroes Series]
'A [Samoan] village maiden in festive attire'; Plate I, Augustin Krämer, *Die Samoa-Inseln* (Stuttgart, E. Schweizerbartsche Verlagsbuchhandlung [E. Nagele], 1903), vol. 1 (p.643).
'A Young Woman of Otaheite, Dancing'; in John Hamilton Moore, *A New and Complete Selection of Voyages and Travels* (London, Alexander Hogg, 1780?), vol. 2, n.p.
Professor Tcherké zoff (Photo by Bruce Harding, MBCPS).

First published © 2004 Serge Tcherkézoff, Macmillan Brown Centre for Pacific Studies, The Journal of Pacific History Inc.

This edition © 2008 ANU E Press

Table of Contents

In memory of the Samoans who discovered the Papālagi	vii
Acknowledgements	ix
Introduction	1

Part One: the Samoan discovery of Europeans (1722-1848)

1.	June 1722, the Dutch 'discovery' by Jacob Roggeveen	15
2.	May 1768, the French 'discovery' by Louis-Antoine de Bougainville	23
3.	December 1787, Lapérouse: first incursion on land	29
4.	Lapérouse, the Ignoble Savage, and the Europeans as 'spirits'	51
5.	The turn of the century: from Edward Edwards (1791) to Otto von Kotzebue (1824)	69
6.	Commercial vessels. Another French visit: Lafond de Lurcy	81
7.	The late 1830s: Dumont d'Urville and Wilkes; Jackson and Erskine	91
8.	Conclusion	109

Part Two: Methodological comparisons

9.	'On the boat of Tangaroa'. Humanity and divinity in Polynesian-European first contacts: a reconsideration	113
10.	Sacred cloth and sacred women. On cloth, gifts and nudity in Tahitian first contacts: a culture of 'wrapping-in'	159
11.	The Papālagi ('Europeans') and the Sky. Etymology and divinity, linguistic and anthropological dialogue	187

Conclusion: Ethnohistory-in-the-field	203
Illustrations	211
Bibliography	223

In memory of the Samoans who discovered the Papālagi

Europeans have been losing their way in the Pacific from the beginning when early explorers made up for navigational errors by claiming inhabited islands as new discoveries. Never mind that the islanders had simultaneously discovered the explorers, no doubt with a fair bit of despair and surprise, but since it took years for islanders to learn the tiny scratches that the visitors called writing, the European claims had a head start in the history books. ... Curious Caucasians could sail in to a new port in the good old days without permission and be hailed later as daring explorers who broadened the horizons of mankind. Islanders doing the same today are known as overstayers. They are not hailed as daring and are very quickly sent back over the horizon (Ulafala Aiavao 1994).

Acknowledgements

Part One of this study was drafted in a preliminary form while I was a Research Scholar at the Macmillan Brown Centre for Pacific Studies in 2001 (January-April). During the time that I was again hosted as a Scholar by the Centre in 2002 (February-March, July-October) and when I visited the Centre in 2003 (January-February), Part One was enlarged and Part Two was written. So to a very great extent this work is the outcome of the hospitality I have enjoyed. I express my deepest gratitude to the Centre and its staff for this wonderful opportunity: the Centre's successive Board Chairs (and also Acting Directors in 2002), Professor Peter Hempenstall and Dr John Henderson; the Director in 2001, Dr Ueantabo Neemia-Mackenzie, and the new Director Professor Karen Nero. Peter Hempenstall's and John Henderson's familiarity with Samoan studies (colonial history, political science) was of great help to me. I owe a special debt of gratitude to Dr Bruce Harding, Research Associate, who was kind enough to take a deep interest in my Samoan studies and who offered to undertake the heavy task of editing the awful Frenglish of the first draft of almost the whole book, and of designing, together with Moana Matthes, the cover. In all matters his generosity was beyond imagining. Many thanks to Moana Matthes for her hospitality towards the incoming scholars, as the administrative officer with responsibility for the Centre: it was much more than administrative hospitality, it was, every day, friendship and hospitality in the 'Pacific way'. My special thanks go to *The Journal of Pacific History*, Brij Lal, Peter Hempenstall, and Karen Nero who made possible the publication of this study, and to the various people who, in addition to Dr Harding, helped with translating and editing; in France, Karin Johnson-Sellato who did a preliminary editing of Part One and carefully translated into English the quotations from Lafond de Lurcy and from Dumont d'Urville; in Canberra, Dr Stephanie Anderson who translated chapter 9, and parts of chapter 10 and the Conclusion, all of which I had written in French, and then edited the whole final manuscript before it went to the *JPH* board; Jennifer Terrell for the final checking and formatting.

The Macmillan Brown Centre would not be the significant research institution that it is, and this study could not have been achieved in such a short time, without the Macmillan Brown Library—certainly one of the best world-wide for Polynesian studies, with its rich historical collection (begun by Professor Macmillan Brown) and its mission to add to its collection most of the contemporary items published in even the remotest places of the Pacific. I am extremely grateful to its dedicated members, Max Broadbent, the Chief Librarian, and his staff, who were always very helpful, and traced items as old as Forster's 1772 translation of Bougainville's *Voyage*, and the original twenty volumes, in French, of one of Dumont d'Urville's expeditions, when I had not expected to find these works among the rare books of the library. My thanks go also to the librarians of the Central Library of the University for allowing me to read the Schouten narrative of 1619 in the Rare Books section. Thank you, too, to my fellow anthropologists from the Sociology and Anthropology Department, Dr Patrick McAllister and (in 2001) Dr Claudia Gross, who welcomed me to their seminars and thus contributed, together, with my colleagues at the Centre, to making me feel at home on the campus of Canterbury University. Claudia Gross also devoted a considerable amount of time to reading Part One of the manuscript as part of a review process, and I would like to thank her very much for her enthusiastic support and for her very useful suggestions. My thanks, too, to Michael Goldsmith for his supportive review, and to Tom Ryan for his preliminary reading of Part One.

The book was finalised during my stay at the Research School of Pacific and Asian Studies, The Australian National University, as an Australian Research Council Linkage Fellow (2004), in the Gender Relations Centre. My deepest thanks to Margaret Jolly for this wonderful opportunity.

In its preliminary form in 2001, which consisted only of Part One, the main aim of this study was to trace the origin or the Western misconceptions about Samoan sexuality. It was dedicated to Professor Freeman who was the first to form the hypothesis, in his book of 1983 (p. 227), even if it was just a brief note, that there is no reason to think that pre-Christian Samoa would have been substantially different from Samoa in later periods in terms of the sexual rules pertaining in adolescence given what is known of the 19th and early 20th centuries. Although we disagreed and argued about the reconstruction of the causes that led Margaret Mead to produce her distorted conclusions about the ethos of Samoan adolescence, we certainly agreed on the ethnographic critique of Mead's writings about Samoa. In its present form, this study is mainly dedicated to the Samoans who, from 11 December 1787 and onwards, sometimes paid a heavy price for discovering the existence of the Papālagi ('Europeans'). *Mo oe Logona-I-Taga John Derek Freeman! Mo outou o fanau o le lau eleele na fetaiai ma tagata Papalagi i aso anamua faapea foi aso nei*. This book is also dedicated to my son Tuvalu Junior Rokeni Fuimaono. His passion for Samoan history has been a strong encouragement to provide his generation with a sketch of this forgotten past.

Addendum 2008: Many thanks to Stewart Firth, Margaret Jolly, Vicki Luker, Jenny Terrell, and Darrell Tryon who contributed to the decision for this reprint by ANU E Press. And to Duncan Beard who did a wonderful new edition, at such short notice, for the volume to be ready for the ceremonial event of October 2008 when I was booked to present to the Samoan people, with the help of the French Embassy in Wellington, the full English translation of the French historical texts narrating these early encounters (deposited at NUS and Samoa National Archives).

Introduction

Women and gods, barter and gift-giving: an anthropology of historical encounters

This book narrates the first encounters between Samoans and Europeans, adding some Polynesian comparisons from beyond Samoa, to advance a hypothesis about the interpretations made by the Polynesians at the time of the nature of these newcomers to Pacific waters. Bearing on encounters of historical and cultural significance, it discusses the ways we can address the analysis of such events. In order to do so we must go back two centuries and reconstitute as far as possible the point of view of those who—European narratives say—'were discovered', but who, in fact, had to discover for themselves these other peoples whom they called *Papālagi* (in Western Polynesia), *Haole* (Hawaii), *Popa'a* (Tahiti) or *Pakeha* (Aotearoa-New-Zealand). Thus, it is an anthropology of these encounters, a 'history's anthropology' or an 'ethnohistory' as Greg Dening (1966, 1988) would call it.

The book is the outcome of two different research projects. The first one, larger in scope, relates to the studies of the so-called 'first contacts' in Polynesia: the very first contact and the subsequent early encounters between Polynesians and Europeans. This field readily reveals the bias of studies undertaken from a Eurocentric point of view. The Samoan case appears to provide a clear illustration of the benefits that an anthropological orientation can inject into these studies. The second more specialised project was carried out when it became necessary to introduce a study of pre-missionary Samoa to the so-called 'Mead-Freeman debate' which bears on the rules and values regulating adolescent sexuality in 'Samoan culture'. As both research projects made use of the same material they logically converged to become a single book.

This material comprises European narratives written between 1730 and 1850. It so happens that a good part of the crucial narratives have been authored by French voyagers: Bougainville, Lapérouse, Lafond de Lurcy, Dumont d'Urville. Some of these texts are not well-known or are difficult to find; two of them have never been translated into English. The reader will judge if it has been worth bringing them to light and if they allow us to reconstruct something of the other side of the encounters: the Samoan side. This attempt is by way of a humble return, or more precisely a kind of *ifoga* (see chapter 1, section 4), from a French researcher, in remembrance of the fact that it was French seamen who made the first intrusion on Samoan land by *Papālagi* (December 1787).

1. First contacts in Polynesia

Methodology and the Samoan case

For the Pacific region, the sources regarding first contacts are essentially accounts written by European travellers. One can quite easily imagine the extent to which these accounts, especially those published in the form of a book which was intended for a large public, foreground interpretations based on prejudices and preconceptions. Their preconceived views blinded the authors themselves, these first voyagers, and prevented them from understanding the whole range of acts and behaviours of the indigenous population. In particular, several contexts were the occasion of gross misunderstandings. Let me immediately evoke the two principal contexts in which these occurred.

In the first context, the local inhabitants brought some objects to the visitors who understood this as a proposition to 'barter' goods. The visitors attempted to put a value on the goods presented in order to make a commensurate reply with their own 'trinkets' which they had intentionally brought with them to 'impress the savages'. As soon as the exchange appeared to the Europeans to be unfair, or when the inhabitants dared to climb on board ship and then seized everything they could and jumped into the sea, the encounter became a 'theft' committed by savages whose 'character' was obviously 'treacherous'.

The second context of misunderstanding was caused by the inevitably male-dominated view of the voyagers. The crew members were of course male and they always had their eyes on the 'women' of the island they were visiting. Their sole interest in the women was as possible sexual partners (with highly differing degrees of appreciation according to the 'colour of the skin' of different women as the voyagers saw and classified it). They made no distinction between adult and adolescent females. In particular, they saw in every 'woman' the sexual complement of a man, thus reducing all relationships of gender to one level. They were unaware of the fact that, in many societies, and certainly in Samoa, a man and a young woman who came forward in front of the visitors could more often than not be a brother and sister, or a father and daughter, rather than a husband and wife.

A complete misunderstanding about rules of 'nakedness', where European taboos of the time were projected indiscriminately onto the inhabitants, together with the close association between nakedness and sexuality that prevailed in European ideology, meant that the indigenous population was generally qualified as 'lascivious, lewd' and the females seen as engaging in 'wanton behaviour' (since in every presentation of women they were more or less 'naked'). The European visitors were unaware that, on the contrary, such behaviours took their meaning as part of very formal dances where the fact of presenting oneself in the finale without clothing was a mark of 'respect' (see chapter 10) towards visitors who were compared to sacred chiefs and seen as envoys of the divine world (chapter 9). Moreover, as we shall see in a number of cases, the very specific occasions on which the indigenous adults proposed to the visitors that they take a woman (in fact an adolescent girl) in order to have sexual relations with her were reduced by our visitors simply to a question of sexual hospitality, when in fact it was certainly a matter of a sacred proposition of marriage. This followed a pattern in which a family offered one of its daughters to a high chief with a view to obtaining progeny and, through this, a tie of kinship to this illustrious lineage.

The project of arriving at a detailed history of the genesis and hardening of European prejudices, with regard to the colour of the skin, to the exchange of goods, and to sexuality among Pacific peoples, necessitates a wide re-evaluation of European ideology which is currently in progress.[1] At the same time, it is necessary to rewrite or, often, to commence writing (where nothing has been done up until now) the history of the first contacts case by case and, as far as possible, to do so from the point of view of the indigenous peoples. Marshall Sahlins has already begun doing this for Hawaii, Anne Salmond and her team for Aotearoa-New-Zealand, Greg Dening for the Marquesas, Tahiti and Hawaii, and Jean-François Baré for Tahiti, while Nicholas Thomas has added numerous comparative remarks and has also worked on first contacts in the Marquesas Island(s).[2] But, until now, only two articles had appeared in relation to Western Polynesia (Linnekin 1991, Grijp 1994). So the present study, which is centred on the first contacts made in Samoa, opens the door to research in this field.

How can one write or rewrite this history when our sources are biased accounts related by voyagers? My approach will be to combine the results of two different types of analysis which I shall term (i) the *internal* analysis (dealing with original documents such as sea captains' journals) and (ii) the *ethnographic* analysis (integrating ethnographic data derived from a later period).

The internal analysis offered here is an examination of voyagers' original accounts—a procedure that requires examining both published and unpublished materials such as logs and journals. More often than not, even published materials have yet to be scrutinised: some journals have been published in specialised editions which have remained largely unknown (or at least have not yet been carefully studied from this perspective), as is the case for the expeditions of Bougainville or Lapérouse. The internal analysis, then, consists of separating out that which, in an account of historical events and encounters, is a *description* and that which is already an *interpretation*. One could argue that a neutral

---

[1] Tcherkézoff (2001a: chapters 2-8; 2003a; n.d.; in press-1).
[2] Sahlins (1981, 1985a, 1989, 1995), Salmond (1991, 1997), Dening (1980, 1984, 1988, 1992, 1996, 1998, 2004), Baré (1981, 1985), Thomas (1990, 1997); Thomas and others have also edited numerous early accounts (Thomas, Guest and Dettelbach 1996; Thomas and Losche 1999; Lamb, Smith and Thomas 2000; Nero and Thomas 2002).

description does not exist, that every description is already, *de facto*, an interpretation. This is only partially true. While this is certainly the case for any work—a book or journal—considered in its entirety, it does not necessarily hold true for a page—sometimes only a sentence—where one may find a few lines that simply describe a scene preceding an interpretative passage which contains an explanation of what took place. We shall see that this kind of distinction is possible regarding the material relating to Samoa, especially in the case of documents from Lapérouse's expedition. This has also proved possible regarding the material relating to Bougainville's visit to Tahiti in a study recently completed (Tcherkézoff in press-1).

The second type of analysis makes use of subsequent ethnographic work, both from the 19th century and from the contemporary period, in order to suggest possible reasons for the various actions carried out by the Polynesians during their 18th-century encounters with Europeans. This reinterpretation obviously yields results that are very different from the interpretation of Polynesian behaviour made by these first Europeans. The voyagers usually only stayed for a few days, less often for a few weeks, and they did not speak the language of the inhabitants. But it is their accounts of these short sojourns which have underpinned the European tradition of interpreting 'Polynesian customs'. This interpretative tradition took root in so-called science in Europe as early as 1775 with the regrettable consequence that it continues to inform/deform the anthropological interpretation even of data collected recently.[3] Shortly after these early encounters, some of the first long-staying residents (beachcombers, then the first missionaries) left accounts that were now based on an intimate knowledge of the language and on observations made over periods that sometimes lasted for several years (Campbell 1998). Furthermore, in certain contexts, the continuity of the cosmological scheme and of some of the vocabulary is quite noticeable, persisting from the time of the early dispersal of first Polynesians, as proved from comparison of data collected from far-flung Polynesian regions (Kirch and Green 2001). Hence, in some cases, the recent work of professional ethnographers may be put to direct use to interpret ancient facts, once these latter have been extracted via the method of internal analysis from the original over-interpreted narratives of the voyagers.

These combined analyses, the internal and the ethnographic, will thus constitute my methodology in the quest to arrive at an anthropology or ethnohistory of the early encounters between Samoans and Europeans.

Polynesian methodological comparisons

To this study of first contacts in Samoa, which forms Part One of this book, three shorter studies are added for comparative purposes in Part Two. The first of

---

[3] As can be seen most clearly in recent discussions on 20th-century Samoa (Tcherkézoff 2001a, 2003b).

these takes up the whole question raised by the 'Sahlins-Obeyesekere debate' over the Hawaiian and pan-Polynesian interpretation of the nature of the first Europeans, and discusses the past Polynesian conception of chiefs and gods, with comparative examples from the Cook Islands, Tahiti and elsewhere. Polynesians had seen Europeans neither as 'humans' nor as 'gods' in the Western Judeo-Christian sense, but as material manifestations of spiritual beings sent by the gods-as-principles-of-sacredness, and who, just as these gods could do at will, took on whatever human appearances and attributes they chose. The central point is that, ontologically, Polynesian gods were an invisible principle that could take temporary visible forms ('images', *ata*) of all kinds, each of which was only a partial realisation of the underlying, substantive principle. Now it is the case that Europeans have been treated by Polynesians as if they were such images, temporary visible forms of the particular divine principle. Sahlins has rightly insisted on this point, but it has been missed by his critics who have thought, quite wrongly, that he had simply attributed to the Hawaiians a conception expressed by the bare equation: Cook=Lono=a god (in the Western sense).

Most of the early and recent Western misconceptions about the Polynesian interpretation of Europeans at the time of contact, and much of the recent misreading—among anthropologists (see below chapter 9) and linguists (chapter 11)—of Sahlins's texts about Captain Cook, rest on a lack of understanding of the past Polynesian system of representing by 'images', *ata,* the world of 'godly', *atua*, entities. Material images of a 'god', *atua*, are themselves said to be '*atua*', but they remain partial and temporary manifestations of the *atua*-as-a-principle. The clarification of this point is crucial to the precise formulation of the hypothesis about the Polynesian interpretation of the nature of the first Europeans who appeared in the Pacific in the 16th to the 18th centuries.

The second study presented in Part Two (chapter 10) considers the specific role of gifts of cloth (barkcloth, fine mats, etc.) in first contact situations, particularly in Tahiti. Europeans had no conception at all that what they saw merely as 'cloth' could, to the Polynesians, be the most ritually efficient and sacred object, specifically designed to attract and make visible the godly forces. They therefore entirely misunderstood the relation between this central role of cloth in ritual and acts of dressing/undressing in dances and formal presentations. When the Polynesians who were undressing themselves were females, the European visitors could only imagine that they were witnessing outbursts of 'lascivious, lewd and wanton' behaviour. In fact, the relation between sacred cloth and the body of the (young) female was of a very different kind. Much of the misunderstanding about clothing and nudity directly resulted in implanting or reinforcing the false idea that Polynesian cultures actively promoted sexual liberty.

Finally, the third study in Part Two (chapter 11) brings us back to Samoa. It discusses how Europeans—the missionaries initially—misinterpreted the etymology of the Samoan word *Papālagi* used to denote the Europeans. The point at issue is the European view—but one attributed to the Polynesians—of the European visitors as 'sky-bursters', the missionaries claiming that this was the etymology of the word *Papālagi*. Here, as would happen again later with Gananath Obeyesekere's interpretation, a particular Eurocentric ideology based on Christian theological concepts produced a schema that was then projected onto a falsely constructed 'Polynesian' worldview, resulting in a gross ethnocentric misinterpretation. It is deeply ironic that it is in fact quite possible that the word *Papālagi* referred initially to 'cloth' and was coined in the context of the first exchanges of cloth, during the earliest encounters (between Tongans and the Dutch), as a recent study by two linguists has suggested (Geraghty and Tent 2001). And this etymological hypothesis refers us back to the theme of the preceding chapter: gifts of cloth, by both parties, played a central role in European/Polynesian first contacts.

The first exchanges of cloth and other goods produced a reciprocal illusion about the nature of the Other. For the Europeans, Polynesians were 'treacherous partners in barter'; for the Polynesians, Europeans were linked to the spiritual world of *'atua'* things and entities. Indeed, this book could have borrowed its title from a paper written years ago by the late French anthropologist Daniel de Coppet: 'First barter, double illusion'.[4] De Coppet's article (1973) described the 16th-century arrival of the Spaniards in the Solomon Islands, the first barter, and called for an anthropology of ceremonial exchanges in past and present Melanesian social organisations to be developed. May this book also pay homage to his memory.

2. The origin of Western misconceptions about Samoan adolescent sexuality

My second reason for writing this book is quite different. The anthropological field of Samoan studies has gone through a rather agitated period during the last twenty years in the wake of the so-called 'Mead-Freeman' debate. Numerous arguments and counter-arguments have been exchanged about the validity of Margaret Mead's assertion, published in her first book *Coming of Age in Samoa* (1928), that the Samoan ethos of the 1920s implicitly favoured sexual freedom in pre-marital sexual relations (Mead 1928; Freeman 1983, 1999; Tcherkézoff 2001a). The debate has had some beneficial consequences, and some much less so. Among the latter, there was a quite unfortunate side effect: a Western misconception about the historical transformations in the *fa'aSāmoa* ('Samoan

---

[4] *'Premier troc, double illusion'*. Daniel de Coppet was my first teacher of anthropology. He passed away while I was in New Zealand working on this book.

customary') social regulations concerning sexuality. In particular, an unexpected extension of the debate touched upon reconstructing pre-Christian Samoa: it immediately fell back into the two-centuries old Western cliché about unrestrained 'traditional Polynesian sexuality'.

Derek Freeman's criticisms in addressing Mead's book—factually well-grounded when addressing specific contexts of Samoan social life—were advanced within an unacceptable framework of quasi-sociobiology, anti-culturalism and methodological individualism (Tcherkézoff 2001b, 2001c). Freeman, writing in 1983, had no hesitation in condemning the entire disciplinary field of social and cultural anthropology, from Durkheim and Boas through to post-modernism, and, predictably, most of the professional anthropological community were outraged and replied with every possible argument that they could muster. But the numerous reviews highly critical of Freeman's book that appeared through the 1980s and 1990s neglected to clarify one issue: a salutary opposition to Freeman's model did not require a defence of Mead's ethnographical account of Samoa. Mead's account appears flawed by many instances of misinterpretation when it is set against more detailed ethnography relating to the Samoan representations of gender and sexuality (Tcherkézoff 2003b: 277-442).

Among the authors who opposed Freeman's thesis, several tried to adopt an historical approach. Eleanor Leacock (1987) and Lowell Holmes (1987) particularly, in brief accounts, and James Côté (1994, 1997) in more extended works, claimed that Mead's statements about the 'extensive tolerance' and 'great promiscuity' of 'pre-marital sex relations' in Samoa in 1926[5] are validated, at least partly, from what is known of the distant past. According to these authors, it is well established, from early missionaries' observations, that pre-Christian Polynesian cultures largely admitted 'free sexuality'—and sometimes 'institutionalised' it—for the adolescents and even, in some contexts, for all the adults. This terminology is applied to the Samoan case by Côté (1994: 76-7), a psychologist and sociologist whose knowledge of Samoa is solely derived from the writings of missionaries and early ethnographers (John Williams's journal of 1830-32 and all the post-1850 literature). Leacock also based her remarks on these writings. Holmes had done fieldwork in Samoa long before this debate, but he mainly studied the chiefs' system and not the Samoan representations of gender and sexuality. Other authors have referred to this 19th-century literature as well (Shankman 1996, 2001, n.d.; Mageo 1994, 1996, 1998, 2001). In some cases we see that the point of view is more balanced. A thorough examination of these sources would require a more detailed discussion than I am able to undertake here (Tcherkézoff 2003b: 307n., 391n.).

---

[5] I quote from Mead's reports written in the field, in early 1926, which formed the basis of the generalisations that she would make a year later in the introductory and concluding chapters of her book on Samoa published in 1928; see references in Tcherkézoff (2001b: note 22).

But, generally speaking, too much attention has in the past been given to the *opinions* expressed by the 19th-century observers, and not enough attention to the *ethnographic data* found in these sources. A detailed study of the relevant data shows that, in spite of the opinions, interpretations and final remarks proffered by these observers, all the ceremonies and local regulations described in this literature point overwhelmingly towards a strict enforcement of pre-marital virginity, *including in families of low rank*, for the whole period from Williams's arrival in 1830 up until the 1930s (Tcherkézoff 2003b: 345-442). As for the opinions and decisive judgements that we find in this literature, we know how much the missionaries and early 'consuls' were themselves biased by certitudes which they derived from their reading of the early voyagers' accounts. As I have undertaken an analysis of the post-1830/1850 literature on Samoa elsewhere (*ibid.*), my aim here will be to clarify the issues raised by the 18th- and early 19th-century writings which are the source of all subsequent misinterpretations.

Since Côté's 1994 book aimed primarily at providing a general overview of the whole Mead-Freeman debate, it was widely circulated and welcomed by a number of supportive reviewers. Besides presenting the various opponents and their arguments about the validity of Mead's conclusions for the 20th century, Côté devotes no less than three chapters (4 to 6), totalling fifty pages, to a historical analysis of Samoan sexual rules and practices in which he upholds the claim of a free-sex pre-Christian Samoa, presenting it to a relatively large audience. For Côté, the contemporary Samoan attitude of valuing pre-marital virginity for all women can only be the result of missionary influence, because free sexuality undoubtedly prevailed in earlier times. (The only exception that Côté and other supporters of Mead's analysis recognised, as Mead also did, was the case of the '*taupou*, the daughters of high chiefs', whose virginity was severely guarded). Côté writes:

> From these many accounts [by the missionaries who constantly referred to Samoan 'promiscuity'], there can be little doubt that sexual behaviour in Samoa before it was Christianized was more casual for virtually everyone, including young females. The denial of this by Freeman and some contemporary Samoans can be understood in terms of the concerted efforts of missionaries and the local pastors to create, and then maintain, a hegemony of Victorian sexual values and practices (1994: 82).

But Côté goes further and also raises the issue of the early voyagers' writings. He quotes Robert Williamson (1939: 156) who, at the beginning of the 20th century, on Seligman's instructions, wrote vast treatises on Polynesia based entirely on the literature—as Côté does now on a smaller scale (unfortunately these treatises by Williamson [1924, 1933] are still considered to be a great scholarly achievement and a reliable source):

Introduction

Finally, Williamson (1939/1975) carried out an extensive review of all of the early accounts of Polynesian cultures ... With respect to premarital sex in general, he said that in Samoa:

'According to Turner and Brown [early missionaries], chastity ... was more a name than a reality ... *D'Urville says that girls were entirely free to dispose of their persons till married, and Lapérouse tells us that girls were, before marriage, mistresses of their own favours, and their complaisance did not dishonour them*' (p. 156) (Côté 1994: 80; my emphasis).

Through Williamson, Côté is thus calling on, in addition to the missionaries' writings, early voyagers' accounts of the 'South Seas', namely those of Dumont d'Urville and Lapérouse.

Côté seems unaware of how much these early French voyagers' views of Polynesian women, whether Tahitian, Marquesan or Samoan, conformed to a preconceived template from the time that Bougainville's myth of the 'New Cythera' took hold. The misconception started after the French 'discovery' of Tahiti in 1768 and became 'common knowledge about the South Seas' as early as 1775 in all European capitals (Tcherkézoff in press 1). It still played a major role a hundred and fifty years later in the choices made by various publishers for the designs of the book cover of the successive editions of Mead's work on Samoan adolescence (Tiffany 2001). Some of the strongest evidence for a generalised bias is the recurrence of a rhetorical dualism throughout those accounts, from the 1770s until the 1950s. On the one hand, the Polynesian women are always 'as beautiful as Venus', 'of a very fair skin, almost white', and described (after 1769) as customarily raised only to master the 'art of love'. On the other hand, the Melanesian women are said to be 'ugly' and are described only as hard workers at the service of men (see Jolly 1992, 1997a, 1997b, n.d.). This rhetoric had long been at work in European narratives as part of the broader stereotype that devalued all peoples of 'dark skin' and that invented the 'white Polynesians' long before the word 'Melanesia' was coined by Dumont d'Urville to discriminate the 'black race in Oceania' from the 'coppery race'. Such rhetorical dualism can be traced as far back as 1595 (Tcherkézoff 2003a).

Côté is right: Lapérouse and Dumont d'Urville did write that 'girls were entirely free ... till married', and Williamson drew his conclusions from the two French voyagers' accounts. But the only statement that really needs to be made is that *these two French accounts of 1787 and 1838 constitute the origin of the Western misconception of Samoan adolescent sexuality*. With them begins the Western myth which will continue with the missionaries, then with E.S.C. Handy and Mead, up until the contemporary proponents of *Coming of Age in Samoa*. But the genesis of the Western myth about Samoan adolescence was already itself the result of previous misinterpretations published after the 'discovery' of Tahiti (1767-68) and Hawaii (1777).

Besides the problem of his lack of awareness of the hegemonic Western myth about a sexually liberated Polynesia—a myth which has biased all French observations in Polynesia from 1769 to the 1850s—Côté's allusive reference to Lapérouse's and Dumont d'Urville's generalising conclusions about sexual freedom is certainly not sufficiently grounded in empirical fact to permit a valid conclusion to be drawn from the voyagers' narratives. We need to look more closely at the available literature. Instead of being satisfied with quoting some brief conclusions arrived at by two early observers, we must look in detail *at the facts* actually described that led these two observers to form these conclusions; and we must also look exhaustively at the writings of *all the other early observers*, from the earliest contact with Samoan people in 1722 until the late 1830s, after which the missionaries were firmly established and the arrival of commercial boats was a common occurrence in Apia harbour. On what actual observations did the two French navigators base their conclusions? And what were the conclusions of the other travellers who navigated the Samoan waters before and after these French captains?

The game of short quotations taken out of context can be a never-ending source of conflict. What should we do with this other conclusion arrived at by another French captain? Gabriel Lafond de Lurcy stayed in Samoa, mainly in Apia, in 1831 (before any missionary influence could be established) and wrote few years later:

> The [Samoan] women were the joyous children of nature described with such charm by Bougainville and Lapérouse. All seemed to suggest that they would be found with little virtue, but my task as a historian forces me to add that the only favours they accorded our seductive lovelaces on board were inconsequential frustrations (Lafond de Lurcy 1845, quoted in Richards 1992: 38).

Instead of bandying about short quotations taken only from the conclusions of the travellers, let us try to find out what these travellers had actually been able to see when they arrived in Samoan waters. The passages mentioning a female presence must not be taken in isolation from the rest: the first encounters at sea, the first exchanges of gifts, the first misunderstandings, the first acts of violence... Detailed study of the context of Lapérouse's and Dumont d'Urville's stays in Samoa will show precisely how this European misconception of Samoan sexuality arose.

As the Samoan case illustrates what happened on many other Polynesian islands, this study of the early European visits to Samoa is also a part of the larger work of unveiling the origins of the Western myth of unrestrained Polynesian sexuality and how the myth was constructed. And the study of the Samoan discovery of Europeans and of the ceremonial and violent acts which the Samoans devised for this encounter is a part of the wider comparative study of the pan-Polynesian discovery of Europeans, a study which aims to elucidate the various offerings—including the sexual offerings—and acts of violence that were enacted by the Polynesians in these first contacts with Europeans.

PART ONE

The Samoan discovery of Europeans (1722-1848)

*aux Samoas, comme partout, il est des hommes
que tourmente un instinct voyageur*

(Gabriel Lafond de Lurcy, 1831)

Chapter 1

June 1722, the Dutch 'discovery' by Jacob Roggeveen

1. Introduction

During the 17th and 18th centuries, various Dutch expeditions ventured into the Pacific, searching for new routes to the East Indies and new lands where gold or spices would be abundant. Small islands did not present any interest other than as sites for brief restocking of provisions such as wood, water, or fruit. When indigenous people were encountered, they became a target for the guns of the visitors the moment that their gestures could be interpreted as a sign of hostility. The Spaniards had opened fire on indigenous people in the 16th and 17th centuries. After Mendaña's massacre in the Marquesas in 1595, news of these dreadful creatures—the Spaniards—must have spread through Eastern Polynesia. And after LeMaire and Schouten's musket firing on canoes in north Tonga in 1616, the awful news of this deed must likewise have spread through Western Polynesia. We know that the memory of such extraordinary encounters can last many generations. As we shall see in chapter 11, the Tongans explained to Cook in the 1770s that some '*Papālagi*' had already come to their shores: undoubtedly this was Tasman in 1643 (and/or LeMaire even earlier).

The last of the Dutch expeditions conformed perfectly to the rule of brutality when it 'discovered' Rapa Nui in 1722 on Easter Day, hence naming it 'Easter Island', and fired on the Pascuans. It also happened to be the first expedition to sight the Samoan Islands, in June 1722. The expedition was under the command of Jacob Roggeveen, 'President', and consisted of three ships, the *Arendt* (Captain Jan Koster), on which Roggeveen sailed; the *Thienhoven* (Captain Cornelis Bouman); and the *Africaansche Galley* (Captain Roelof Rosendaal). This third ship was wrecked on the reef of one of the Tuamotu atolls in May 1722. Roggeveen's journal has been made more accessible through Andrew Sharp's translation from the Dutch (Sharp ed. 1970: for Samoa, see pp. 150-6). Sharp also mentions the relevant entries of Bouman's log. In the 18th century, the story of the expedition was widely known only through the sometimes imaginary account of a young officer, Carl Friedrich Behrens, whose narrative was published in German and in French (Behrens 1739). Concerning the discovery of Easter Island, Behrens's narrative contains crucial supplementary pieces of information, but he has nearly nothing to say regarding contact with the Samoans.

'First Contacts' in Polynesia

2. The narrative

On 13 June 1722, the Dutch expedition arrived at the easternmost part of the Samoan archipelago, sighted the uninhabited Rose Island atoll (this name given much later by a merchant ship) and, apparently, was able to land and get 'so many greens that the whole crew ate to their satisfaction four times and the sick [suffering from scurvy] six times'. From there they saw the island of Ta'ū and, on 14 June, came near the coast. 'Two to three canoes' came by and 'had some coconuts, which we exchanged for 5 to 6 large rusty nails'.

The comment on the 'exchange', quite common in the narratives of early voyagers, must not lead us to think that this kind of exchange was already an established practice for the Polynesians. When the description is more precise, we see that, in every case, the Polynesians spontaneously gave an offering of food, probably a first-fruits type of offering: coconut, fish, fowl, fruits, a plantain branch. The trade-minded Europeans, who could not understand that this was a form of sacrificial offering, interpreted it immediately in terms of barter and gave in return some glass or iron trinkets. The same misunderstanding occurred with the sexual presentation of young girls in Tahiti in 1767-1769 and rapidly transformed a religious act into one of sexual commerce.

The Dutch noted the dense forest covering the slopes, and the 'painting' that covered the 'Indians [...] from the thighs downward to the legs' (Sharp ed. 1970: 151). It was of course the tattoo, on the same part of the body as we know it from the 19th century and today. We can now see, in retrospect, that for nearly *three hundred years*, the part of the body that is tattooed has remained the same, and has remained quite specific (pelvis, thighs, and knees, with nothing on the face or the chest) in comparison with the practices of other Polynesian peoples.

The Samoans wore only 'a girdle round the waist to which a lot of long broad leaves or rushes, or of another plant, was fastened'. This garment has been described by all later observers as the usual garment for fishing, plantation work, and all other kinds of work activities (Te Rangi Hiroa 1930). The formal and indoor garment was barkcloth (*siapo*), but this dissolved if soaked in water.

No anchorage could be found at Ta'ū and the Dutch steered towards the two other islands of the Manu'a group, Ofu and Olosega. A party came near the shore on the sloop:

> The Upper Mate of the said ship Thienhoven rowed with the sloop towards the shore or the beach in order to take soundings, and having come there he says that the King sitting in a canoe, and having by him a young woman of 18 to 19 years, whose neck was encircled by a string of oblong blue beads, asked the Mate by signs if he had any such, pointing to the said string, whereupon the Mate, by nodding his head, said yes, but indicated by his hand towards the ship that the beads were

there, and he would bring them to the land. That this was the King he concluded from this, because when the King came near the sloop a thousand and more Indians were on the beach, armed with spears, bow and arrows, and he gave them a directing sign with his hand that they should go away, which was obeyed in a blink of an eye, all retreating into the trees (Sharp ed. 1970: 152).

Bouman adds:

> The old man gave my Mate when he saw that he intended to go to the ship as a present a branch with 6 half-grown coconuts and they parted as good friends, and the inhabitants came also to the side of our ships in their canoes, having only some coconuts and 4 to 5 flying fish, which I bartered from them together with a small mat for 4 to 5 strings of glass beads. I tried to get some of them into the ship, but they would not come aboard (ibid.: note 2).

Bouman recognises that the coconuts from the Chief were a 'gift' but again treats the coconuts handed over by the other Samoans in terms of the bartering logic.

Behrens's narrative contains only one additional remark. Many canoes surrounded the canoe of the man 'who seemed to be the Master of the country'; beside this man, 'a young woman was sitting; her body was all white'.[1] We know that at that time, as well as throughout the following centuries, European travellers keenly noted in the first instance the colour of the locals' skin, then their size, and finally other physical aspects (a physiology that also included judgements on beauty and on the 'character' or 'temperament' of the 'nation' encountered: 'honesty', 'treachery', etc.) (Tcherkézoff n.d.). Behrens also notes that most of the indigenous people appeared to him to have fair skin, but some were more 'red' or 'brown'. Fifty years later, the French (Bougainville and Lapérouse), as well as the English on other islands (Cook in Tahiti, etc.), would also note these various 'colours' of the skin and make hypotheses about it.

No anchorage was found and the Dutch moved on. In the next two days they sighted Tutuila in the distance and, later on, Upolu. Although many were eager to visit those islands, the President was not inclined to do so. He was worried by the fact that the season of the southeast trade winds, on which they needed to rely in sailing to the west of 'New Guinea', would soon end and give way to the dreaded westerlies. The search for an anchorage could take four days or more and he did not want to allow for such a delay. Thus, the Dutch left the Samoan waters without any further contact than these two brief encounters at sea, off Ta'ū and Ofu-Olosega.

---

[1] See the French text in Behrens (1739), and the original German text (from Behrens 1737) in the quotation by Krämer (1903: vol. 2, Part 1; translated into English in Krämer 1995: II: 3-4).

3. Interpretations

Although the facts are few, the lesson from that very first contact is rich. The only woman in sight was an adolescent sitting beside the main Chief, on a canoe that came to meet the visitors. We do not know if she made any specific gestures or if she remained motionless. She could have been a young wife of the Chief. But, if we are to judge from similar situations in the 19th and 20th centuries, a young female accompanying a chief (*ali'i pai'a*) who comes to greet visitors or enemies was a daughter or sister (real or classificatory), one of those girls referred to in the later literature as 'village maiden: *taupou*' (more precisely, in Samoan honorific vocabulary, a *tausala, augafa'apae, saotama'ita'i*). This person bore a specific title which represented a sacred complement to the Chief's title. More precisely, the 'dignity' (*mamalu*) of a High Chief's title was always made of a 'mutual agreement' (*feaga'iga*) in the sense that it was constituted by two aspects: the *tamatane* name—the Chief's name—and the *tamafafine* name—the sacred female's name. The two sides representing these two aspects were respectively the progeny of the sons and the progeny of the daughters of the founding ancestors, and they cooperated in well-defined ways to maintain the 'dignity' of the title.[2]

If Behrens's noting of the particularly fair colour of the girl's skin is valid, it would be a further proof that this girl was a *tausala*, as those high-ranking official virgins were kept very secluded inside their houses. Later ethnography has noted this pan-Polynesian practice as it applied to high-ranking females. The thinking behind it was for the girls to avoid sunburn and remain as white as possible (and even enhance their whiteness by getting very fat and having the skin distended). The practice had both a cosmological and a social reference. Cosmologically, the light of the sun was valued over darkness as the sign of life (*ao* versus *po*). Socially, avoidance of the sun was a sign of superior rank. The sun's rays blind other people, obliging them to keep their eyes down and bow their heads. Dark skin denotes someone who is working outside and thus is exposed to the sunlight (fishing, tilling the garden, preparing the food), while fair skin denotes the person of chiefly rank who stays inside and is served food by others.[3]

---

[2] Schultz (1911) was the first to make this clear; for more recent literature, see Schoeffel (1978, 1979, 1995), Aiono (1986, 1992), Tcherkézoff (1993, 1997a: first part, 1999, in press-2).

[3] James Cook was probably the first to note this distinction, after his first stay in Tahiti in 1769. He mentions, in his first *Voyage* (Beaglehole ed. 1955: 123), that the 'various kinds' of skin colour of the Tahitians are due to their relative degrees of exposure to the sun: 'They are of various colours, those of the inferior sort who are obliged to be much exposed to the sun and air are of a very dark brown, the Superiors again who spend most of their time in their Houses or under shelter are not browner than people who are born or reside long in the West Indias nay some of the women are almost as fair as Europeans.' Sahlins (1985a: chapter 1; 1995) provides several examples from the Hawaiian ethnographic literature about the particular relationship between the high chiefs and the sun. In chapter 9 we shall return to the question of 'light', as the physical principle of Polynesian social hierarchy, versus darkness, which makes everyone alike (this is why there is no hierarchy inside the dark world of spirits and

4. Blue beads, 'life-giving' gifts and the mythology of the Papālagi

The Dutch noticed that the girl beside the Chief had her 'neck encircled by a string of oblong blue beads' and that the Chief pointed at it while looking at his visitors. Augustin Krämer, the famous German ethnographer who had sojourned in Samoa in the 1890s, mentions the early contacts in the introduction to Volume 2 of his *Samoa Inseln* and comments on the blue beads noticed by the Dutch (Kramer [1902] 1995: II: 6). He considers that they were not a native object, because, in the 19th century, the only local object of that colour (fragments of nautilus shell) was used as the centrepiece of the ceremonial head-dress but not in necklaces. He therefore assumes that the beads were of European origin and that the Samoans had obtained them from the Tongans, who themselves received them from the Dutch expeditions of 1616 and 1643.

We shall see several confirmations of this later on. When he came to Samoa in 1791, Captain Edwards observed: 'we saw a few of the natives with blue, mulberry and other coloured beads about their necks, and we understood that they got them from Cook at Tongataboo' (Thompson ed. 1915: 56). Lapérouse noted in 1787 that the Samoans were very fond of these beads, as did Otto von Kotzebue in 1824, while Lafond de Lurcy added in 1831 that a necklace of these beads *could be used for saving one's life in a war* when given by a prisoner to the victorious side. Indeed, the Samoan practice of *togiola* (literally 'life[-giving] gift/payment') is well affirmed in legends, and still operates today: it involves the giving of fine mats in a special presentation called *ifoga,* where the person guilty of murder, manslaughter or a severe breach of taboo and who is asking for mercy, entirely covers himself with one of these mats (Tcherkézoff 2002).

Thus, it seems that the Samoans, even before seeing the Europeans, the *Papālagi*, for the first time, had already elaborated a representation of the power inhering in some of the *Papālagi* objects. Actually the whole story of the life-giving value of these beads could have originated even before Cook's arrival in Tonga. In 1616, LeMaire and Schouten fired on a canoe in north Tonga (near Samoa), killing several people. The canoe was apparently carrying twenty people or so, including women and children. The Dutch opened fire because the canoe did not stop its course in front of their ship after a first warning shot had been fired into the air. But immediately after they had done so, they manoeuvred so as to get near to the survivors and, feeling pity, as well as curious to make contact, they helped those who were in the water to get back on board their large canoe which was still afloat. They even attended to the wounds of those who had been shot, and they gave them some trinkets of the kind that European

---

goblins). This socio-cosmological theme, clearly attested to in the 18th and 19th centuries, seems to extend further back if we are to judge from mythological comparisons from throughout Polynesia (Tcherkézoff 2003b: 36-54).

expeditions had carried with them, since the early voyages, to be used in bartering with the 'Indians' for food (Schouten 1619: 100-4).

I would favour one hypothesis about how the trinkets were received and understood by the Tongans: the survivors could only have concluded that these objects, given to them after initial gunfire that killed some of their companions, were a 'life-giving' sign handed over by these superior creatures. After LeMaire and Schouten in 1616, Tasman, in 1643, had also distributed such trinkets (Moyle ed. 1984: 78, note 133). LeMaire handed over linen, beads, nails, hatchets while Tasman also distributed satin, knives, copper wire, looking glasses, an earthenware dish, a drinking glass, tailored clothing such as a hat, shirt, and so on (Ferdon 1987: 281-5). These Dutch visits introduced the glass beads and opened up an era lasting in Samoa until the 1830s in which sacred value attached to these beads, after which new European objects—fabrics, tools, salted beef, bread—were to replace beads in local ceremonial exchanges. It is also probable that it was actually during these early encounters with the Dutch that the word '*Papālagi*' was coined and then rapidly diffused through the Tonga-Fiji-Samoa region (see chapter 11).

Thus, the first contact with the Samoans in 1722 was not, from the Samoan point of view, entirely a first contact. Samoans already knew something about the *Papālagi*. They probably knew about the muskets: how else might we interpret the King's order to his people to retreat behind the trees while he approached the Dutch? They certainly knew about the blue beads: how else might we explain why they immediately asked the Dutch for more of them?

The people from whom they could have heard stories about the *Papālagi* are the nearby Tongan islanders. It is not surprising that an event in Tonga would have been recounted all around the region. The pioneer missionary John Williams noted in 1830 the Samoan use of the word '*Papālagi*', but we know that the expression had been in circulation in Western Polynesia since at least the time of Tasman's passage through Tongan waters in 1643, as the Tongans repeated it to Captain Cook when the British arrived (see chapter 11). We know from various legends describing wars and marriages that the relations between East-Fiji, Tonga, and Samoa have been constant for a very long time (Kaeppler 1978, 1999, n.d.). In 1777, a member of Cook's third voyage noted while in Tonga the nature of the Tongan relationship with Samoa: Samoans were established in Tonga and vice versa.[4] We shall see that, in 1824, Kotzebue noted how Samoans spoke Tongan to him; that, in 1831, Lafond de Lurcy himself saw the big canoes of the Tongans coming regularly to Samoa. Between 1840 and 1842, the beachcomber John Jackson, who stayed at Ta'ū and later at various Fijian islands,

---

[4] While in Tonga he heard Samoan words such as 'Tamaloa, A chief man [*tamaloa*], Tamae'ty, A Chief Woman [*tama'ita'i*], Solle A common man [*sole*]' (see Beaglehole 1967: II: 957-8, Anderson's journal)].

noted how frequent were the visits and the war alliances between Fijians, Tongans, Samoans, and Uveans.[5]

---

[5] See Jackson (1853: 413, 423, 453, 461, 465): a Tongan chief visiting Taveuni; a Fijian chief preparing a local war replies to another Fijian chief asking for help that he will come with his men, among whom there are Tongans, Samoans, and Uveans; in Rewa, Jackson witnessed the arrival of a Tongan boat from Lifuka in the Ha'apai (and with the Tongans he saw an African-American man who worked as a cook on a European boat and who deserted while in Tonga).

Chapter 2

May 1768, the French 'discovery' by Louis-Antoine de Bougainville

1. The narrative[1]

The French round-the-world expedition led by Louis-Antoine de Bougainville was among the first to open up a new era of voyaging in wich discoveries were sought as much for mercantile profit as for the new scientific study of the 'System of Nature'. This was the second opportunity that Samoans had to see European ships, apart from the supposedly few Samoans who had earlier seen European ships sailing in Tongan and Fijian waters. Nevertheless Bougainville, when he sighted the Samoan islands, thought he was the first European to do so. Behrens's account, the only one published from the Dutch expedition of 1722, did not give any precise nautical information for the location of the islands that he described in his text. Because Bougainville admired the dexterity of the Samoans as they manoeuvred their canoes around the French ships, he called his island discovery *l'Archipel des Navigateurs*, the 'Archipelago of the Navigators'.

The sources for the following discussion are Bougainville's voyage narrative published in 1771 (an immediate success, and published in English as early as 1772), Bougainville's journal, and also the various journals written by his companions, including the naturalist Philibert Commerson, the young volunteer Felix Fesche and Prince Nicolas de Siegen-Nassau.[2]

Bougainville's journal indicates that on 3 May 1768, when he reached the Manu'a group (the three easterly islands of the Samoan archipelago: Ta'ū, Ofu, and Olosega) there were already a number of canoes visible in the distance. On 4 May Bougainville passed between Ta'ū on one side and Ofu-Olosega on the other when a canoe with five men on board approached his ship. The men held up coconuts and 'roots'. Bougainville noted that the Tahitian navigator he took with him (after departing from Tahiti in mid-April), a man who could find his way among islands several days' distance from Tahiti, found nothing he recognised in this archipelago and could not make himself understood by the Samoans. The Samoan canoe would not come near the ship, and when

---

[1] Where I cite the French text below the English the quotations are my translations from the French original (Bougainville 1771). Where only the English is cited, the quotations are taken from Johann Reinhold Forster's very accurate translation, published in 1772 (Bougainville 1772b; the pages relating to Samoa are pp. 278-84).

[2] See Bougainville (1771, 1772b); Taillemite (ed. 1977: I: 334-35, for Bougainville's journal; II: 98, 250-1, 333, 400, 476, for the journals written by Fesche, Vivès, Caro and Commerson).

Bougainville had one of his small boats put to sea, with the intention of getting nearer to it, the Samoans turned back. Fesche's journal records that, after this first attempt, Bougainville hotly pursued the Samoan canoe with one of his ships. The Samoans began to shout and jumped into the sea with their coconuts and fowls, also releasing a bird that they had with them (we know from later ethnographic accounts that chiefs were always accompanied by tame birds when they were journeying: the birds were the messengers of the gods).

2. Three hundred years of a tradition: the design of Samoan tattooing

Fesche went on to note the 'painting' (tattooing) on the thighs. All the journals from this expedition confirm that the painting—sometimes said to be of a 'blue' colour, sometimes 'black'—began at the waist (*depuis la ceinture de la culotte*) and went half way down the thighs (*jusqu'à moitié de la cuisse*); Commerson, the most accurate observer, because he was the naturalist of the expedition, adds that the painting could also be seen on the navel and lines running along the ribs 'as flames' (*ils ont de plus au nombris* [sic] *et sur les costes des espèces de flammes*). All of this corresponds precisely to the pattern observed minutely in the second half of the 19th century by German ethnographers and reproduced in great detail in their books.

One might think that the lack of change in the Samoan pattern of tattooing through the 20th century and up until this very day (see precise descriptions of year 2000 patterns in Galliot 2001), is due to the fact that the pattern had been recorded in books at the end of the 19th century and, since then, has been reproduced in exactly the same way. But we can see that there had, in fact, been internal continuity, in the absence of models recorded externally, at least from the early 18th century (as noted in the Dutch accounts) till the end of the 19th century. Thus the continuity of patterns over 150 years was demonstrated before the patterns were reproduced and published by the ethnographers at the beginning of the 20th century.[3]

3. An 'ugly woman'

Shortly afterwards, more canoes came, '8 or 10', each large enough to carry eight people. After some time, they came near the ship. In one of them Bougainville noted the presence of an 'old and ugly' woman (according to his published text). But the journal says: 'A woman who came in one of the canoes was extremely ugly' (*une femme venue dans une des pirogues était affreuse*).

---

[3] This is a welcome example, and certainly not unique, that can be used to counter a certain post-modernist view which holds that ethnographers always tend to create an illusory permanence in the social systems and cultural styles of non-Western societies and erroneously call it 'tradition' when these rarely last more than a generation (see the discussion and the references in Tcherkézoff 2003b: 515-17).

She might still have been a ceremonial virgin (*tausala*), and not particularly 'old', but a woman who appeared to Bougainville quite different from the Tahitian women, hence 'ugly'. We shall see how Tahiti was the absolute reference for beauty—in women and in 'Nature' in general—according to Bougainville, and how, by comparison, he described everything he encountered in Samoa in negative terms. The descriptive term 'ugly' could have induced Bougainville, when he revised the text for publication two years later, to add 'old'. Besides, the hypothesis that this was all a ceremonial presentation is supported by another remark in the journal. It is said that some of the Samoans had garlands of flowers around the neck (*nous leur avons vu des colliers de fleurs*). Of course, in this ceremonial context, the woman could have been an elder woman of high rank, or a medium, or something similar.

4. First exchanges: iron and cloth

The Samoans did not want to board the ship, although they were invited to do so; instead, they offered their produce and crafted goods from their canoes. According to Bougainville, the gifts were yams, coconuts, fowl, a nice looking blue bird in a cage, necklaces of painted seeds (which suggests the well-known necklace of red-dyed pandanus fruits used for chiefs, as this is the only type of necklace which matches the description—others are made of shells, bones/teeth, or flowers), and pieces of turtle shell. The bird and the painted necklaces are definitely kinds of ceremonial gifts which were, and still are, never used in ordinary barter (information derived from 19th-century German sources, such as Krämer 1994-95 and my contemporary notes).

They also gave barkcloth, which Bougainville found 'much coarser' (literally: 'much less nice', *beaucoup moins belles*) than the 'Tahitian cloth', 'dyed with ugly red, brown and black colours'—we see how easily Bougainville could use the adjective 'ugly'. They also offered some large fishing hooks, which again Bougainville found 'bad', literally 'badly made' (*mal faits*); also 'some mats, some lances'. When the Samoans failed to admire the iron tools, the French again thought that Samoa could not be equated with Tahiti:

> [From the published narrative:] They didn't want iron and preferred small pieces of red coloured cloth to the nails, knives, and earrings which have met with such success in Tahiti.
>
> (*Ils ne voulurent point de fer; ils préféraient de petits morceaux d'étoffe rouge aux clous, aux couteaux et aux pendants d'oreilles qui avaient eu un succès si decidé a Tahiti.*)
>
> [From the Journal:] *Au reste ces Indiens n'ont aucune connaissance du fer et n'ont paru en faire aucun cas. Plusieurs ont examiné des couteaux proposés en échange et n'en ont pas voulu. A Cythère, la premiere demande des insulaires était aouri.*

[which can be translated as] Besides, these Indians don't have any knowledge of iron and didn't attach any importance to it. Several of them have examined the knives that we were offering them in exchange for their goods and did not want them. [But] in Cythera [Tahiti] the first article demanded by the natives was aouri [iron].

But the Samoans very much appreciated and valued the gift of cloth. In his journal, Bougainville noted that, when the French were showing them the red material, one Samoan was even brave enough to dive from his canoe and catch a rope hanging from the ship, with the apparent intention of climbing on board; but he did not succeed as the ship was moving too fast.

The officer Caro also noted that the Samoans seemed to be ignorant of the use of nails when the French presented them with some nails in exchange for the fish they were offered. But we can ask ourselves the following question. Was it not possible that the Samoans did know about their existence (Roggeveen had given them some 'rusty nails'), but simply did not yet see the decisive advantage of knives and nails over their iron-wood, bones, and shell tools, all of which were very efficient? The knowledge of iron in Western Polynesia dated at least from the Dutch voyages—and maybe even earlier, given the Spanish wrecks in the Tuaomotu islands, if we assume that there could have been exchanges throughout Polynesia in the 16th and 17th centuries (from one island network to the next, via the Cook Islands).

But the question of cloth was different: the Samoans knew for certain about the value of European cloth from what they saw in Tonga and from the stories told by the Tongans from their own dealings with the Dutch. They knew the decisive advantage of European cloth compared to their barkcloth. The former did not dissolve when wet from the rain or from the sea. Besides, the bright red colour was attractive throughout Polynesia. Regalia like the *maro ura* in Tahiti or the Samoan *'ie ula* (roll of red feathers), as well as the fringes of Samoan fine mats (*'ie tōga*), were made from an accumulation of red feathers. The barkcloth was most often painted with the red-brown dye extracted from the bark of the *'o'a* tree.[4] The heavenly house of the great Samoan creator-god Tagaloa was the Red House (*Fale Ula*). But the red feathers, obtained from a specific parakeet species, were rare; the birds were rare in Samoa and were very difficult to catch. In Fiji these birds were more numerous. Hence the Samoans bartered for their feathers from the Fijians, through the Tongans (Kaeppler 1978, 1999, n.d.). The surgeon Vivès tells us that one of the French threw a gift of clothing into the sea, and a Samoan immediately took it, rolled it up, and swam with it to the coast (swimming on his back), although the coast was very far away. (The French

---

[4] The *Bischoffia javanica* (Te Rangi Hiroa 1930: 297). This dye was explicitly compared to the life-giving blood of the bride (Tcherkézoff 2003b: 365).

apparently did not bring with them the blue beads that were also greatly valued by Samoans).

5. The Tahitian reference

Bougainville concludes:

> I do not believe that these men are so gentle as those of Tahiti: their features were more savage (Bougainville 1772b [Forster's translation]: 280).
>
> (Je ne crois pas ces hommes aussi doux que les Tahitiens; leur physionomie était plus sauvage.)

He adds that his Tahitian guide, who had embarked in Tahiti, predictably 'manifested all his contempt in front of such people' (*a temoigné le plus grand mépris pour ces insulaires*). We have already seen how Bougainville found the first woman he saw 'ugly', the barkcloth 'much coarser', the colours of the dyes for the barkcloth 'ugly', the fish hooks 'badly made', and how he commented with derision on the fact that Samoans did not attach any importance to iron tools.

Thus, the French immediately compared Samoa to Tahiti, where they had stayed a month earlier. It is well known that Bougainville had made of his 'Nouvelle-Cythère' (Tahiti) the most perfect habitat of 'Natural Man': he referred to the Tahitians as a people who had maintained their kindness and innocence since the time of the Creation (the Noble Savage ideal-type). This was due to his total misunderstanding of the sexual presentations of girls who had been brought to him and to his crew in Tahiti; I shall return to this when discussing Lapérouse's narrative. From then on, steering westwards, he only found people who seemed to him to be 'less' of everything. He applied this judgement of inferiority to the physical appearance of the men and women, as well as to their goods (barkcloth, fish hooks) and their lack of interest in iron.

Bougainville thus inaugurated a narrative genre that would be continued by the other French captains. It was even reinforced after 1787, when the Samoans also acquired a reputation as 'murderers' via Lapérouse's account.

6. Departure

The next day, 5 May, the French ships stood in front of Tutuila. Many canoes passed by 'and the signs made by the Indians seemed to invite us to land' (*les Indiens semblaient nous inviter par leurs signes à aller à terre*); but the reef barrier seemed to render it impossible and Bougainville decided to resume his course in the Pacific. In the distance he saw the eastern end of Upolu, but the fog was very dense and so he continued on his route. Thus ended this brief two-day interlude of contacts at sea, only the second recorded contact that Samoans had yet experienced with Europeans.

Some islands in the Samoan archipelago had not been visited by the first expedition (Roggeveen's), nor even by the French during this second contact episode: for instance, the large island of Savai'i would have to wait for Captain Edward Edwards's expedition in 1791 to see *Papālagi* passing by its shores for the first time (chapter 5). But judging by early 19th-century observations, the demonstrable unity of the language throughout the archipelago observed from 1830 onwards, and the existence of a kinship system where marriage ties are widespread as each village was (and often still is) an exogamous unit, the practice of constant inter-village and inter-island visiting that lay at the heart of Samoan life in those years allows the supposition that news of any contact with the *Papālagi* on one island would have spread to inhabitants of the other islands within a few years if not a few months.

Chapter 3

December 1787, Lapérouse: first incursion on land

(The 'young girls', the origin of the Western myth and a comparative hypothesis about the Polynesian sexual presentations)

With the arrival of Jean-François de Galaup de Lapérouse we come to the first Samoan/European contact on land, and to the first of the two authors who are Williamson's and Côté's key witnesses for the theory of a free sex pre-marital life among Samoan girls. We saw in the Introduction how Côté found to be crucial Williamson's statement that 'Lapérouse tells us that girls were, before marriage, mistresses of their own favours, and their complaisance did not dishonour them'. Indeed, as regards this quotation, as for all others from Lapérouse in his volumes on Polynesia, Williamson was accurate. The question, though, is why he had noted that very passage, among dozens of pages from Lapérouse's narrative. Lapérouse did indeed write this very sentence in his journal. It can be found in a concluding part of his narrative of his encounter with the Samoan people. But the preceding lines, omitted by Williamson (and apparently not checked by Côté), contain a surprise and lead us to a very different conclusion: young and weeping girls were forcibly dragged by adults into a chiefly house, where they were held firmly in the arms of an elder and sexually offered to the French. It seems that in Williamson's case the Western myth of Polynesian sexuality had once again informed the selection of ideas just as it did at much the same time for Margaret Mead. Actually the myth was already at work in Lapérouse's case: influenced by his reading of Bougainville's chapter on 'New Cythera' (Tahiti), Lapérouse misinterpreted in terms of female 'favours' what he saw (and/or what he had been told by some of his officers) during his brief landing in Samoa.

Lapérouse had the commendable habit of sending a copy of his journal to France from his main ports of call. Thus, although he and all his expedition disappeared in 1788 in the Solomons (Vanikoro) (shipwrecked on a reef in a storm; no survivors were ever found and material traces of the expedition were not discovered until forty years later), the French Navy was in possession of the journal of the expedition, from early 1786 when Lapérouse entered the Pacific until his last call at Botany Bay in January and February 1788, thus shortly after his passage through the Samoan islands in December 1787. His journal was published with some alterations by French authorities in 1797 (edited by Général

Millet-Mureau). In 1985, a scholarly edition was published by John Dunmore of Massey University and Maurice de Brossard of the French Navy and the *Académie de marine*. The editors were able to go back to the original manuscript. An English translation was published by Dunmore in 1994 (volume 1) and 1995 (volume 2).[1]

1. Lapérouse's conclusion about Samoan 'customs': the women's behaviour

After his chapter describing daily events, Lapérouse wrote a concluding chapter describing his encounter with the Samoans. His summary of the contents, given on the first page of the chapter, says that his remarks will bear 'on the customs and practices of these people, their crafts and the country's products. Basis of a belief that they do not all share the same origin...' ([Lapérouse] Dunmore ed. 1995: 415). Lapérouse speaks first of the names and position of the islands, and refers first of all to Bougainville's comments. (We thus know that Lapérouse had carefully read the narrative of Bougainville's circumnavigation of 1766-9). Then he summarises Roggeveen's voyage from his reading of Behrens's narrative through the quotations that are in 'Président de Brosses''s work of 1756. This was the great compilation, used by all captains of the second half of the 18th century.[2] Lapérouse then proceeds to describe the physical appearance of Samoan men, 'the tallest and most robustly built we have met', and how they are 'painted or tattooed in such a way that one could almost believe they are clothed' (Dunmore ed. 1995: 419). Then he describes the women (we shall return to the passage in its entirety). His last lines about Samoan 'women' concern the 'girls' and contain the words highlighted by Côté via Williamson: Whatever navigators who preceded us might say, I am convinced that at least in the Navigators Islands girls are mistresses of their own favours before marriage, their complaisance casts no dishonour on them, and it is more likely that when they marry they are under no obligation to account for their past behaviour. But I have no doubt that they are required to show more restraint when they are married (*ibid.*: 420).[3]

Lapérouse then goes on to describe 'crafts', notes how the art of plaiting fine mats is prevalent in comparison with making barkcloth (called in Samoan *siapo*),

---

[1] Dening (1998: 41-7) has emphasised the great achievement that these publications represent, and the contribution that they make to the researches of ethnohistorians of the Pacific.
[2] In 1756, Charles de Brosses, a jurist, geographer, President of the Parliament of Dijon in Burgundy, and a reader of all prior voyagers' accounts (in all languages), had published two large volumes that were a compilation and a study of these previous voyages in the Pacific (de Brosses 1756; Ryan 2002).
[3] *Quoiqu'en puissent dire les voyageurs qui nous ont précédés je suis convaincu qu'au moins dans les isles des Navigateurs les jeunes filles avant d'être mariées sont maîtresses de leurs faveurs, que leur complaisance ne les déshonore pas, il est plus vraisemblable qu'en se mariant elles n'ont aucun compte à rendre de leur conduite passée. Mais je ne doute pas quelles ne soient obligées à plus de réserve lorsqu'elles ont un mari* ([Lapérouse] Dunmore and de Brossard eds, 1985: II: 477).

carefully describes the houses,[4] then tries to characterise the language and the origin of the Samoans.

We see that his final sentence about 'girls as mistresses of their own favours' is presented as a sheer hypothesis: 'Whatever navigators who preceded us might say' (i.e., 'even if prior navigators said nothing of the kind'; Lapérouse is referring of course to Bougainville's and Behrens's accounts), 'I am convinced…', 'it is more likely…', 'I have no doubt…'. Why was he 'convinced'? One reason is of course his reaction to certain events. We shall return to this in what follows. But there may have been a more general reason: Lapérouse assimilated the Samoans to the Tahitians and thus interpreted everything in a biased way. The assimilation followed two complementary paths. Firstly, Lapérouse reflected on the language area and noted a certain unity. Secondly, as to the women and girls, he had in mind Bougainville's narrative recounting the numerous 'Venuses' seen in 'New Cythera'.

2. Interpretation (i) — Samoa and Tahiti: 'dialect of the same tongue'

On the following page, when Lapérouse discusses the language and the origins of the people, he says that Samoans seem to belong to the same language area as Tahitians. 'At first', Lapérouse says, the language of the people met on those 'Navigators Islands' seemed to have 'no similarity with our vocabularies from the Society and Friendly Islands' (Tahiti and Tonga). We remember that this was Bougainville's impression as well. Lapérouse continues: 'but more careful

---

[4] Although his general conclusion is that Samoans 'spend their days in idleness or engaged in tasks that have no other purpose than their clothing and their luxury', Lapérouse admired 'the elegant shapes of their houses… axes made of a very fine and very compact basalt shaped into adzes; and they sold us for a few glass beads wooden dishes affixed to three feet holding them up like a tripod and which seemed to be painted with the finest varnish…they make some paper-cloth (*étoffe-papier*) similar to that of the Society and Friendly Islands; they sold us several lengths of a single reddish-brown colour. It seems that they do not prize it very much and have little use for it, the women prefer mats (*nattes*) that are extremely well plaited and I saw only two or three men whom I took to be chiefs who had instead of a grass skirt a length of material (*une pièce de toile*) wrapped around them like a skirt, this cloth is woven with a true thread drawn no doubt from some ligneous plant, like a nettle or flax, it is made without a shuttle and the threads are woven through absolutely as with the mats, this cloth has both the suppleness and the strength of our own, is very suitable for their canoe sails and cannot be compared in respect of its advantages to the paper cloth of the other islands which they also manufacture but seem to disdain' (Dunmore ed. 1995 : 420-1 ; Dunmore and de Brossard eds, 1985 : II : 477-8). His description of the house he was taken to during his landing of 10 December (see below) is very precise and corresponds exactly to what we know about a *fale tele* from 19th-century sources. The floor was made of pebbles, the Samoans 'stretched out the finest and freshest mats on the ground' to welcome the French. 'I went into the best hut which presumably belonged to the chief and was extremely surprised to find a vast latticed room as well and indeed better made than any in the environs of Paris. The best architect could not have given a more elegant curve to the two ends of the ellipse ending this hut, a row of columns five feet from each other ran along the edge, these columns were only tree trunks very elaborately worked between which the Indians had placed some fine mats that could be raised or lowered with ropes like our roller-blinds and arranged with the utmost skill like fish scales, the rest of the house was covered with cononut-tree leaves' (p. 394).

study convinced us that they speak a dialect of the same tongue.' It confirmed, Lapérouse adds, 'the view held by the English' (*ibid.*: 421).

What was this view? Lapérouse does not expand on this, but we can easily guess. The conclusion from Cook's first voyage (1769-71), reinforced after the second voyage (1772-75), was that there was a strong similarity of language and customs throughout the region, and this lead to the attribution of a common origin to the various people of Tahiti (and neighbouring islands), Tonga, New Zealand (Maori), the Marquesas and Rapa Nui (Easter Island). J. R. Forster, the naturalist who accompanied Cook on his second voyage, had elaborated these ideas in his report which was published in 1778.[5] The very first mention of this idea in France appeared in Bougainville's chapter on 'Tahitian Language' (*Vocabulaire de l'ile Taiti*), in the concluding pages that were added to the second edition of his *Voyage autour du monde (Voyage around the World)*:[6] 'the British have found that the language of New Zealanders (Maori) is more or less the same as the language of the Tahitians' (Bougainville 1772a: II: 434; my translation).[7] In autumn 1771, Bougainville had already received this information from the British, since Cook's first expedition returned to London in July 1771 (Banks came to Paris to meet his fellow naturalists).[8] Bougainville (1772a: *ibid.*) added that one can also make comparisons with the words noted by the Dutch in north Tonga (on the islands they called '*Îles des Cocos*'). He also mentioned a French linguist, de Jebelin ('*M. Court de Jebelin de l'Académie de la Rochelle*'), who had just sent him a '*mémoire*' on Tahitian language, based on the lists brought back by the French, mainly from their extensive conversations with 'Aoutorou' on board ship while they were sailing back to Europe, and on the vocabulary lists

---

[5] Forster's book of 1778 has been republished in a scholarly edition (Thomas, Guest and Dettelbach eds 1996). For a detailed analysis of Forster's theories on that topic, see Tcherkézoff (n.d.).

[6] The *Voyage* was first published in March or April 1771 (Bougainville 1771) and republished in French with additions the following year (Bougainville 1772a), while the first edition was translated into English and also published in 1772 (Bougainville 1772b).

[7] Bougainville's first edition of 1771 was probably published in March. The final manuscript was approved by the Royal Censor authorities on 15 January 1771. This decision was transmitted to the Publishing Register authorities on 27 February and registered on 2 March. The speed of this process suggests that the French were eager to have the book appear as soon as possible and leads one to think that it was printed immediately after registration. The French were clearly in a hurry as they thought that 'Banks' first voyage around the world' expedition (as Cook's first expedition was then called) would be returning soon. They knew that the expedition was supposed to observe the transit of Venus in Tahiti in 1769, on the advice of Wallis, the 'discoverer' of Tahiti, who came back to London just before Cook left. This first edition already included the final chapter on the Tahitian language (Bougainville 1771: 389-402). But only the second edition, in 1772, includes this final observation by Bougainville: '*Cependant les Anglois dans leur dernier voyage ont constaté que le langage des habitants de la Nouvelle Zélande est à-peu-près le même que celui des Taitiens.*' (1772a: II: 434). Obviously, Bougainville heard about this after Cook's return, thus after mid-July 1771. (My thanks to Marc Kurt Tabani, Curator of Ethnological Collections at the Bibliothèque Nationale de France, who verified these dates, with the help of Jean-Dominique Mellot, Curator at the Bibliothèque Nationale, 'Département de la reserve', and consulted the first edition at a time when I only had access to the second edition at the Library of our Centre de documentation de la Maison Asie-Pacifique in Marseilles.)

[8] Personal communication from Tom Ryan (June 2001).

of the British made during Cook's first voyage. According to this *mémoire*, Tahitian has 'a very strong analogy' with the 'Malay language' (*avec le Malais*) and 'as a consequence [we can be sure that] most of the islands of the South Seas had been peopled by immigrations which came from the East Indies' (*ibid.*: 435).[9]

Bougainville had built on an earlier and very general hypothesis proposed by de Brosses in 1756 about the supposed conquest by Asians of an 'old race' of 'black and frizzy-haired' people. De Brosses himself was influenced in this by Buffon. Thirty years later, Lapérouse pursues the same theme. We can note that Lapérouse, in the 1780s, had himself approached Buffon, by then quite elderly, when Lapérouse was in Paris preparing his expedition (Dunmore 1985: 192). Thus, in December 1787 Lapérouse, as he indicates in his narrative, is immediately interested when he notices that a 'young servant from Manilla' who is on board 'could understand [the Samoans] and explain to us the greater part of the islanders' words'. He then makes the hypothesis of 'Malay colonies'. It is known, he says, that:

> all the languages of the Philippines are derived from Malay, which language more widely spread than Greek or Latin is used by the innumerable peoples who live in the South Sea in the islands of both hemispheres; I consider it proved that these various nations are merely Malay colonies which in very remote periods conquered these islands ([Lapérouse] Dunmore ed. 1995: 421).

After remarking on the unknown date of the 'Malay' conquerors' arrival (but which probably occurred, he says, at a time much earlier even than 'the so-called antiquity of the Chinese and Egyptians'), he expands into a theory of 'two very distinct races', for all the South Seas, thus following a tradition established by de Brosses in 1756, by Bougainville in 1772 and by Forster in 1778 (Tcherkézoff 2003a). He then applies it to the 'Navigators Islands':

> Basis for a belief that they do not all share the same origin, and that the natives of these islands were[,] before the mixing of the two nations[,][10] dark and frizzy-haired like the inhabitants of New Guinea and the Hebrides, their form of government maintains their ferocity...

> I am convinced that the indigenous people of the Philippines, of Formosa, of New Guinea, New Britain, the Hebrides, the Friendly Isles &c in the southern hemisphere: and of the Carolines, the Marianas, the Sandwich Islands in the northern hemisphere were these frizzy-haired men who

---

[9] *Ce mémoire par lequel il me paroît prouver que la langue de Taiti a la plus grande analogie avec le Malais, & conféquemment que la plupart des îles de la mer du Sud ont été peuplées par des émigrations forties des Indes orientales.*

[10] *Motif de croire qu'ils n'ont pas touts une origine commune, et que les indigènes de ces isles étaient avant le mélange des deux nations noirs et crépus comme les habitants de la Nouvelle-Guinée et des Hébrides, la forme de leur gouvernement entretient leur férocité* (Dunmore and de Brossard eds 1985: II: 471).

still live deep in the interior of the Luzon islands and of Formosa, whom it was impossible to subjugate in New Guinea, New Britain, and the Hebrides and who, defeated in the islands further east, which were too small for them to find a refuge in the centre of the said islands, intermarried with the conquering people and gave rise to that very dark race of men whose colour retains ten shades more than the skin of those families presumably distinguished in their countries who made it a point of honour not to marry beneath them. We were particularly impressed by these two very distinct races in the Navigators Islands and do not attribute any other origin to this (*ibid.*: 415, 421-2).[11]

Lapérouse is convinced that, in ancient times, Samoans were 'like the inhabitants of New Guinea'. The violence that they were still displaying to this day (he is referring to the 'massacre' during the last day of the encounter, on 11 December) shows that 'their form of government maintains their ferocity'. Nevertheless, they had been a 'Malay colony' for a long time, like the rest of Polynesia, following the 'mixing of the two nations'. Therefore it was to be expected that one would find some 'similarity' (in language and hence in customs) between the 'Navigators Islands' and the 'Society and Friendly Islands'.

3. Interpretation (ii) — they 'offered their favours': extension of the myth from Bougainville to Lapérouse

We thus have good reason to think that, when Lapérouse interpreted what he thought he had observed about Samoan 'girls' and 'women', the Tahitian reference was uppermost in his mind. This may explain why he immediately interpreted some gestures in terms of female 'favours': the 'girls' would be 'mistresses of their own favours' and the 'women' themselves were 'offering their favours'. Twenty lines earlier, before the conclusion about the girls being 'mistresses of their own favours', Lapérouse begins to describe the women, right after his description of the men which I have already quoted: The women also are very tall and before their springtime has ended they have lost the shapes and that gentle expression, which Nature has never withheld from these

---

[11] I have quoted James Cook, who had noted in Tahiti, in 1769, that the 'various kinds' of skin colour are due to the relative exposure to the sun, according to the type of work done. Implicitly, this social class model proposed an alternative explanation to the tradition, dating from the first Spanish observations and generalised in the mid-18th century by de Brosses, that theorised a multiracial peopling of the Polynesian islands by successive groups of 'light'- and 'dark'-skinned people. But Cook was not an intellectual like Forster, or even Bougainville or Lapérouse, and did not broaden this remark into a comparative discussion of earlier theories. Forster (1778), like Buffon and de Brosses, attributed the colour variation in human groups to ancient climatic adaptations, thus still leaving the way open to interpret the variety of groups encountered in Polynesia as the result of successive migrations of different 'races' (in the sense of 'varieties of humanity' which had originally become different through climatic influences). As we can see, Lapérouse kept to this idea, which persisted until the advent of the racist theories of the 19th century represented by Dumont d'Urville's 'Melanesia' and similar classifications. The major change was that the idea of ancient climatic adaptation was replaced by a new belief in original and immutable physical differences among human groups.

uncivilised people but which it seems to leave with them for only an instant and reluctantly. Among a very large number of women I found only three who were very pretty; the rough impudent expression of the others, their indecent gestures, the off-putting way they offered their favours...(*ibid.*: 419).[12]

We shall see later how Lapérouse ends his sentence. But, for the moment, let us reflect on this expression: 'offered their favours'.

Lapérouse in Mauritius

We must remember that Lapérouse was among the navigators who had read Bougainville before departing for the Pacific. In the 1770s and 1780s, Bougainville's version of Tahiti was the absolute reference—in most of Europe, but certainly for all French captains—and Lapérouse, like any other captain of a Pacific expedition, sailed with this narrative firmly in his mind. Perhaps even more so than other captains, because Lapérouse had personally met those who had been in Tahiti with Bougainville.

In Mauritius ('*Isle de France*'), where Lapérouse stayed in 1772, he met some of Bougainville's companions from the 1766-69 circumnavigation and discussed the events of their voyage at length with them. Several of Bougainville's companions were living there, including the famous naturalist of the expedition, Philibert Commerson. His '*Post-Scriptum sur Tahiti*', published in the main Parisian newspaper in 1769, which described Tahiti as paradise on earth, started off the whole myth of the 'New Cythera' as a Garden of Eden (Tcherkézoff in press-1). In Mauritius, 'La Pérouse had numerous opportunities to discuss the great voyage of exploration with them' (Dunmore 1985: 86-7). As it happens, Commerson had disembarked from Bougainville's ships at Mauritius in November 1768, while the expedition was on its way back to France, and it was from there that the famous *Post-Scriptum* had been sent. He worked as a naturalist on local projects in this French colony, and was still there four years later when Lapérouse arrived in 1772 (Lapérouse was an officer serving on the French vessel *Belle-Poule* which was bringing a new Governor to Mauritius [Dunmore 1985: 75]).

First contacts in Tahiti: the Western myth and the ethnography

Let us turn back briefly to this other French 'discovery' of 1768 (Tcherkézoff in press- 1). In Tahiti, on the third day of Bougainville's tacking off the coast (before he even attempted a landing), a group of Tahitians brought an adolescent girl out with them and had her climb on board; once there, she took off her

---

[12] *Les femmes sont aussi très grandes et ont perdu avant la fin de leur printemps ces formes et cette douceur d'expression, dont la Nature n'a jamais brisé l'empreinte chés ces peuples barbares mais qu'elle paroit ne leur laisser qu'un instant et à regret. Parmi un très grand nombre de femmes je n'en ai vu que trois très jolies; l'air grossement effronté des autres, l'indescence de leurs mouvements, l'offre rebutante qu'elles faisaient de leurs faveurs ...* (Dunmore and de Brossard eds 1985: 477).

barkcloth (obeying the adults who accompanied her, as we learn from the journals) and appeared to the French on the deck 'such as Venus shewed herself to the Phrygian shepherd' (Bougainville 1772b: 219). This sentence, which became the most famous of Bougainville's book of 1771, together with the *Post-Scriptum* from Commerson, sparked the myth about the 'lascivious' customary education of Tahitian—and later all Polynesian—adolescent girls that spread throughout Europe. It gave the idea that the girls *were offering themselves* quite willingly.

Then, when the French landed, they were conducted into a chief's house where, with complete ceremonial decorum, they were asked to take a young girl sexually. The journals provide some crucial details that were never published. We learn that the girl was presented to the visitors in the middle of a circle of adults who chanted (prayers?) and held a green bough in their hands (as a sign of fecundity and as an offering to the superior entities?). We learn too that the girl was crying. The significance of the green bough (a branch of plantain) can be inferred from the Tahitians' behaviour in front of their own sacred chiefs, as observed a few years later by James Morrison, the first European visitor to stay a long time in Tahiti. The presentation of a green bough paved the way for making offerings to a superior, as can also be seen from other scenes, such as the gifts of barkcloth presented to Cook and Banks in May 1769 (as I shall describe in chapter 10). The presence of the green bough indicates the formal and indeed ritual (sacrificial) character of the whole scene which, contrary to what Bougainville wrote in his book, cannot thus be reduced to any kind of sexual 'hospitality'.

These details are supplied in the journals and logs of the companions and officers who accompanied Bougainville. But the captain did not include this information in his published account and only mentioned that in 'every house' of this island where the French entered those favours were 'offered'. He thus led the European reader to believe that all of this was purely sexual hospitality, from a people who had made sexuality their main value and thus their main offering. The French made no attempt at all to decode the ceremonial and ritual context in which the sexual offering occurred and concluded for the most part that they had found in Tahiti a people who had remained 'as Eve before her Falling': a place in which the sexual act was 'naturally' done, constantly practised and 'staged in public' (*en public*).

Had Bougainville been able to land in Samoa, he might have met with the same experience—the presentation of girls—as his successor, Lapérouse, and he might have rated both his New Cythera and his Navigators' Islands as two remnants of the 'Garden of Eden'. (We leave aside the crucial difference that, in Tahiti, everything went peacefully for Bougainville because, a few months before his visit, the Tahitians had experimented with the cannons of Wallis via their attempt to attack and seize the Europeans' boats, thus learning what a European response to aggression could be—but Bougainville was not aware of the earlier visit, thinking himself to be the 'discoverer' of the island of Tahiti, and therefore interpreted Tahitian society as 'naturally' peaceful.) In any event, Lapérouse's account mirrors what Bougainville would have written: there were the same misinterpretations about this Samoan custom of presenting girls, Lapérouse painting it as sexual hospitality, 'offerings' (with a touch of a 'selling') of 'favours' for European goods, within a customary setting in which 'it can be observed' that there are no restrictions on pre-marital sexual activities. The two gross misinterpretations of these sexual encounters were (i) to see in these ritualised contacts a form of sexual 'hospitality' or a 'selling of favours' and (ii) to conclude from the encounters that, between themselves, the local people behaved in the same way, thus implying that a custom of 'free pre-marital sex' for all adolescents prevailed in these societies.

Thus, we can trace two trajectories of the Western-inspired myth. The more recent of the two runs from Lapérouse to Williamson and through to Côté as a proponent of the Meadian Samoa: Lapérouse's account contains the two sentences that suggest the idea of a free sex life for females in Samoa. The older trajectory runs from Bougainville to Lapérouse to Williamson, for the influence of Bougainville's book was twofold. First, Lapérouse's interpretation was produced out of, or at least found its assertiveness in, what he had read in Bougainville's account of sexual presentations in the Polynesian region. And secondly, the fact that in the 1930s Williamson picked out these sentences and not others in Lapérouse's account, is again a direct consequence of the Western myth of adolescent sexual freedom in Tahiti. By the time that Williamson was working on his compilation, this myth was being transformed into one that was applicable to the whole of Polynesia (with the help of Handy's fanciful 'ethnology' of the Marquesas and Mead's equally fanciful description of Samoan adolescence, both published in the 1920s).[13]

4. Interpretation (iii)—women as 'worthy of the ferocious beings…'

Besides mentioning the 'favours', Lapérouse portrayed the Samoan women as making 'rough impudent' faces and 'indecent gestures'. We can see here a major point of discontinuity between Bougainville and Lapérouse: the transformation of the Noble Savage into the Ignoble Savage. I shall return to this in the next chapter, when I discuss the 'massacre'. Let us only note here how Lapérouse ended his sentence about the 'favours offered':

---

[13] For the role played by Edward Craighill Smith Handy and for the references to his publications, see Tcherkézoff (in press-1 and 2001a: chapters 3-4).

'First Contacts' in Polynesia

> Among a very large number of women I found only three who were very pretty; the rough impudent expression of the others, their indecent gestures, the off-putting way they offered their favours, everything made them in our eyes seem worthy of being the wives or the mothers of the ferocious beings surrounding us (*ibid.*: 419).[14]

Lapérouse wrote these lines and, probably, the whole concluding chapter about his Samoan visit, after his departure from Samoa, either at sea or during his stay at Botany Bay. He had in mind that the scenes of 'offered favours' were followed by the 'massacre' of his men. Lapérouse thus portrayed these women as 'indecent' creatures *precisely* because it made them 'worthy' of the picture of men as 'ferocious beings' and 'barbarian murderers' (as Kotzebue was to say after reading Lapérouse; see chapter 5). Firstly, the implicit reference to Bougainville's Tahiti led Lapérouse to interpret everything in terms of 'offered favours'. But he had insisted on this for various reasons; one of them was diametrically opposed to Bougainville's views.

Lapérouse's conclusion appears to be biased on two counts, as it took on the Noble Savage myth (in the attention paid to female 'favours') and transformed it into its contrary. It became a discourse on the Ignoble Savage type of Pacific society, where free sex was linked to the brutality of a pre-civilised age. It was opposed to the Noble Savage type of society elaborated by those such as Bougainville, Commerson and Banks for whom free sex was a sign that people had remained within the happy and innocent state of the primordial Creation.

It is this doubly biased discourse, expressed in the concluding lines where—as usual—the description of events is replaced by judgements and interpretations, that Williamson deemed to be representative of Samoa. It is also the discourse that Côté would like us to retain today as a perfect summary of pre-Christian Samoan culture!

5. Events—the real scene observed by Lapérouse: the sacred marriage of virgins

Internal analysis

The reference to Tahiti led Lapérouse to interpret some events in a particular way and thus to convey a certain image of women, which he filled out in his last pages and which he therefore wanted to be conclusive. We need now to seek out a description of these events. Fortunately, Lapérouse's narrative does give us some pieces of information. So far, we have quoted the first and last lines

---

[14] *Parmi un très grand nombre de femmes je n'en ai vu que trois très jolies; l'air grossement effronté des autres, l'indescence de leurs mouvements, l'offre rebutante qu'elles faisaient de leurs faveurs, tout les faisait paroître à nos yeux bien dignes d'être les femmes, ou les mères des êtres féroces qui nous environnaient* (Dunmore and de Brossard eds 1985: 477).

of his passage on 'women'. In between, Lapérouse suddenly becomes more precise:

> ... everything made them in our eyes seem worthy of being the wives or the mothers of the ferocious beings surrounding us. As the story of our voyage can add a few pages to that of mankind I will not omit pictures that might shock in any other kind of book and I shall mention that the very small number of young and pretty island girls I referred to soon attracted the attention of a few Frenchmen who in spite of my orders endeavoured to establish links of intimacy with them; since our Frenchmen's eyes revealed their desires they were soon discovered; some old women negotiated the transaction, an altar was set up in the most prominent hut, all the blinds were lowered, inquisitive spectators were driven off; the victim was placed within the arms of an old man who exhorted her to moderate her sorrow for she was weeping; the matrons sang and howled during the ceremony, and the sacrifice was consummated in the presence of the women and the old man was acting as altar and priest. All the village's women and children were around and outside the house, lightly raising the blinds and seeking the slightest gaps between the mats to enjoy this spectacle. Whatever navigators who preceded us might say, I am convinced that at least in the Navigators Islands girls are mistresses of their own favours ... (*ibid.*: 419-20).[15]

These lines are clearly quite different in kind from those that mark the beginning and the end of this particular passage. For a brief interval, Lapérouse did not interpret but simply described what he saw or what he had been told by some of the people of the de Langle party who had visited another village. Through ethnographic analysis we can compare this short piece of ethnography with other data.

The 'women': comparison with Tahiti

The 'indecent gestures' of the 'women' might well have been signs to the Frenchmen indicating what the 'young girls' had been brought for. Lapérouse does not mention any actual sexual encounter with those 'women', neither in this concluding chapter nor in the previous description of daily events (as we

---

[15] *Comme l'histoire de notre voyage peut ajouter quelques feuilléts à celle de l'homme je n'en écarterai pas des tableaux qui seroient indescents dans tout autre ouvrage et je raporterai que le très petit nombre de jeunes et jolies insulaires dont j'ai déjà parlé eut bientôt fixé l'attention de quelques Français qui malgré mes ordres chercherent a former des liaisons d'intimité avec elles ; comme les yeux de nos François exprimoient leurs désirs ils furent bientôt devinés ; des vieilles femmes negotierent cette affaire, l'autel fut dressée dans la case du village la plus apparente, toutes les jalousies furent baissées, les curieux écartés ; la victime fut placée entre les bras d'un vieillard, qui lexortoit à moderer sa douleur, car elle pleuroit ; les matrones chantoient et hurloient pendant la cérémonie, et le sacrifice fut consommé en présence des femmes et du vieillard qui servoit d'autel et de prêtre. Toutes les femmes et enfants du vilage étaient au tour et en dehors de la maison soulevant legerement les jalousies et cherchant les plus petites ouvertures entre les nattes pour jouir de ce spectacle (ibid.).*

shall see). What about 'the off-putting way they offered their favours'? Here again, it could in fact be a mistaken interpretation of the sexual gestures these women were making, that is, the gestures may not have meant that the women offered themselves but may have been made as a non-verbal explanation of how the Frenchmen should behave with the 'girls'. This hypothesis can reasonably be put forward since this is precisely what happened during the first Tahitian contacts in which descriptions were sufficiently detailed to discriminate between the adults' movements and the 'young girl's acting (Tcherkézoff in press-1). In any event, we need some hypothesis of the sort in order to explain this encounter on Samoan land, since the one and only description by Lapérouse of a sexual act (the 'sacrifice' in the 'prominent hut') *concerned only*, in his account, 'the very small number of young and pretty island girls I referred to'.

The 'girls' and the 'sacrifice': comparison with Samoan ceremonies of 1830-1850

Now, turning to the 'young girls' and the 'sacrifice', the description is self-evident. The 'victims' were the 'girls'. Each girl was 'weeping'. She was presented by the 'old women', and then 'placed in the arms of an old man' (an orator *tulafale*?) who spoke with her. She was apparently held by the orator during the operation, since this 'old man' is said by Lapérouse to have himself been the 'altar' on which the 'sacrifice' was made. She was presented in 'the most prominent hut', which seems to indicate a high stone base (*pa'epa'e*), which in turn identifies the house as belonging to the main chief of the area (from 19th-century data, e.g. Krämer 1994-95). All the blinds were lowered, and the women 'sang and howled'.

This exactly matches the description of a 19th-century Samoan marriage ceremony where the young bride is a virgin and is ceremonially deflowered. There are two types of description. In one of them the bride is presented on the sacred ground of the village, in front of everyone, and is deflowered manually by an orator (of the groom's family) or by the groom in the case of high chiefs. In the other she is deflowered behind the blinds of the house, with no clear indication of whether the man who performs this rite is an orator, *tulafale,* or the bridegroom.[16] Let me quote from the first detailed descriptions available, from the early 1830s (the first missionary visit) and the 1850s, passages which show clearly what was involved.

> John Williams's account of 1830-1832 tells us how girls could be held by older people while the defloration ceremony was performed. The bridegroom is seated in front of his group, on the central and sacred ground (*malae*) of the village: The female now prepares herself to meet him which in general is attended with considerable delay. The

---
[16] See the discussion in Tcherkézoff (2003b: 350-72).

preparation is mostly attended with furious crying & bitter wailing on the part of the young woman while her friends are engaged in persuading her that what is about to take place will not hurt her. She at length consents & is taken by the hand by her elder brother... If she does not consent to go she is dragged by force to him. She is dressed... [with] scented oil... finely wrought mats edged with red feathers...on arriving immediately in front of her husband she throws off her mat and stands before him perfectly naked. He then ruptures the Hymen of the female with two fingers of his right hand... [when everyone sees the blood, the women of the girl's family] throw off their mats & commence dancing naked... If the female objects to submit to the above ceremony which is sometimes the case persons are employed to hold her—some to hold her down others to hold her arms others her legs. She is thus held in the lap of another person while the husband ruptures the Hymen. On some occasions the parties bed immediately after the ceremonies are concluded (Moyle ed. 1984: 255-6).

This last sentence describes the same procedure that had been used for the 'marriages' with the French in 1787. We can easily imagine how, in 1787, the 'girls' were terrified when they were brought in to be married to these unknown and awesome creatures. Hence, for that 'first contact', the marriage ceremony took the form described by Williams when 'the female objects to submit...'.

Lapérouse's remark about the 'matrons singing and howling' could refer to what William T. Pritchard (son of a pastor and 'consul') observed in the 1850s:

All her mats were taken off by the old duennas; who then slowly paraded her, naked and trembling, before the silent gaze of the multitude, then she was seated, with her legs crossed, on a snow-white mat spread on the ground, in the centre of the square, or *malae*. There the chief approached her and silently seated himself also cross-legged, close to and directly facing her. Then was the critical moment. Though perhaps more than a thousand spectators looked on, of all ages and both sexes, not a word—not a sound was heard. Then, placing his left hand on the girl's right shoulder, the chief inserted the two forefingers of his right hand into the *vulva*, while the two old duennas held her round the waist from behind. In a moment, the chief's arm was held up, the two fingers only extended, when her anxious tribe watched eagerly for the drops of blood to trickle down—the sight of which was the signal for vehement cheers...

Once more, the old duennas loud in songs that told of rivers flowing fast water no banks could restrain, seas no reefs could check—figurative allusions to the virgin blood of the chaste bride—once more those stern old duennas led their trembling and bashful girl, still naked as before, to the gaze of the cheering and excited multitude, to exhibit the blood that trickled down her thighs. Cheers of applause greeted her, which were acknowledged only by the tears which silently stole down her cheeks.[17]

'The blinds lowered': comparison with ethnography of the 1930s-1980s

Lapérouse's observation that 'all the blinds were lowered' is also very important. As far as I know from my discussions with Samoans in the 1980s, there were only two cases where something would be conducted inside a house with (all) blinds lowered. One was a defloration ceremony for marriage (some of the old people remembered cases from the 1930s). The other was a 'meeting with the spirits' (*fono ma aitu*) (which was attested at a village level until the 1960s), when chiefs of the village, faced with making an important and difficult decision, met at night and sat silently for hours, seeking inspiration from the superhuman world. In the morning they were supposed to emerge from the meeting convinced of the kind of action that needed to be taken. Such meetings, which require those attending to sit in silence, are called *tapua'iga*, from *tapu*: people put themselves in a state of taboo (Tcherkézoff 1995a, 2003b: 189-90). They can also be enacted in the daytime but inside a closed house, and could also, and still can, be organised by a small family group for a matter concerning only themselves.

In all other cases, even when there is a storm, Samoans have told me that some of the blinds—at least one—should always remain up because if all of them are lowered 'it becomes very dangerous'. It seemed to me, from their tone and the way they abruptly started speaking very quietly, that having all of the blinds lowered afforded an opportunity for the 'spirits' (*aitu*) to enter the house, which would thus cause great danger to the people staying within it—but this intrusion by the spirits was a necessity in the case of ancient marriages and of *tapua'iga* meetings.

Although paradoxical, it should be understood that a closed Samoan house, with all of its blinds down, is in fact open to the spirits' agency. The 'sacred ring' which gives the house its significance in terms of genealogical and territorial history is the circle of posts supporting the roof. When there is a formal meeting, each chief leans against one of the posts of the ring, sitting cross-legged. Chiefs of lesser rank sit in between the posts and their titles are exactly that:

---

[17] The description was published by W. T. Pritchard in his 'Notes on Certain Anthropological Matters respecting the South Seas Islanders' (Pritchard 1864: 325-6) and is cited by Danielsson (1956: 116-17). In his well-known book *Polynesian Reminiscences*, published two years later, Pritchard did not include this description, as 'amenities of decorum' forbade it, and only alluded to it: 'The ordeal by which the virtue of the chiefgirl of Samoa was tested was as obscene as severe, and the amenities of decorum forbid the description here' (1866: 139).

'between-the-posts chiefs'. The ring of posts is the sacred circle of titles that defines a village and that can be enacted any time chiefs meet in any house. When the blinds are up, the 'space between the posts' (*va*—significantly, the word is also used in the general sense of 'social relation') is significant because it is *visible*. Each man must then choose his point of entry into the house and his sitting position according to his rank in relation to the rank of the other men seated there.

From these elements, we can hypothesise that, when *all of the blinds* are down, the sacred ring—which is the 'sacred circle' defining all Samoan social contexts of belonging to a group as these relationships can be 'seen' in 'daylight' (*ao*) (Tcherkézoff 1997a, 2003b: chapter 2)—is no longer active. Then things have returned to the 'night' side of the world, where the sources of life are located, but are hidden, and must be seized from the gods and the spirits, as was the case for a marriage (the marriage finding its meaning only with the procreation of a child) and for a *tapua'iga* meeting.

December 1787: the first marriages with Papālagi

Thus, apparently, the scene described by Lapérouse belongs to this very specific context where young virgin brides were presented for 'marriage'. This context had been adapted by the Samoans in order to make a sexual presentation to the first European men who appeared on their land. The Europeans were seen as '*Papālagi*', beings in some measure endowed with super-human powers (chapters 9, 11). The young girls were presented to them, perhaps according to a mythical logic of theogamy, the strategy being to bring about the creation of sacred progeny.

But, whatever the motives of the Samoan chiefs who had these girls brought forward, there is nothing in that very specific scene which could allow us to conclude with Lapérouse that, in the local custom, girls were free to give themselves sexually. The scene described by Lapérouse strongly contradicts any idea, from the girls' perspective, of a search for sexual pleasure. The French tell us that the girls were 'young', felt great 'sorrow' (or 'pain': *modérer sa douleur*), were 'weeping', were directed by old people, and were held by adults during the procedure.

Thus, Lapérouse makes the same mistake as Bougainville in Tahiti, who thought that the French were welcomed *as ordinary men*, as travelling visitors, and that the behaviour of the Tahitians towards them, in the presentation of girls, was indicative of everyday behaviour between Tahitians. Indeed, one of Bougainville's companions, Felix Fesche, even went so far as to suggest, in his journal, that what he had seen of the presentation of girls offered to him and his friends allowed him to explain to his French audience the conduct of 'a marriage ceremony between Tahitians' (Tcherkézoff in press-1).[18] Lapérouse's often-quoted conclusion about young girls' sexual freedom (reproduced by Côté via Williamson) is therefore completely unfounded. As we have just seen, this refutation can already be supported by evidence contained in the two pages where Lapérouse wrote about the 'favours' bestowed by the women. Now we must also look at Lapérouse's previous chapter, where he describes the daily events during his stay and includes a narrative from his officer, Jean-François Tréton de Vaujuas (Dunmore ed. 1995: 386-414). In this narrative, we shall find an important observation relating to the sexual encounters: the presence of 'very young girls'. Moreover, the content of this preceding chapter allows us to make a precise reconstruction of the whole visit. I shall limit my analysis in this chapter to any episode that mentions a sexual offer made by women or girls. Other aspects of the visit will be discussed in chapter 4.

6. Daily events: the presence of women and 'very young girls'

After some first contacts had been made at sea in the Manu'a group and at Tutuila on 7 and 8 December, the expedition dropped anchor on 9 December at 4 p.m., in a small bay on the north coast of Tutuila. As the bay was not well protected, the French decided to anchor there only for a short time. Lapérouse remained on board and his officer, M. de Langle, commanding three small, armed boats, attempted a short landing ('staying an hour', *ibid*.: 391). Offerings (food, birds, etc.) were brought by the Samoans, and the French returned to their ships. In the early morning of 10 December, a second landing was made at the same place in order to get fresh water. Two armed longboats, followed this time by Lapérouse himself in another boat, made the landing. But de Langle ' decided to go in his small boat for an excursion to a second cove approximately one league from our watering place' and 'returned delighted, enchanted by the beauty of the village he had visited'. Meanwhile, at the watering place, the French established 'a line of soldiers between the Indians and the shore', while filling up the casks at the river:

> Messrs de Clonard and Monty established the most satisfactory order, a line of soldiers was placed between the Indians and the shore, we invited them all to sit down under the coconut trees lining the coast less than 8 *toises* from our longboats. They numbered about two hundred, with among them many women and children, each one had with him some hens, pigs, pigeons, parakeets, fruit and they all wanted to sell them at the same time, which created a little confusion.
>
> The women [*les femmes*] some of whom were very pretty, offered with their fruit and poultry their favours to anyone who was prepared to give

---
[18] See the English translation of Fesche's journal in Dunmore (ed.2002:259).

them beads;[19] soon they crossed the line of soldiers who pushed them back too weakly to stop them; their behaviour was gentle, merry and beguiling; Europeans who have sailed around the world, and especially Frenchmen, have no weapons against such attacks; they went through the ranks, the men came closer, then there was some little disorder, but Indians armed with sticks, whom we took to be chiefs, re-established order; each one returned to his post and trade began anew to the great satisfaction of buyers and sellers (*ibid.*: 393).

We cannot tell from the use of the word 'women' whether this included girls (I shall return to the account of Vaujuas for de Langle's landing). But we do know that it is was common practice in the English and French narratives of the time to include in the category of 'women' any girl, whatever her age, who seemed to the visitors to be making sexual proposals, or who was brought by adults making sexual gestures that indicated why the girl was being presented.[20]

What are we to make of the 'women' demanding beads? We need to keep in mind that we are examining the very first contact on land. We know from the Hawaiian and Tahitian cases that the initial attitude of the Polynesians was to present young females without specifically expecting a definite material gift in return. And although they did not ask for anything in return, they still tried by whatever means they could to force the visitors to accept their sexual offer.[21] It is only when they noticed that the Europeans—for whom such a presentation could only be understood in terms of sexual trade—were constantly handing over material gifts in return, that the Polynesian leaders understood the European trade mentality and then brought forward older girls and women as well to engage in the 'trade' proposed by the Europeans. In the Samoan case, because of the high value they placed on the beads traded by the Europeans and the stories of previous contacts with *Papālagi* (through Tongans or directly in 1722 and 1768), this first contact on land was not a completely new discovery for the Samoans, hence their demand for beads.

But was it really 'in exchange for favours'? We must be careful about this. For Lapérouse, as for every European traveller, there was no doubt that any presentation of females was sexual in intent and was used by local inhabitants as 'trade' for obtaining material gifts. But we know from later descriptions (Edwards, Lafond de Lurcy) that the beads were considered by Samoans to be of great value and even a life-giving gift. Therefore it was not, for the Samoans'

---

[19] The French text is : *Les femmes dont quelques unes étoient très jolies offroient avec leur fruits et leurs poules leurs faveurs à tous ceux qui voudroient leur donner des rassades; bientôt elles traverserent la haye des soldats ...* . 'Rassade' is an old French word for coloured beads. 'Donner des rassades' is also used by Lapérouse in another passage to refer to gifts given to the chiefs ('Donner des rassades...Ces présents distribués', p. 461).

[20] See, for example, the narratives for Tahiti (Tcherkézoff in press-1).

[21] For Hawaii, see Sahlins (1985a: 2); for Tahiti, we have Fesche's Journal (Taillemite ed. 1968: 16 n.1).

part, a matter of profane greed for a decorative shining object. The whole context (including the question of the 'young age' of the 'girls' presented) cannot be reduced to a sexual trade in which women were merely satisfying (or were used by men to satisfy) a greed for European goods. More likely, the 'women' were asking for beads while the presentation of a 'young girl' for sacred marriage was being made or planned. This kind of demand conforms to what would be described in the 19th century as expected marriage gifts given by the male side (the category of *'oloa*) when the groom was a European. He was expected to provide all kinds of European goods and tools of the type introduced by the first adventurers and merchants.

Lapérouse also raises a different topic, that of a Samoan who struck a French soldier (I shall return to it later). In the following line, Lapérouse tells us how he himself, and presumably a group of his men, took the time to visit a village that was 'a couple of hundred paces away' from the watering place; he gives a very precise description of the spatial arrangement and of the houses, thus providing us with clear evidence that Samoan architecture as we know it today dates back at least to the 18th century.[22]

After filling the casks, and after the extensive tour of the nearby village, the French party went back to the ships. Nothing in the description allows us to decide if it was during this reception at the village that Lapérouse and his companions were presented with the scene described in the concluding chapter as the 'sacrifice' performed in the 'prominent hut'. It could instead—or also— have been at the next village where de Langle and his men spent the day as the presence of a village in this next cove is mentioned in the narrative. Or it could have happened the next day, on 11 December, when de Langle and his men returned to this village in the next cove, while Lapérouse stayed on his ship.

De Langle, who was in command of the second ship, had returned from his own excursion and told Lapérouse that before setting sail he would like to bring his ship in nearer to the next cove in order to take on a greater quantity of water and let his sailors, who were suffering from scurvy, get some rest on land. Meanwhile, night was approaching and there was no time left to attempt the landing. It was decided to wait until the next morning.

---

[22] 'While all this was going on quite peacefully, and our water casks were being filled, I thought I could walk a couple of hundred paces away to visit a charming village situated in the middle of a forest of trees that were heavy with fruit and which one could call an orchard; the houses were placed along the circumference of a circle some 150 toises in diameter, the centre of which was empty forming a wide public place covered with the finest grass; the trees shading it and the houses preserved a delightful freshness; women, children, old men had accompanied me, they all pressed me to enter their houses, and stretched out the finest and freshest mats ...' (Dunmore ed. 1995: 394). There follows a precise description of a *fale tele* (see note 4 above). We should note this very first description of a Samoan village, with *the pattern of a circle* (Tcherkézoff 1997a: 322, 327-8; 2003b: chapter 2, 5), centred on a *malae* consisting only of a grassy ground. The well-known 1850-1890 descriptions of villages and ceremonial houses by missionaries, 'consuls' and German ethnographers correspond to what Lapérouse had already observed in 1787.

At dawn on 11 December, de Langle and about sixty men landed with their longboats. This is where the so-called 'massacre' took place. Lapérouse stayed on board his ship, and later was given an account of what happened by the survivors who managed to get back to the ships. His journal cites only the narrative of Vaujuas, one of the officers who was with de Langle. Vaujuas reported that in the cove the same arrangements had been made as on the previous day during the water-fetching expedition when Lapérouse was present:

> We peacefully rolled out, filled and reloaded the water casks, the natives allowing themselves to be fairly well contained by the armed soldiers, there were among them a certain number of women *and very young girls* who made advances to us in the most indecent fashion, of which several people took advantage. I saw only one or two children there (*ibid.*: 407; my emphasis).[23]

Soon after, stones began to fly and the attack was launched.

These are Vaujuas's only lines on the topic of sexual encounters. If we relate these lines to Lapérouse's description of the 'sacrifice' in the 'prominent hut', we must conclude that the French 'took advantage' of the 'advances' of the 'girls' only. We can then interpret the 'advances' made by the 'women' as sexual gestures inviting the French to 'take advantage' of the girls. If the women were really 'offering' their own favours, there is no reason why the French would not have accepted them. And there is no reason why Lapérouse would have omitted to mention it in his concluding pages and decided to mention only the sexual act with the 'girls'.

Lapérouse adds nothing more than the lines already quoted from his final chapter. Thus, we cannot know whether his precise description of the 'sacrifice' within a 'prominent hut', with an 'old man' as the 'altar', which is given only in those concluding pages, refers to his own landing on 10 December or to what he was told by men of de Langle's party. In the latter case, it may refer to their first excursion on 10 December to the 'next cove' and/or to the landing on the following day whose events we have just seen described by Vaujuas. The hypothesis that the description does in fact relate to 11 December is supported by the fact that, in all his narrative, the only time when Lapérouse, through his quotation of Vaujuas, admits that some of the French sailors 'took advantage' of the sexual 'advances', relates to that day. A further argument is that Vaujuas talks about 'women *and very young girls* who made advances' (my emphasis), and that Lapérouse, when he describes the 'sacrifice' in his concluding chapter, mentions that the only females offered were 'young girls'.

---

[23] *Il y avoit parmi eux un certain nombre de femmes et de filles très jeunes qui de la manière la plus indescente nous faisoient des avances dont plusieurs personnes ont profité* (Dunmore and de Brossard eds 1985: 461).

7. A comparative hypothesis for Polynesia concerning the 'young girls' and the sexual presentations in first contacts

The mention of 'very young girls' (*filles très jeunes*) may appear surprising. In my view, it must in fact be a crucial piece of information that can assist us to interpret the whole context. But this view is built on a limited comparative study and it is offered here with due reserve as a working hypothesis that has yet to be tested against other existing data on first contacts in Polynesia.

If what these accounts can tell us about Samoan beliefs and practices concerned only sexual advances and a search for sexual pleasure, if indeed the goal were just to attend to the sexual desire of male travellers who had been deprived of female company for some time, then the presentation of young—therefore inexperienced—*and weeping* girls would be somewhat surprising. Similar scenes to those recorded in Lapérouse's narrative can be found in reports describing Tahitian, Maori, Tongan and Marquesan cases of sexual presentation.[24] The obvious conclusion is that the 'women' were bringing and presenting the 'girls', and that the girls were not presented for a kind of sexual hospitality offered to European sailors. Why were they presented? One possibility (is there any other?) is the kind of 'theogamic' scheme that has already been mentioned. Here I am following Sahlins's well-known hypothesis for Hawaii (Sahlins 1985a: chapter 1). But why the '(very) young' girls?

The Tahitian and Hawaiian, as well as the Samoan, data on *ritual dances* indicate that, in following a mythical theme, *only young girls who were virgins* were presented to the gods—and later to the *Papālagi* when these creatures appeared on the scene. Why such a presentation to the gods? Because in Polynesia the pre-contact mythical idea of a divine pregnancy, rightly identified by Sahlins as the central aspect of the mythical structure that Polynesians applied to the historical conjuncture of the first encounters with Europeans, had two characteristics which historians and anthropologists have tended to overlook. One of these was an essential requirement. It was also accompanied on occasions by another, paradoxical, aspect.

The essential requirement was the virginity of the girls. More exactly, the girls must not yet have given birth. Here, too, a specialised discussion is necessary. The critical issue—very far from any masculine Eurocentric representation of 'female purity'— concerned certain cosmological theories about the fecundity of the female blood within a 'closed' body, with a symbolic link between the blood in the veins, the hymeneal blood, and the menses. Bligh was told in Tahiti that when a girl of high rank married, the *first child* was the result

---

[24] In every case the girls' sorrow is noted; in every case the girls are brought in by adults; where the presence of the women is noted, the women both assist and sing; in the Tahitian case and one of the Tongan cases, the virginity of the girls is explicitly stated (Tcherkézoff in press-1). The only recorded case of the girl being held by older people while the sexual act is completed occurs in Samoa.

of a god's action (and not of the husband's). Cook and Banks were given to understand that girls were allowed to stay in the Tahitian dancing schools only as long as 'they did not have any connection with [a] man'. The question was not the integrity of the female body seen from a masculine Eurocentric point of view, but the ritual work of producing 'sacred children' through a first giving birth (the Samoan *tamasā*, the Tahitian *matahiapo*, etc.).

The other and paradoxical aspect was, apparently, that this mythical presentation of females to the gods was disconnected from the physical reality of pubescence. The girls were often rather young, for the reason just given, but, sometimes, they could be extremely young: the age range of '8 to 10 years old' is mentioned occasionally, in Tahiti and elsewhere (for instance, Dumont d'Urville noted it in the Marquesas, as we shall see in chapter 7). This applied to the dances and, apparently, some of the presentations to the *Papālagi* (Europeans). There are some indications that families tried their hardest to get their daughters into the dance schools (in fact schools where students received instruction about the entire cosmological system, as is well known in relation to the Hawaiian performance, the *hula*) as soon as possible. We can see that it did not matter greatly if the girls were of a very young age, since, as long as the scene was limited to dancing with the male gods and to the mythical idea of virgin birth (girls impregnated by the rays of the sun, etc.), the presence of pre-pubescent girls obviously did not present any practical contradiction to the mythical template.[25] But in the scenario of the first contacts with Europeans, things became different.

I hypothesise that, at the initiative of the chiefs and/or orators, *this whole* cosmogonic context, a complex mythical structure, was transposed onto the scene of the encounters with the *Papālagi*, and this therefore included those aspects of the female agent (the '(very) young' age) which have not been taken into account in previous discussions of the first encounters between Polynesians and Europeans.

But, at the time, the European visitors, who understood the scene only in terms of sexual hospitality offered to them, were astonished to see the young age of (all or some of) the girls presented. Of course, they could rationalise this observation in only one way. It gave them a further reason to conclude that the

---

[25] It is possible that real presentations of very young girls to chiefs also took place. One of Margaret Mead's informants mentioned sexual acts with girls under ten years old (Tcherkézoff 2003b: 371). This discussion leads to another point: in Samoa (but there is no reason why Samoa should be a unique case) there was also a belief, recorded in the 19th and 20th centuries, that the marriage ceremony (defloration) could provoke the beginning of menstruation, if the bride was pre-pubescent (*ibid.*: 373-84). Somehow, the very flow of hymeneal blood itself and the act of smearing it on the sacred cloth was symbolic of menstrual blood and of the divine action which had brought life to the girl's blood. Significantly, a belief clearly attested to in the 20th century, in Samoa, and also in Eastern Polynesian, was that the days on which impregnation was thought possible were right at the end of the menstrual period (*ibid.* and Hanson 1970).

main goal of the children's education, according to the 'customs' of the islanders, was the proper or even 'artistic' performance of sexual acts; in effect, an apprenticeship to what would later become the 'main preoccupation' and activity of their adolescent and adult lives. John Hawkesworth was an even more active proponent of this particular misinterpretation than Bougainville and his companions: in 1773, when he was given the task of editing for publication the manuscript of the narrative of Cook's first expedition, he unfortunately re-phrased Cook's and Banks's observations, noted in 1769 in Tahiti, to accord with this view. Being himself a director of a school, Hawkesworth misinterpreted what he read in terms of a whole educational-cultural value specific to these societies. Shortly afterwards, from his reading of Bougainville's book and Cook's narrative *as rephrased by Hawkesworth*, the French philosopher Voltaire concluded in 1775, and made it known to all Europe, that, since the French and the British 'observations are identical', this vision of the 'Tahitian custom' must indeed be true. The Western myth of Polynesian sexual freedom was then ready to spread in every direction. Twelve years later, Lapérouse's interpretation was already a consequence of that myth. Furthermore, the interpretations of Williamson a hundred and fifty years later and of Côté more than two centuries later, are no less due to the cultural misreading which created the Western myth of 'Polynesian sexuality'.

There is no further information on our topic to be found in Lapérouse's narrative and we can let his ships sail away. After 11 December, Lapérouse stayed for the next two days 'tacking in front of the bay' where the attack happened. On the morning of 14 December, he set sail for Upolu and had to cruise along the coast for the next days because of the lack of wind. Brief contacts were made at sea (see next chapter). On 17 December, he was in front of Savai'i. No canoes came out to make contact with his ships. On the evening of that day, the French lost sight of land and sailed towards the islands of 'Cocos' (north Tonga).[26]

---

[26] As this book was going to press the following came to my notice. For the shipwreck of the Lapérouse expedition on the reef of Vanikoro and the debate about the existence of survivors, see the recent archaeological findings (including the location of what appears to have been the camp of some survivors) by Jean-Christophe Galipaud (IRD, Noumea) et al. in *Lapérouse à Vanikoro: résultat des dernières recherches franco-salomonaises aux îles Santa Cruz*, Association Salomon (ed.), Noumea, Centre IRD, 2002, 113pp.

Chapter 4

Lapérouse, the Ignoble Savage, and the Europeans as 'spirits'

In the preceding chapter all recorded references to female sexual 'offers' were collated and discussed. The analysis of this material on the one hand provided conclusive evidence that, in the final pages of his account relating his encounter with the Samoans, Lapérouse was in fact describing a marriage ritual and not sexual hospitality, and, on the other, showed that there were no grounds to support the hypothesis of customary sexual freedom during adolescence.

But additional information about the encounter is necessary in order to provide an exhaustive study of the interactions between the Samoans and their *Papālagi* visitors. So let us now see what happened during the encounter in other contexts from day to day. The usual elements are present here as well: the offerings made to the *Papālagi*, the barter proposed by the Europeans and the eruption of violence.

1. Contacts at sea in the Manu'a group: 'barter' with men or 'offerings' to awesome creatures?

Barter and 'theft'

At the first meeting at sea, in the Manu'a group, the Samoans gave 'some twenty coconuts and two blue sultana hens'. In the same way as the Dutch in 1722, the French only understood the transaction as 'a little barter with us'. This is why they were not only rather surprised 'to obtain so little', but why they also became immediately convinced that the Samoans 'were, like all the South Sea islanders, untrustworthy in their trade'. This judgement was made because the Frenchmen noticed that, several times, the Samoans took the goods handed to them and rowed away as 'thieves', 'without handing over the agreed compensation. In truth these thefts were of minor importance and a few bead necklaces with small pieces of red cloth were hardly worth complaining about' (Dunmore ed. 1995: 387). Circumscribed by their vision of 'barter' and 'compensation', the French could only interpret the attitude of these Samoans as 'theft'. Hence the negative conclusion: 'untrustworthy in their trade'. The French were quite unable to conceive that, from their perspective, the Samoans were undoubtedly making *offerings* to these *Papālagi* and were glad to receive *gifts*—and even sacred gifts since these objects (the beads and the red cloth) were so highly prized, as we already know from Roggeveen's and Bougainville's narratives.

'First Contacts' in Polynesia

From the Spanish visits in the 16th century up until the various visits in the mid-19th century, the 'South Sea islanders' were categorised as 'thieves' by the Europeans. They could make no other interpretation of the fact that the islanders received from their visitors—and often seized for themselves when they climbed on board—a number of *Papālagi* objects and hastily jumped into the water or rowed away with their pickings. They could not imagine that this behaviour of seizing and snatching was in line with the mythological and ritual structure of the annual raid that the people perpetrated on the first fruits and on all signs of life send by the gods. The goods of the *Papālagi* were signs of life and fertility, but they had to be snatched because, in the whole of pre-Christian Polynesia, gods always had to be forced to surrender a part of their powers to human beings as they would not do this willingly. In Tonga, Tahiti, Hawaii and Aotearoa-New Zealand, the festive cycle linked to the seasons always included a ritual raid on the first fruits.[1] *Kava and cloth*

Shortly afterwards, the French noticed that a speech was addressed to them: 'an elderly Indian's harangue, who was holding a branch of kava in his hand and making a fairly lengthy speech' (*ibid.*: 388). Lapérouse's identification of the branch must have been accurate because, as we shall see, Vaujuas's report on the events in Tutuila also clearly mentions that the branches of *Piper methysticum* were used to welcome the French. This gesture on the part of the Samoans proves to us beyond any doubt that their attitude towards the *Papālagi* was an attitude of offering and not of bartering. From 19th-century and recent sources, we know that in Samoa a branch of kava was and is handed over only within the most ceremonial contexts, and then only to highly revered superiors: to sacred chiefs of the village or chiefs visiting from another village.

How did the French respond? By 'throwing him a few pieces of cloth' (*ibid.*) For them it was a way of showing thanks for what they took as a welcome and 'a sign of peace'. Lapérouse explains that he knew from his previous reading of 'several accounts of voyages' that such a presentation (the presentation of any kind of branch) was a sign of peace. Although he does not specify, he may have referred to Bougainville's and Cook's accounts relating to Tahiti, where the presentation of 'green branches' (mostly young banana trees) had been interpreted by the voyagers in that way. We can imagine that the Samoans, too, saw some logic in the transaction. It so happens that, according to their custom, the presentation of a branch of kava to the sacred chiefs was and is reciprocated with gifts of cloth (fine mats and barkcloth).

---

[1] For Tonga, see Ferdon (1987: 94) and Douaire-Marsaudon (1993: 813-38); for Tahiti, see Babadzan (1993: 235-51, particularly 245-6); for Hawaii and Aotearoa-New Zealand, see Sahlins (1985a: 112-20; 1985b; 1989; 1995: 22-31, 206-7). The corresponding context in Samoa was probably the *palolo* festival (the collecting of sea worms which come to the surface once a year).

Later on more canoes came 'to offer new exchanges': 'five hens, several items of their clothing, six sultana hens, a small pig, but above all the most charming turtle dove we had ever seen... [there follows a detailed description] this little animal was tame, ate in your hand and from your mouth' (p. 389). The description, which is quite precise, corresponds exactly to the multi-coloured fruit dove *Ptilinopus Perousii* (as it was named by the naturalist of Wilkes's expedition in 1838 with due reference to Lapérouse [*ibid*.: note 2]): it is the Samoan *manumā* (also called *manulua* and close to the *manutagi*). Again, the gift of this tame dove shows us the way in which the Samoans interpreted the nature of their visitors. From what we know in later years, this animal was restricted to high chiefs, being used by them as a sacred pet—these birds represented the link between gods and humans—and not as food.

Lapérouse adds, rather surprisingly, that his officer M. de Langle 'bought two dogs from the Indians, which were judged very tasty' (p. 390). Unlike the previous items, dogs were not used as gifts between Samoans (again, as far as we can judge from the 19th-century sources). But, through the Tongans, and from everything which had been passed on to them concerning the recent visits of the *Papālagi* (who came from Tahiti and who used only Tahitian words; Lapérouse did so himself, see p. 388), the Samoans may have known that, according to Tahitian custom, the gift of a dog was welcomed (we shall see another occurrence of this during the visit of Kotzebue).

Iron and beads

A final note about the contacts in the Manu'a waters brings us back to an observation made by Bougainville: 'we never persuaded them to accept our axes or any iron tool and they preferred a few glass beads which could be of no practical use to them to anything we offered by way of cloth or iron' (p. 390). Lapérouse is of course wrong to combine iron and 'cloth': his own observations and Bougainville's account had shown how much European 'cloth', and certainly the highly prized red cloth, was appreciated by the Samoans. But the remark about the lack of interest in iron, *in comparison with the great interest in glass beads*, is consistent with the observations made by Roggeveen and Bougainville.

Lapérouse adds finally that

> they sold us a wooden vase filled with coconut oil, which had exactly the same shape as one of our earthenware pots and which a European worker would never have believed could be made without a turning-lathe; their ropes were round and woven exactly like several of our watch-chains; their mats were very fine but their cloth inferior in respect of the colour and texture to those from Easter Island or the Sandwich Islands (p. 390).

Here again we find the barter theme: they 'sold us...'. We note, too, that Lapérouse follows Bougainville in devaluing Samoan barkcloth in comparison to the Tahitian barkcloth. From an ethnographic perspective, we can note that, among Samoans in 1787 (as will be observed in other Polynesian cultures), coconut oil was a valued offering as part of a category of gifts *used to wrap up the body* ('cloth': fine mats, barkcloth) and to make the body shine (which was pleasing to the gods). Indeed, later ethnographic information recorded in Tahiti and Samoa shows that cloth and oil were given to gods, to ancestors and—in Samoa—to the bridegroom's family during the marriage ceremony.

2. First landings (Tutuila, 9 December and 10 December) and first incidence of violence

'They bartered for beads… priceless diamonds'

The next contact was at sea off Tutuila. In the late afternoon of 8 December, writes Lapérouse, 'three or four canoes came alongside that very evening, they brought us pigs and fruit which they bartered for beads'. On the morning of 9 December, 'a large number of canoes had come laden with coconuts, pigs and other fruit which we bought with beads; this great abundance increased the desire I had of anchoring' (p. 391). Before nightfall a bay was found where anchor could be dropped. De Langle, commanding three armed boats, landed: 'the Indians lit a great fire to light up the assembly, they brought birds, pigs and fruit, and after staying an hour our boats returned to the ships'.

The next morning, 10 December,

> a hundred canoes were around the frigates with all kinds of provisions which the islanders were prepared to barter only for beads. For them these were priceless diamonds and they scorned our axes, our cloth and all our other trade goods' (p. 392).

Lapérouse landed with two long boats filled with empty casks to get water. The 'Indians' were now

> about two hundred, with among them many women and children, each one had with him some hens, pigs, pigeons, parakeets, fruit and they all wanted to sell them at the same time, which created a little confusion. The women, some of whom were very pretty, offered with their fruit and poultry their favours…

We are now familiar with the following passage: although Lapérouse had lined up his soldiers and kept the Samoans at a distance from the longboats and the watering party, even so these women 'soon crossed the line of soldiers'. The French did not resist ('Frenchmen have no weapons against such attacks') and there was 'some little disorder but Indians armed with sticks, whom we took to be chiefs, re-established order' (p. 393). A little later, Lapérouse again mentions that the Samoans 'had sold on our market over two hundred wood-pigeons as tame as puppies, that wanted to eat only from one's hand; they had also bartered the most charming turtledoves and parakeets as tame as the pigeons' (p. 394).

The presence of parakeets is confirmation of the ceremonial nature of these gifts. These birds (certainly the *sega*) were not raised as food, but for their feathers. A roll of red parakeet feathers (*'ie ula*) was for Samoans a most highly valued gift. In the 19th century, Augustin Krämer describes how, for example, these rolls were prepared, along with kava and food, and taken by a chief's orators to the family of his wife in another village (Krämer 1995: II: 98, 182n.). The final destination of the feathers was to adorn the fringe of the beautiful fine mats, here again an object used only for sacred gifts (Tcherkézoff 2002).

A 'real act of hostility'?

Meanwhile, a Samoan man managed to steal into the water, and 'he had climbed onto the back of our longboat, picked up a mallet and struck several blows on the arms and backs of our sailors'. Lapérouse, in front of this 'real act of hostility', decided that 'I should teach them to have a better opinion of us by punishing this Indian for his insolence'. He ordered 'four of the strongest [of his men] to throw themselves at him and hurl him into the sea' and had three pigeons 'bought' and 'thrown up in the air and shot down in front of the crowd' (p. 393).

What we should notice about this 'act of real hostility' is that, apparently, the Samoan man did not plan an attack in a European military sense; otherwise he would not have come alone and unarmed. Most probably it was an act of bravado staged for the benefit of his peers, or sheer curiosity about the physical nature of the newcomers: to dare to board a *Papālagi* boat, to touch them, to see if they could bleed... We must remember that this moment is the very first time that *Papālagi* had landed on Samoan land. It is the first time that they were quite near, they were no longer out there on the decks of their great ships, lofty and menacing, but standing on land or sitting in canoes (the longboats used for landing). This Samoan man was not the only one to make such an attempt. Lapérouse was told later by his companions that 'stones had been thrown at Mr Rolin, our senior surgeon; an islander pretending to admire a sword belonging to Mr Moneron had tried to snatch it from him' (p. 395, no details are given).

A 'chief' on board

After this close contact, some of the Samoans dared to approach the ship. At midday, when Lapérouse returned to the ship, after his extensive tour of the nearby village (no details are given besides the description already quoted of the houses and of the *malae*), he found there on the quarter-deck 'seven or eight Indians, the eldest of whom was presented to me as being a Chief'. The officers explained that they could not have prevented those men from coming on board unless they had used extreme violence against them, and that knowing that Lapérouse's orders were to avoid bloodshed, they let them do so. (Nevertheless, some violence may have occurred, if we are to believe one story told in the late 1790s to a beachcomber; see below, in relation to George Bass's visit in 1802). 'He added moreover that since the chief had come aboard, the other islanders who had preceded him were much quieter and less insolent'. If we can make an inference from other descriptions of encounters in Eastern or Western Polynesia, the mention of 'insolence' in the European narratives always referred to two kinds of behaviour on the part of the islanders: snatching things on board and/or touching the body of a European.

Lapérouse tells us that he gave 'a great number of presents to this chief' and had his men fire through planks and at pigeons, but 'it seemed to me that the effect of our weapons did not make much of an impression on him' (p. 396). The French thought that the Samoans were utterly ignorant of the fatal powers of muskets. This is of course an absurdity. If that were the case, the noise, the holes in the planks and the bleeding pigeons falling from the sky would have provoked precisely a reaction of terror that could not have been disguised. Much more probably the Samoans were perfectly aware, again through their connections with the Tongans, of the firing powers of the *Papālagi*, and this demonstration was no surprise to them. The Dutch and the British had made many such demonstrations for the benefit of the Tongans.

3. Second landing: the fateful day of 11 December 1787

'The happiness in such an enchanting site'

While Lapérouse was giving his presents to the chief, on that afternoon of 10 December de Langle came back to the ship and described his discovery of another cove that seemed extremely attractive. We must remember that, up to this moment, the French vision of Polynesia was heavily influenced by Bougainville's narrative on Tahiti. The manner in which Lapérouse commented on what he had seen up until then in Samoa makes this quite clear:

> What imagination could conjure up the happiness one would find in such an enchanting site, a climate requiring no form of dress; breadfruit trees, coconuts, bananas, guavas, oranges &c growing quite naturally offered these fortunate inhabitants a pleasant and healthy nourishment; hens, pigs, dogs living on surplus fruit allowing them to vary their diet. They had such wealth and so few needs that they scorned our iron tools and our cloth, and wanted only beads—with a surfeit of real goods they hankered only after frivolities (p. 394).

Thus, Lapérouse accepted de Langle's plan to bring a contingent of Frenchmen back to this cove.²

'Massacre Bay': twelve Europeans and thirty Samoans

The next day, a group of 61 men landed at the cove. Lapérouse had decided to stay on his ship. Until the survivors of the 'massacre' came back, Lapérouse did not know what was happening, as the cove lay out of sight. For de Langle, the difficulties began immediately. It so happened that the tide was unexpectedly low and, instead of manoeuvring in a large bay, as he had seemed to do the day before, the French officer had now to navigate a very narrow channel. The officer Vaujuas, who was with de Langle and who survived the attack, noted in his narrative that on arriving near the shore the French were welcomed by the Samoans who 'threw into the sea several branches of the tree from which South Seas islanders obtain their intoxicating liquor' (this clearly refers to kava: p. 406). Again, this gesture tells us much about the Samoan interpretation of the newcomers.

The casks were filled under the protection of a line of soldiers as was done during the first landing. Vaujuas adds that the Samoans were 'allowing themselves to be fairly well contained by the armed soldiers' and everything went 'peacefully' (p. 407). This is where he inserts the lines that we have already seen: 'there were among them a certain number of women and very young girls who made advances to us in the most indecent fashion, of which several people took advantage' (p. 407; no further details).

But when the French boarded their longboats again they were unable to move, probably because of the added weight of the casks. The boats were stuck fast. At least this was the case for the group that had landed with de Langle and who had brought the longboats very near to the shore, while another group, commanded by Vaujuas and Mouton, stayed further from the shore and afloat. The sailors who were with de Langle had to stay put and wait for the tide to come in. The other group waited with them. On seeing this, the Samoans waded into the water near where the boats were stranded; the water reached only to the men's knees. Moreover, a number of Samoan canoes, which had gone out to the ships for 'bartering', were now coming back to the cove. The French found themselves surrounded by several hundred Samoans. Shortly after, stones began to fly.

De Langle, as well as many others in his group, 'had only time to fire his two shots' and 'was knocked over' by the stones. Those who could not escape were

---

² The idea was also to get some more fresh water, although the supply for that day was good, and to bring back some provisions for the sailors suffering from scurvy; de Langle also wanted to put some of these sick sailors ashore, in the hope of restoring them to health more rapidly. At the time it was still believed that, at sea, it was the lack of the air found on land, and not only the lack of fresh food, that was the cause of the sickness (see *ibid.*: 432 note 1).

then clubbed. Eleven or twelve men died while the others who could make it to the farther longboats escaped; thus some fifty men made their way back to the ships. Besides the eleven or twelve dead among the French, some thirty Samoans fell, according to what Lapérouse learned from the survivors. But he did not record the Samoan losses in his main report of the incident, which he devoted entirely to expressing his sorrow for the fallen Frenchmen. This is why it is rarely mentioned; Lapérouse only alludes to it, among other things, in a letter written when staying at Botany Bay.[3]

4. The precious beads, again

Lapérouse's and Vaujuas's interpretations

According to Lapérouse—who had not been present and had to rely on the narrative of the survivors—the Samoans were busy climbing on the longboats that had been seized and 'breaking up the thwarts and everything else to look for the riches they thought we had, none of the islanders took much further notice' of the other boats, which were thus able to escape (pp. 399-400).

Vaujuas's description adds an important detail here, where once again the role of the beads appears central:

> Towards the end [of filling up the casks], the number of natives increased and they became more troublesome. This circumstance caused Mr de Langle to give up his earlier intention of buying some provisions, he gave the order to get back at once into the boats. But before then (and this I think is the primary cause of our misfortune) he had given a few beads to some kinds of chiefs who had helped to keep the islanders at a little distance; we were sure however that this pretence at policing was only play-acting, and if these alleged chiefs have any authority it is only over a very small number of men. These gifts being made to five or six individuals aroused the others' displeasure. From that moment a general murmur arose and we were no longer able to control them; however they let us get back into the boats, but a number of them followed us into the water while the others were picking up stones from the shore (p. 407).

Then, according to Vaujuas, de Langle fired into the air and tried to have the boats pushed into the water. The immediate result was that some of the Samoans held on to the cables, trying to retain the boats, while others began hailing stones on the French.

Lapérouse's interpretation was that the Samoans wanted to seize everything that the boats contained, but from the additional information in Vaujuas's narrative we can infer that this desire was probably exacerbated—or indeed

---

[3] The letter was appended to the 1797 publication of the narrative; I found mention of it in Jocelyn Linnekin's article on Lapérouse and the theme of the Ignoble Savage (1991: 7).

triggered—by the Samoans' observation that the landing party had brought with them their famous beads.

A Samoan view? The recipient of the gift

Let us take the interpretation a little further. It may well be that it was not just the showing of the beads, but also, or mainly, the way these beads had been distributed by de Langle that had played a critical role. It is almost certain that the Samoan men whom the French saw 'policing' the crowd during the filling of the casks were either the *taule'ale'a* of the village (unmarried non-chiefly men constituting 'the strength of the village' as they are called, who are in charge of the collective work and indeed are responsible for maintaining order) and/or some *tulafale* of low rank (orators). No high chief would have performed this low-status job of policing the crowd. That these men were chosen by the *Papālagi* to receive beads might have raised within the crowd the idea that everyone could, or indeed should, get some.

Furthermore, the idea of taking their sacred goods violently from the *Papālagi* was not something illogical according to the ritual ideology of the time.

5. A Samoan view? 'Killing' a Papālagi and a raid on the life-giving goods

This attempt at interpretation must also take into account what happened shortly after the fight. Lapérouse wished to make a punitive expedition and to destroy the whole village. In fact this proved impossible. He was unable to come in near enough to the cove with his ships. As for the idea of attempting another landing in the longboats, it was abandoned once the survivors explained to him that the stones used by the Samoans were thrown 'with such skill and strength that they had the same effect as our bullets and had the advantage over our muskets shots of following each other much more quickly' (p. 402). Nevertheless, the French spent two days tacking off the bay, full of anger. So we can well imagine how astonished they were to see that 'five or six canoes came from the coast with pigeons, coconuts and pigs to offer to barter with us'. As Lapérouse warns his reader, this 'will sound incredible' (p. 403). He decided to avoid firing his cannons at the men in the canoes; they stayed for a long time and only departed when Lapérouse, who wanted to disperse them, ordered his men to fire into the water near their canoes.

'Incredible'! How could 'murderers' return to engage in barter as if nothing had happened? Lapérouse may have been less surprised if he had known that shortly before, in 1778, a similar event had happened in Hawaii. After the Hawaiians killed Captain Cook on the shore, they rowed to the ships and asked when he would come back to visit them (Sahlins 1985a: 122). Their thinking was that Cook was not just a man but a certain temporary embodiment of their god Lono (see our chapter 9).

The whole context of these violent encounters can no longer be interpreted according to the instrumental European point of view that sees the battles generated by the contact situation as competition for goods or land. It must now be looked at from the Islanders' point of view. The *Papālagi* boats were bringing superhuman goods, they were 'boats of Tangaloa' (the great creator), as ritual chants expressed it in the Cook Islands (see chapter 9). The goods of the *Papālagi* were signs of life, and the way to gain possession of them was to snatch them in a raid.

Of course, this discussion about the Polynesian view of the *Papālagi* and about the pre-contact annual ritual cycles in itself requires a detailed study of various sources. At least, though, this hypothesis which links the *Papālagi* boats and goods to the pre-contact ritual cycle with its raids on the first fruits is more useful than the various attempts dating from the 19th century that were made, mostly by the English missionaries of the London Missionary Society (LMS), to 'explain' the Samoan attitude on that fateful 11 December 1787. Let us now turn to a review of these attempts.

6. The missionaries' interpretations: thieves from elsewhere

While in Samoa in the 1840s, the missionaries heard vague accounts memorised by the Tutuilans, which blamed another group of Samoans for the massacre (Krämer 1995: II: 16-18, Linnekin 1991: 18-20). As the story went, this offending group had supposedly come from another island and just happened to be at the cove where de Langle landed. One of these men had tried to 'steal' something from the boats and had been hit by the French. He had returned to shore and called his comrades. Or, in another version, he had been shot dead and the event had aroused the anger of his group. The missionaries were prepared to believe any such story, because it was impossible for them rationally to reconcile the opposed attitudes that were supposed to have characterised a single group of villagers: the initial attitude of 'welcoming' (including the supposed sexual welcoming) and the final attack and outright 'hostility'. Hence the idea that the incident involved two different groups. The first missionary to tell the story would have been the Rev. Archibald Murray who passed it on to Captain Bethune, who had visited Samoa in 1837-38 (but left no detailed narrative). The following year he in turn passed it on to Commodore Wilkes (Linnekin *ibid*.).

Later, the Marist priests, who of course remained faithful to the French view, recalled the initial interpretation as suggested by Lapérouse: the cause had been greed for European goods (Krämer *ibid*.). Theirs was a more developed 19th-century version of the 17th-18th-century cliché about the South Seas Islanders as 'thieves'. And they allowed for alternative nuances. Father Padel had asked questions—but sixty years after the event. According to him, there were Samoans who held that the reason for the attack was greed for the garments worn by the French. But he himself supported the other interpretation: that an individual and unplanned fight, probably because of a 'theft', had led to a general fight between the two groups.

7. A Samoan view? The Papālagi as 'spirits' and the virgins in the first line of battle

Padel added another comment, noting that some of the Samoans had told him that the French ships had been considered a piece of 'the land of spirits' (*terre des génies*). Hence, thought Padel, the feelings of the islanders must have been a mixture of 'admiration and terror' (*admiration et terreur*) so that in this tense context a small fight gave way immediately to a generalised fight (Monfat 1890: 84).

> Thirty years later, enlarging the scope of this discussion, Mgr Vidal, who stayed in Samoa in the 1880s, commented on Padel's interpretation. He held that for the Samoans the people on the ships were indeed 'spirits' ('*esprits*/aïtou') and hence dangerous beings; thus violence was an expected outcome: As soon as they [*Papālagi* ships] were seen from far away, the inhabitants gathered on the shore. They would sit and form half a circle; in the middle, a young girl of rank who enjoyed a reputation for chastity was chanting and moving her fan, as if she was moving the ships away, and she was uttering sacred words: 'Go away, go away from our peaceful land, you malignant spirits' (Monfat, *ibid.*).[4]

We have no way of ascertaining the conditions under which these stories were recorded by the Marists nor the exact phrasing of their indigenous informants. Nevertheless, the idea that in the first contacts the *Papālagi* were considered by the Samoans as some kind of spiritual beings is consistent with the kind of offerings that had been presented to them (we have already noted the presence of sacred birds and branches of kava).

As for the ceremonial virgin's chant, the description is too different from any of the Western clichés about the South Seas to be a sheer invention. But most significantly it is consistent with some later ethnographic data. The girl was chanting while the rest of the people 'sat' in a 'circle': it is likely that they were holding a *tapua'iga*, the silent gathering which I mentioned when discussing the lowered blinds of the marriage house and which was always required in the

---

[4] *Les Samoans, convaincus que l'universalité par les hommes se concentrait dans leurs îles, tenaient pour des génies (aïtou) les hommes des vaisseaux qu'ils voyaient passer au large. Aussitôt qu'on les avait signalés, tous accouraient sur le rivage. Ils s'y rangeaient en demi-cercle; au milieu, une jeune fille noble, ayant une bonne réputation de vertu, chantait en agitant un éventail, comme pour éloigner le navire, des paroles sacrées: 'Eloignez-vous, éloignez-vous de notre paisible terre, aitous malfaisants!'*

context of a difficult endeavour. Her central role and her words are also congruent with what we know of the role of ceremonial virgins in case of war: they would stand *in the front line* to attract the attention of the protective deities of the group and/or to be taken as wives by the enemy in case of defeat, thus allowing a massacre to be avoided and war to be transformed into alliance (Schoeffel 1979, 1995; Tcherkézoff 2003b: 395-7). We could also note Lapérouse's first observation when he entered Samoan waters. After a night in the channel between Ta'ū and Ofu-Olosega before any canoes had approached the ship to make offerings, the following day he noticed that there was a large group of Samoans, seated in a circle, who were observing them: 'when we were to windward of the island [of Ta'ū] we have seen some houses and a fairly large group of Indians seated in a circle under some coconut trees who seemed to be enjoying quite calmly the spectacle we offered them' (Dunmore ed. 1995: 386).

Finally, the conclusion that the Polynesians did not wish to have the *Papālagi* on their shores, or at least did not wish to have them there for long, is consistent with some of the data recorded about other first contacts. There are descriptions of how the Tahitian and Hawaiian chiefs did indeed try to have their visitors' stay shortened (Tcherkézoff in press-1). The presence of the *Papālagi* certainly inspired both 'admiration' *and* 'terror' in the Samoans, as Vidal expressed it. But once that sense of 'admiration' was fulfilled through receiving (or seizing) the *Papālagi* objects (and, in a number of cases, through having girls impregnated by the *Papālagi* powers), the possibility that these creatures, who delivered death (they had shot dead a number of their fellows) as well as life, would stay forever or for a long time was quite understandably a source of 'terror' for them. This was not the kind of religious terror and awe that leads to prayer and submission, as in the attitude shown towards the great gods, the main *atua* such as Tagaloa. Rather, it was the kind of terror that leads to combatting an enemy, and *this was precisely the Samoan attitude towards their 'spirits' (aitu)*. This attitude was recorded several times by the early LMS missionaries: people would call the *aitu* to come and 'fight' when they attributed some misfortune to the spirits' actions.[5]

If we assume that the Samoans considered the French to be some kind of *aitu*, then a feeling of terror leading to fighting may have arisen among them. Perhaps it grew even stronger when they saw that the French, although they had boarded their longboats now that the episodes of gift-giving (and possibly impregnation) were over, *were not moving away*. The French were just waiting for the tide, but to the Samoans it might well have looked as if their visitors were there to stay.

---

[5] See Stair (1897: 181-2, 228-9, 231, 265-6). In 1983 I was told by eye witnesses that such things occurred in the 1970s.

8. Other interpretations

The story of a beachcomber

We should also take careful note of what a beachcomber from Tonga, who came to Samoa in the late 1790s, told George Bass, the first visitor to arrive in Samoa after Lapérouse (Bass was getting supplies for Botany Bay and came once, sometime in the period from 1802 to 1806. The beachcomber related an incident that was said to have taken place on Lapérouse's ships: a Samoan chief had several times offered a roast pig to one of the French officers, but as the latter was busy with his work, he became annoyed with the Samoan and struck him with his sword, causing him to bleed (Linnekin 1991: 16). In contemporary Samoa, to strike a chief offering a pig would indeed be an immediate declaration of war. If we pay any credit to this story, it may be remembered that the attack in the cove began *after* the return of the numerous canoes that had been 'bartering' at sea with the ships, and therefore after this deeply offending incident. But this could only have been an additional reason for the Samoan assault on the stranded party. The main context that we should keep in mind is the European (mis)handling of the beads and the Samoan will to seize those signs of life.

Augustin Krämer's interpretation: 'Où est la femme?'

Augustin Krämer, the noted German Samoanist of the late 19th century, offered his own interpretation of the killing (1995: II: 16-18). Kramer had formed the impression, during his various trips in the archipelago, that the Tutuilan boys, by comparison with the men of the other Samoan islands, were particularly violent: 'among the Samoans indeed those of Tutuila are the most savage and brutal'. He also thought that these boys could not accept the fact that the girls had been 'sold' by their relatives to the French, and so a fight had started immediately. In fact, it seems that this interpretation had been proposed by some earlier European visitors, in relation to certain 'stereotypes of French national character' (Linnekin 1991: 16). It provides an interesting case of a European, non-French, projection of their own negative feeling towards the stereotype of the French male as sexual conqueror onto the Samoan males. And indeed, this stereotype was already well-entrenched by that time: one of Bougainville's companions, Felix Fesche, wrote in 1768 that, in front of the Tahitian women, he and his mates had to keep up their reputation as ardent lovers that Frenchmen enjoyed all over Europe.[6]

Interestingly enough, Krämer adds that, from what he could observe in Samoa in the 1890s concerning the behaviour of female adolescents, he could not

---

[6] ...*la galanterie et de la bouillante ardeur si généralement reconnue dans les françois*, Journal de Fesche, in Taillemite (ed. 1968: 12-13 note 2).

possibly accept Vaujuas's suggestion that the girls offered themselves willingly. In 1787, the girls whom Vaujuas wrote about must have been forced to act as they did. They would have to have been 'sold' by their 'greedy' parents, and all of this must have angered the young men.

There are several steps to Krämer's interpretation. First, Krämer himself reveals the preconception informing his interpretation that the problem had arisen from the sexual offers purportedly made by the young girls. As he sees it, 'in the South Seas', female sexuality is frequently at the root of conflict:

> It is well known that Samoans are thieves, as will be enlarged upon further below under Jurisprudence [Krämer is introducing his second volume of ethnography]. Accordingly one must not consider acts of violence among them impossible, such as Cook, the *Duff* and the *Port au Prince* on which Mariner served, suffered among the Tongans. However here it would indeed seem to me that, as is unfortunately so often the case especially in the South Seas, the issue was in part 'où est la femme?' [in French in the text: 'where is the woman?']. For de Vaujuas states p. 256: 'Il y avait parmi eux un certain nombre de femmes et de filles très jeunes qui s'offraient à nous … (There were among them a certain number of women and very young girls who offered themselves…)' [Krämer quotes the 18th-century publication of Lapérouse's narrative] (Krämer 1995: II: 16).

Krämer then advances his argument about the violent character of the Tutuilans who would have been angered to see that the girls were sold. Finally, he is able to conclude that 'the blame must be sought on both sides'.

We can, of course, discard all of this as a fantasy on the part of the German Doctor, *but we must remember his observation relating to the 1890s*: in his time at least, young women could not be seen offering themselves to strangers. In Krämer's account, these 'excesses' (the 'girls who offered themselves' alluded to by Vaujuas)

> must have enraged the Samoan young men. For this was not a case of girls voluntarily debasing themselves, as de Vaujuas claims; La Pérouse points that out too clearly [in the previous lines, Krämer quoted Lapérouse's description of the 'sacrifice' in the 'prominent hut']; the young Samoan women do not loosely give themselves to strangers today any more than in former times, but those were forced by their greedy relatives to sell themselves (*ibid.*: 17).

A similar observation about the reserved attitude of Samoan adolescent girls would also be valid for contemporary times (Tcherkézoff 1999, 2003b: chapter 7). Although Krämer reflected male bias in his belief that everywhere and 'especially in the South Seas' the ultimate reason for fighting among men would be '*la femme*', at least he had noted the contradiction between the description of the only sexual scene found in Lapérouse's narrative (where the 'girls' are forced to act as they did) and the remarks by Lapérouse and Vaujuas that the girls 'offered themselves'.

9. Noble and Ignoble Savage…
'I am angry with the philosophers…'

The killings of that fateful 11 December provoked a century of discussions which sought an explanation for the outbreak of violence (Krämer *ibid.*; Linnekin 1991) and also contributed to the creation of the image of the Ignoble Savage . I have already cited Lapérouse's words describing the Samoa he had seen on his first landing: the tone was entirely in the vein of Bougainville's vision of the Noble Savage. But, after the attack at the cove, the impression now conveyed was somewhat different. It was not so much that the Garden of Eden and Land of Abundance theme was abandoned but, rather, that the philosophical conclusions about the 'Savage' which could be drawn from it were different. Jocelyn Linnekin has drawn our attention to a letter written by Lapérouse in Botany Bay two months later:

> I am… a thousand times more angry with the philosophers, who so enthusiastically extol savage nations, than with the savages themselves… Lamanon [the naturalist of the expedition, who was among the 11 dead]…, told me, the evening before his death, that these men were better than ourselves… A navigator… ought to consider the savages as enemies… whom, without sufficient reason, it would be… barbarous to destroy; but whose hostile attempts he has a right to prevent (Linnekin 1991: 8).

Lapérouse thereby inaugurated the transformation of Bougainville's stereotype of the Noble Savage into an equally stereotyped Ignoble Savage, whose image was to persist for many decades. Already, in his narrative, Lapérouse wrote that right after leaving Tutuila where the 'massacre' occurred, he decided to abandon his previous interest in the 'history' (the customs) of the Samoans and to avoid any further landing in the Samoan archipelago:

> I decided that I would land only at Botany Bay in New Holland where I proposed to build the longboat I had on board. But for the advancement of geography I felt that I ought to explore the various islands [of the Samoan group] I would come upon, accurately determine their latitude and longitude, communicate with these people through their canoes which, laden with foodstuffs, travel two or three leagues from the coast to trade with vessels, and I left to others the task of writing their history which like that of all barbarous people is of slight interest. A 24-hour

stay with an account of our misfortunes is sufficient to describe their atrocious ways, their crafts and the products of one of the most beautiful countries of the world (Dunmore ed. 1995: 405).

The tone was left for posterity: Samoans are barbarians with 'atrocious ways' but they nonetheless inhabit a 'most beautiful country'.

The London Missionary Society and the Marists

Linnekin's study of 1991 also showed clearly how Lapérouse's complete narrative, published in France in 1797, was widely read in Europe and immediately translated into several languages. One of the consequences was the publication of numerous fictional or biographical writings about Lapérouse which were in great demand among the general public—the complete disappearance of the expedition in 1788 had created an aura of mystery around the French captain which was to last for forty years. All of this literature of course accorded a central place to the 'massacre' in Tutuila, and heavily exploited Lapérouse's theme of a contrast between a beautiful country and its ferocious inhabitants (Linnekin 1991: 11 and *ff.*). This literary tradition began at the beginning of the 19th century and continued for fifty years.

But, after the late 1840s, the interpretation of this event changed with the advent of the English missionaries. In their writings and commentaries it now appeared that the Samoans had been provoked by the French, a view which they passed on to Commodore Wilkes who visited Samoa in the period when Anglo-French rivalry was increasing in the Pacific. Furthermore, by the mid-1830s Samoa had become a common port of call for commercial vessels and had thus acquired a reputation as a peaceful and hospitable country. Accordingly, after this we find that the dominant theme of the Anglophone literature was that the Samoans were not to be blamed for what had occurred at the cove: they were a peaceful people, and what happened there was due to the French having shot and killed one of their number (*ibid.*: 21).

We have seen that the Marists of the time, even though they still held to the French explanation of Samoan greed for European goods, also inferred a kind of unfortunate escalation, from an unplanned single assault to a general attack, in a context of tension and terror (the Samoan considered the new visitors as 'spirit'-like creatures). Among the Marists, Padel also repeated what he has been told by the Protestants: the theory of the offending Samoan group from another island. But he added a remark that could only have been invented by a French visitor. It shows us that, for the French visitors at least, the 'massacre' was still viewed in the mid-19th century as a recent event. Padel wrote in 1847 to his superior in France: My dear Revered Father,

> ... we left Taïti at the end of August and touched the first islands of the *vicariat central de l'Océanie* on the 7th of september [1846]; the first land

we touched was the island of Tutuila; we stayed there about eight days. We were not really welcomed: our cross on the flag at the top of the mast and the presence of eight catholic priests were more than enough to distress the protestant ministers who are the masters here. Moreover our French identity was a source of fear for the natives; in this island, but in a different bay than our mooring place, Lapeyrouse's second in command and eight or nine sailors have been massacred; hence the name of the place: *baie des Assassins*. Since that time, the natives always fear that the French will come back to avenge the death of their compatriots. Yet those who perpetrated this assassination are not the inhabitants of this island, but some young men of Upolu who were here to make war and who, taken by the feeling of victory as if they were drunk, massacred these men whom they found unable to defend themselves (Padel, letter of 15 April 1847, in Girard ed., 1999: III: 336; my translation).[7]

Of course, one can guess that it was the LMS missionaries, and British beachcombers working with them, who did their best to make Padel and his comrades believe that, as French people, they would not be welcomed by the 'natives'. But apparently Padel took the bait without question.

The Noble and the Ignoble... gender: 'Diana' and 'Hercules'

Let us return to Lapérouse, who decided that he did not want to make any more landings or spend any more time describing the Samoans' 'atrocious ways' of living. It was with this vision of the Ignoble Savage that Lapérouse left Tutuila island and sailed past Upolu and then Savai'i, following his westward route. But his comments on the contacts made at sea off the coast of these Samoan islands reveal an interesting nuance. Standing offshore from Upolu, on the morning of 14 December [we] were surrounded by numberless canoes loaded with breadfruit, coconuts, bananas, sugar cane, pigeons and sultana hens; but very few pigs... [In the afternoon, we were] opposite a very wide plain filled with houses from the hilltops down to the edge of the sea ... roughly in the middle of the island ... The sea was filled with canoes ... As there were women and children among them it was almost a sure sign that they harboured no evil intentions, but we

---

[7] This is the first reference to the event by Padel: it is not yet his own interpretation but only what he hears from the Protestants on his arrival: *Nous sommes partis de Taïti à la fin du mois d'août, et nous sommes arrivés aux premières îles du vicariat central d'Océanie le 7 du mois de septembre; la première terre que nous avons rencontrée, c'est l'île de Tutuila; nous y avons relâché, et y avons séjourné une huitaine de jours. Nous n'avons pas été trop bien reçus dans cet endroit; la croix qui flottait au haut de notre grand mât et la présence de huit prêtres catholiques étaient plus qu'il n'en fallait pour émouvoir les ministres protestants qui y dominent. De plus notre qualité de Français effrayait les naturels; dans cette île, mais dans une baie différente de celle où nous étions mouillés ont été massacrés le second et huit ou neuf matelots de Lapeyrouse, qui donna à ce lieu le nom de baie des Assassins. Depuis ce temps les naturels craignent toujours que les Français ne viennent venger la mort de leurs compatriotes. Ce ne sont cependant pas les habitants de cette île qui ont commis cet assassinat, mais des jeunes gens d'Upolu qui étaient allés là faire la guerre et qui dans l'ivresse de la joie que donne la victoire massacrèrent ces hommes qu'ils trouvèrent sans défense.*

had strong reasons not to trust in it any longer ... they preferred a single bead to an axe or a six-inch nail. Among a fairly large number of women I noticed two or three who were very pretty and one could have thought had served as a model for the charming drawing of the Present Bearer of Cook's third voyage, their hair was adorned with flowers and a green ribbon like a head-band plaited with grass and moss,[8] their shape was elegant, their arms rounded and very well proportioned, their eyes, their features, their movement *spoke of gentleness whereas those of the men depicted ferocity* and surprise. In any one sculptor study the latter would have been taken for Hercules and the young women for Diana, or her nymphs whose complexion would have been exposed for quite some time to the effects of the open air and the sun (*ibid.*: 412-13; my emphasis).

We can see that the Ignoble Savage type, which, after 11 December, came to dominate Lapérouse's characterisation of the Samoans, was largely *restricted to the men*. Lapérouse was certainly influenced by Bougainville's book and the narratives of Cook and Banks (as re-phrased by Hawkesworth). In his references to the Samoan women, the descriptive style continues to resemble Bougainville's. This is another strong indication that we are entitled to take the influence of Bougainville's views into account when we read Lapérouse's and Vaujuas's allusions to the 'favours offered' by Samoan females. Indeed, the Western ideal-type of the lascivious-but-innocent *vahine*, invented by Commerson in 1769 and by Bougainville in 1771, and confirmed by Hawkesworth in 1773, was the vision of Polynesian women that would overwhelm all others in the Western imagination. This was particularly true for the French, even a captain lamenting the 'massacre' of his men.

17 December: offshore from Savai'i, no canoes came out, probably because the French were now more distant from the coast. So ended this memorable French visit to the Samoan islands—the first encounter on land, the first time that Samoans were killed by the *Papālagi*, and the very start of Western misconceptions about the sexual behaviour of Samoan girls.

---

[8] Once again we see the Samoans coming forward with ritual decorum, as in 1722 (the girl with the necklace of blue beads), and as in 1791 (headdresses and necklaces made from flowers, see next chapter).

Chapter 5

The turn of the century: from Edward Edwards (1791) to Otto von Kotzebue (1824)

1. June 1791: Edward Edwards searching for the mutineers

In 1790, the British Admiralty learned about the mutiny on the *Bounty*. Captain Bligh and his companions, who had been disembarked by Fletcher Christian in Tongan waters, made their way in their small canoe to the East Indies and from there back to England. The authorities immediately set up a punitive expedition. Captain Edwards's orders were to search for the mutineers and bring them back alive to stand trial. At the beginning of the 20th century, Basil Thompson located Edwards's journal and published it together with the narrative of the surgeon of the expedition, George Hamilton (only the surgeon's narrative had been published in 1793 and, since then, had never been republished) (Thompson ed. 1915).

Edwards's 1791 Pacific route took the ship *Pandora* through the Tuamotu group towards Tahiti (missing by a few miles the sighting of Pitcairn Island, where Fletcher Christian and his mates had taken refuge, while other mutineers had stayed on in Tahiti). Edwards captured the mutineers who were in Tahiti and took the small boat, a tender, that the men had just built (their plan being to attempt a crossing to the East Indies). He divided his men between the *Pandora* and the tender. Then he left Tahiti with the intention of finding out which of the islands might be sheltering the other mutineers. Those who had stayed in Tahiti did not know where Christian had gone, since Christian himself had not had a precise plan when he left Tahiti. But Edwards searched for the missing mutineers in the wrong direction, constantly westwards, in the Society group, in the Cook Islands, in Tokelau, and then in Samoa.

On arriving in Samoan waters, the *Pandora* lost sight of the tender. The ship sailed to Tonga, came back to Samoa, then sailed to Uvea (Wallis), the Santa Cruz Islands, Torres Strait, and the East Indies. The last part of the journey was made on small boats after the *Pandora* was wrecked on the Great Barrier Reef off the north coast of Australia.[1] Meanwhile, the tender left Samoa for Tonga and then

---

[1] Four mutineers out of the fourteen taken prisoner in Tahiti, and more than thirty members of the initial crew of a hundred and thirty men were drowned. The most famous survivor among the prisoners is James Morrison, whose journal, written in London while awaiting trial (Morrison told his narrative to a minister who wrote it down), has become the main source of information on pre-contact Tahiti.

it too sailed westwards, through the Fijian islands, before reaching the East Indies, where the whole expedition was reunited.

The contacts in Samoa were very brief (Thompson ed. 1915: 49-52, 55-6, 129-31, 136, 166).

2. Contacts at sea

'Had never seen a ship before'

On 18 June 1791, Edwards sighted Savai'i. Sailing along the north coast on the following day, looking for fresh water, he came in contact with 'the natives' (apparently at sea) and was able to ask for information about the location of rivers. He also had contact with a Tongan named 'Fenow' (Finau). Edwards noted that this man was 'a relation of the Chief of that name of Tongataboo Fenow said he had seen Captain Cook and English ships at the Friendly Islands, and that the people of this island [Savai'i] had never seen a ship before they saw the *Pandora*'. Hamilton adds: 'Here we learned the death of Fenow, king of Anamooka, from one of his family of the same name, who had a finger cut off in mourning for him' (a practice observed by many travellers among Tongans, as we shall see in Lafo nd's narrative). 'After trading a whole day with the natives, who seemed fair and honourable in their dealings', the expedition went on to Upolu on 21 June.

Samoans approached in canoes, and Edwards noted that they had 'dye[d] their skins yellow'. This was turmeric, used on ceremonial occasions (van der Grijp n.d.), for example on the bride's skin for the marriage ceremony. The question then arises: had the Samoans applied the dye for the purpose of meeting the *Papālagi*'s boat? Hamilton also notes that 'Some of them had their skins tinged with yellow' and adds: 'Neither sex wear any clothing but a girdle of leaves round their middle, stained with different colours. The women adorn their hair with chaplets of sweet-smelling flowers and bracelets, and necklaces of flowers round their wrists and neck'. If this were so, we must conclude that the presentation was ceremonial, for no such floral adornment of the head and the neck was used for ordinary fishing. Moreover, as the *Pandora* stood in open sea and not in the lagoon, the presence of women cannot be explained by fishing activities, since they did not normally participate in any fishing beyond the lagoon (assuming that what we know of 19th-century practices can be applied retrospectively to the 1790s).

A woman on board

Hamilton continues his narrative:

> On their first coming on board, they trembled for fear. They were perfectly ignorant of fire-arms, never having seen a European ship

before.² They made many gestures of submission, and were struck with wonder and surprise at everything they saw. Amongst other things, they abounded with aromatic spiceries, that excelled in taste and flavour the most delicate seed-cake. As we have never hitherto known of spices or aromatics being in the South Seas, it is certainly a matter worthy of the investigation of some future circumnavigators.³ We traded with them the whole day, and got many curiosities. Birds and fowls, of the most splendid plumage, were brought on board, some resembling the peacock, and a great variety of the parrot kind.

One woman amongst many others [in the canoes] came on board. She was six feet high, of exquisite beauty and exact symmetry, being naked, and unconscious of her being so, added a lustre to her charms; for in the words of the poet, 'She needed not the foreign ornaments of dress; careless of beauty, she was beauty's self'.

Many mouths were watering for her; but Captain Edwards, with great humanity and prudence, had given previous orders, that no woman should be permitted to go below, as our health had not quite recovered the shock it received at Otaheite [where numerous sexual encounters had occurred, followed by venereal disease in the crew; see *ibid.*, p. 123]; and the lady was obliged to be contented with viewing the great cabin, where she was shewn the wonders of the Lord on the face of the mighty deep. Before evening, the women went all on shore, and the men began to be troublesome and pilfering. The third lieutenant had a new coat stolen out of his cabin; and they were making off with every bit of iron they could lay hands on.

It now came on to blow fresh, and we were obliged to make off the land. Those who were engaged in trade on board were so anxious, that we had got almost out of sight of their canoes before they perceived the ship's motion, when they all jumped into the water like a flock of wild geese; but one fellow, more earnest than the rest, hung by the rudder chains for a mile or two, thinking to detain her.

This evening [21 June] at five o'clock, we unfortunately parted company, and lost sight of our tender.

---

² On the contrary, this attitude of fear *once on board the ships* proves that they had heard the stories of contacts with the *Papālagi*. As for the ignorance of firearms, I have already commented on this European misconception.

³ It was probably the *palusami*, cooked coconut cream in taro leaves, which is considered a delicacy, an offering of value (as such it may have been offered to the *Papālagi*), and which has a kind of spicy taste, although there are no 'spices' in Samoan cuisine such as peppers or chillies.

'The savages attacked them'

After cruising for two days in search of the tender, the *Pandora* left for Tonga. Months later, when the crew of the *Pandora* met up with the crew of the tender in the East Indies, they learned that the contacts between the Samoans and the latter continued and took a violent form. Edwards makes no mention of it, but Hamilton notes in his narrative:

> They informed us, [that] the night they parted company with us, the savages attacked them in a regular and powerful body in their canoes; and their never having seen a European ship before, nor being able to conceive any idea of fire-arms, made the conflict last longer than it otherwise would; for, seeing no missive weapon made use of, when their companions were killed, they did not suspect any things to be the matter with them, as they tumbled into the water. Our seven-barrelled pieces made great havoc amongst them. One fellow had agility enough to spring over their boarding-netting, and was levelling a blow with his war-club at Mr. Oliver, the commanding-officer, who had the good fortune to shoot him.
>
> On not finding the ship next day, they gave up all further hopes of her, and steered for Anamooka.

We have no other details about this attack, but we can at least apply to it the same kind of analysis that I used to interpret the violent incident involving conflict between a group of Samoans and members of Lapérouse's expedition.

Tutuila: 'they have murdered them'

The *Pandora* returned to Samoa on 14 July. Due to southerly winds, Edwards had decided to renew the search for the tender and try to obtain some information about the mutineers. Edwards now sighted the Manu'a group. Several canoes approached and some of the Samoans tried to board the ship. He prevailed upon them to do so. The Samoans 'brought very few things in their canoes except cocoanuts [sic], which I bought, and then gave them a few things as presents before they left the ship, and after making the necessary inquiries [about the mutineers] as far as our limited knowledge of the language would permit us…'. Edwards then proceeded to the West, arriving at Tutuila on 15 July: 'We found the same shyness amongst the natives here as at the last islands, but a few presents being given to them they at last ventured on board'. No details are given. Edwards mentions that he made his usual 'inquiries after the *Bounty* and tender and making presents to our visitors', then steered to the west and again neared the shores of Upolu.

Hamilton adds just one detail: 'Here [at Tutuila] we found some of the French navigator's clothing and buttons [which the British probably noticed being worn by some of the Samoans]; and there is little doubt but they have murdered them'. The first edition of Lapérouse's journal was not yet published and it is unlikely that Hamilton would have received a copy from the French authorities. He was therefore just guessing and he was not to know the extent to which the label of 'murderers' applied to the Samoans would soon spread throughout Europe, once the story of the 'massacre' became known following the 1797 French publication of Lapérouse's journal.

The beads

For his entry of 16 July, Edwards notes that his crew 'had frequent communication with the natives, but could get no information' (relative to his search). He then notes the presence of the beads: 'we saw a few of the natives with blue, mulberry and other coloured beads about their necks, and we understood that they got them from Cook at Tongataboo'.

Without adding anything further, Edwards indicates that he stood southwards and was again making for Tonga. Hamilton provides nothing more by way of information. No landing is precisely described and we may infer that all contacts had been made at sea.

3. 1791-1824: the avoidance of Samoan shores

Apparently, for thirty-three years, practically no *Papālagi* boat came to Samoa. The story of the 'massacre' of 1787, widely known after 1797, kept everyone away.

There had been a brief call at Tutuila, in 1802 (Gilson 1970: 67) or maybe a little later (Linnekin 1991: 16), by George Bass, 'supplier of provisions to Botany Bay', formerly a surgeon, who came on a British ship and who 'found the Samoans he encountered friendly and receptive'. This visitor met there an Englishman who had deserted from an American vessel at Tonga (Eua) in 1795 or 1796 (about which no other details are given); we have noted that by that time, Tonga already had a number of beachcombers, but not Samoa. This man told Bass that the Samoans were 'friendly' and that the killings of 1787, which resulted from a misunderstanding, were an isolated event (Linnekin *ibid.*).

From a journal whose author is unknown, we know that in 1823 a call was made at the Manu'a group, by a party in search of provisions, and one man was nearly kidnapped by the Samoans (Gilson *ibid.*), as Jackson was seventeen years later in the same place (we shall return to Jackson's narrative). In 1824, a whaler called at Samoa, also for provisions, and according to Gilson (*ibid.*), it was 'probably the first vessel of its kind to do so'.

Thus, apart from the brief visit of Bass, it seems that after Edwards's visit in 1791 no visitors came until 1823 and 1824, the year which marked the arrival of Kotzebue. Edwards had dared to come because he still had no information as to Lapérouse's fate (we have seen how his surgeon Hamilton had only put forward as a hypothesis the possibility of a murderous attack on Lapérouse's crew) and in fact it was his official duty to visit all the island groups, whatever the cost, in his search for the mutineers of the *Bounty*.

4. April 1824: Otto von Kotzebue. First exchanges

The year that saw the first whaler calling at Samoa for provisions was the same year that a Russian expedition of exploration led by Kotzebue visited the region, although Kotzebue passed by rather rapidly and stayed cautiously out at sea. The Russian captain reminds his readers, at the beginning of his narrative of his encounter with the Samoans, that these people were supposed to be 'most ferocious people... [who] murdered de Langle ... although they [the French] had loaded the natives with presents' (Kotzebue 1830: 258). But, as he suffered no general attack, his own account, once published in English in 1830, made a useful addition to the few whalers' accounts of the mid-1820s-1830s and let it be known that, after all, a peaceful contact with the Samoans was possible.

Kotzebue had already sailed twice around the Pacific, with Krusenstern and with Chamisso. On this first voyage around the world as a captain, he sailed westwards after his Tahitian stay, came in sight of the Manu'a group on 3 April 1824, and turned towards Tutuila, following the route of Lapérouse. He anchored at the same place, off Asu. Expecting to see hundreds of canoes surrounding him, as had been the case for Lapérouse, he was surprised to see just one canoe approaching with only three men on board. He made signs to them to come aboard his ship.

Only one of the Samoans responded. He cautiously climbed along a rope, just to have a look on the deck, but did not jump down. He presented some coconuts and received 'as a counter-gift a piece of iron which he pressed against his forehead as a sign of his gratitude, inclining his head a bit in doing so'. Kotzebue correctly interpreted the 'sign of gratitude'. This is a formal way of receiving a gift and is still practised today. It means that the receiver thereby considers himself to be 'wrapped-in' by the gift of the donor (see chapter 10). It is a way of giving the donor a superior position. One can also think of the 'abasement' rite, *ifoga*, where the self-abasing party places a fine mat over his head (Tcherkézoff 2002).

The Samoan then began a long and impassioned speech, pointing alternately at the land and at the ship. Soon many other canoes arrived: 'we were soon surrounded by the descendants of the barbarian murderers' (Kotzebue 1830: 258). A number of Samoans climbed along the side of the ship but the Russians forced most of them to stay out, with blows and the threat of using their bayonets. Only a few were allowed to jump on board. According to Kotzebue, they immediately rushed to seize everything they could and showed what they had found to their companions who stayed down in the canoes. All of them were shouting.

But there was one of their number on board the ship who adopted a very formal attitude. Several times he raised the gifts above his head, and uttered a number of sentences that made all the other Samoans burst into laughter. Kotzebue believed, wrongly, that he was a chief. More probably he played a kind of clowning role, in the well-known Samoan style of *fale aitu* ('house of spirits'). A further indication that this was the case was the gesture of one of his companions who nipped the bare arm of one of the sailors and made signs which seemed to Kotzebue to suggest 'that such food would be very palatable to him'. Inevitably, Kotzebue then introduces a long passage on the horrors of cannibalism. He was unaware of the fact that the Samoans did not practice cannibalism, but that many of their legends depict spiritual beings (*aitu*) or mythological chiefs who would have done so in the distant past. The gesture witnessed by Kotzebue might again have been a *fale aitu* joke.[4]

Kotzebue also notes that 'the glass beads they obtained from us they immediately hung over their neck and ears' (*ibid.*: 265; no other details). So it seems that the beads were still in great demand. But, apparently, this was also true of iron, since the first gift of a piece of iron was formally acknowledged: the few beachcombers must have made the Samoans aware of the usefulness of iron tools.

5. The presence of 'women': young virgins

About the women, Kotzebue says only:

> In the canoes, we saw a few women who were all very ugly: these disagreeable creatures gave us to understand that we should by no means find them cruel. They were ... as little dressed [as the men were]. Their hair was cut short off [*sic*] with the exception of two bunches stained red, which hung over their faces (p. 266).

His judgement—'ugly, disagreeable'—is of course in the vein of Bougainville's account of Samoa. Kotzebue also came to Samoa after Tahiti, and the approving references to the latter served to cast all the other islands in an unfavourable light. He also had in mind that he was among 'the most ferocious people... who murdered...' and who appeared to practise cannibalism. As well, probably in the light of Lapérouse's account, he was convinced that the 'women' were ready to grant their favours.

---

[4] Similar behaviour on the part of the Kanak people was reported by the French when they arrived in New Caledonia-Kanaky in 1793, and Bronwen Douglas's interpretation is that the gestures, the facial expressions, whistling and the like, showed that an act practised in local wars was here being performed as an ironic display (Douglas 1999a: 81).

It is quite possible that the females made some sexual gestures, which 'gave us to understand…'. But who were these 'women'? The last remark on their hair 'cut short off with the exception of two bunches' gives us the answer. From 1830, the year of the first missionary visit, and through the 19th century, we know with complete certainty that *this very specific style of hairdressing was used only for virgin girls once they were ready to be presented as a bride to a high chief.*[5] We will meet this type of presentation again in the narrative of Captain Erskine.

We can surmise that, had he landed, Kotzebue would have been invited to the same 'marriage' scene that the French of 1787 experienced. In any case, we should remember that the 'women' who, from the canoes, were making some kind of gestures that the Russians interpreted as sexual advances, were virgins presented as brides. This would seem to have applied to all of these 'few women' whom Kotzebue 'saw in the canoes'.

6. More exchanges and moral judgements

In his narrative, Kotzebue then returns to the bartering context. He notes that the 'few fruits' brought by the Samoans 'were exchanged for pieces of iron, old barrel hoops, and glass beads; on the latter especially they set great value'. The Samoans also began to show their wooden clubs and to ask for glass beads, but Kotzebue immediately thought that an attack was being prepared. More canoes were approaching. Some of the Samoans were standing up in the canoes and making long speeches. Kotzebue thought that he heard an 'angry' tone and saw 'menacing gestures', especially when 'at length the screaming and threatening with clubs and doubled fists became general'. He decided to set sail (pp. 266-7).

'Animal-people'

As this point he had been very close to ordering his men to shoot: 'One slight signal from me would have brought death and destruction upon those animal-people' who were screaming and waving their clubs (*ibid.*).

The language of Kotzebue, even if motivated partly by his impression of the 'massacre' which the French had suffered, also reminds us that we are no longer in the 18th century with Bougainville, Cook or even Lapérouse. A new trend characterises the very end of the 18th century and the entire 19th century. It saw the rise to dominance of a racist discourse in which some human 'races' were considered less human than others. This was new and in sharp contrast to the prior meaning of 'races' in the sense of human 'varieties' or 'nations'. For the application of these theories to the Pacific, Dumont d'Urville's invention of the

---

[5] See Schoeffel (1979: 407-10, 426) and Mageo (1994) for references to various sources for this style of hairdressing.

name 'Melanesia' in 1831 (the 'Black Islands', the islands of dark-skinned people), is of course the classic illustration of this major shift in European thought.[6]

Other exchanges and the beginning of the barter

A short stop off Tutuila, again at sea, allowed a number of canoes to come near the ship. The occupants offered their catch of fish. Then Kotzebue anchored off Upolu and the same offerings took place, but no other details are given (p. 268). Then, on 5 April, Kotzebue came near the shore of the small island of Manono, between Upolu and Savai'i.

Numerous canoes arrived, with offerings of fruits and pigs. The Samoans seemed not to understand why Kotzebue prohibited them from climbing on board. They attached their offerings to the ropes that were hanging from the deck. In one hour, '60 large pigs', lots of fowl and 'vegetables and various fruits' were obtained 'for some pieces of old iron, some strings of glass beads, about a dozen of nails. The blue beads seemed to be in highest estimation'. Two strings, and sometimes only one string, of these beads were enough for a large pig (pp. 275-6). The Samoans also brought with them tamed pigeons and parrots, which sat on the hand of the owner.

At some point, a 'great canoe' arrived, surrounded by smaller ones,

> which drew the attention of all the natives. They called out: 'Eige-ea Eige' and hastened to give place. The canoe was rowed by 10 men; in the fore part, on a platform covered with matting, sat an elderly man, cross legged, holding a green silk European parasol. His clothing was a very finely plaited grass-mat, hanging like a mantle from his shoulders, and a girdle round his waist. His head was enveloped in a piece of white stuff (pp. 277-8).

The Chief came on board with three attendants and asked for the 'Eige' (p. 279). He was not tattooed, as Kotzebue noted, which could indicate either that he was the supreme chief of Tonga, *Tu'i Tonga*, visiting Samoa (the word that has been given here for 'chief' was Tongan: *eiki*)—which is doubtful—or a very high-ranking Samoan chief, such as Tamafaiga (Krämer [1995: II: 22] and Gilson [1970: 71] both advance this hypothesis). Tamafaiga indeed reigned over Manono at that time; shortly after this meeting, Tamafaiga was succeeded by Malietoa Vaiinupo who himself received the pioneer missionary John Williams in 1830. No one could touch these very high chiefs and make them bleed (as always happened during tattooing), and the same thing applied to the Tu'i Manu'a, the highest chief of the Manu'a group of Samoan islands.

---

[6] See Blanckaert (1998), Douglas (1999a, 1999b, n.d.); Tcherkézoff (2003a, n.d.), and the following chapter on Dumont d'Urville's visit in Samoa.

The use of Tongan speech to foreigners, something which other visitors to Samoa also noted in the same period, as we shall see, may be due to the fact that the Tongan language was, to the Samoans, the language of relationship with the outside world, since all the non-Samoans in Samoa were either Tongans or European beachcombers who came mostly from Tonga. At that time, even if European visits to Samoa were nearly unknown, Tonga, known as the 'Friendly Islands', had long been an established and, indeed, a much appreciated port of call for Europeans.[7]

Kotzebue tells us that this elderly man made him understand that he was the Chief of the 'Flat Island'. This name is already used a few pages earlier by Kotzebue, who follows Lapérouse's terminology: it was Manono island (p. 271). The Chief had 'three fine pigs, which he called *boaka*, and some fruits' deposited at the feet of Kotzebue (the word used for 'pig' is Tongan). He also took hold of Kotzebue's elbows and raised them, while saying—in English this time—'very good!' The Russian captain gave him hatchets, a coloured silk handkerchief and two strings of blue beads. Using signs, the Chief asked if these items were for him and, being assured that they were by Kotzebue's reply, he jumped up and repeated 'very good, very good'. He put the strings of beads inside a finely woven basket that he had with him and took out of this basket a Spanish dollar. Kotzebue understood that the Chief wanted to know if this could be used to buy more beads.

We can see that the idea of barter and of commerce was now established in Samoa. But it came from Tonga. When Kotzebue asked the Chief where he had got this dollar from, the Chief pointed to the south. Kotzebue thought that this indicated 'Tonga'. The Chief seemed to explain that he had navigated there, that he had met a boat from whose 'Eigeh' he had got the dollar and the parasol. The Chief also indicated by signs that he knew the effect of guns and muskets: he pointed to a gun, said 'puaa' imitating the sound, then closed his eyes and let his head hang down (p. 282).

7. 'Very good waraki' (women)

The Chief then pointed at the shore and took Kotzebue over to the railing. He pointed at 'the women' in the canoes 'whom he called waraki, shook his head,

---

[7] At the end of the 18th century, the international centres in Polynesia were of course Tahiti and Hawaii, and then Tonga. The story of European contact in Tonga dates back to 1616 and 1643 (with the Dutch). It continued with the visits from Wallis (1767); with Cook's expeditions (1773-74, 1777) which brought in all sorts of iron tools, European textiles, and domestic animals as well as new edible plants; and with the French and the Spanish in the early 1790s. The first deserters from American merchant ships appeared in 1795, the first missionaries in 1797. Five years later, there were at least fifteen Englishmen, with firearms, living in Tonga, and some Tongans had already experienced life in Australia (Ferdon 1987: 281-5). If the Samoans were still the sole inhabitants (together with some Tongan visitors or 'adopted' settlers) of the Samoan islands, they had nonetheless heard innumerable stories about encounters with the *Papālagi*. These they heard from the Tongans, and hence most probably in the Tongan language.

and said "not very good". Then he pointed to the island and said in a kind tone: "very good waraki"…'. The word 'waraki' is certainly not a Samoan word nor does it appear to resemble any Tongan word. As this Chief seemed to have had close contact with *Papālagi* in Tonga, he could have heard English-speaking visitors describe the women or girls who were presented to them as 'whores'.

Kotzebue made him understand that he was not interested. The Chief again took hold of his elbows and several times said: 'Marua! Marua!' Then, from the canoes, all the Samoans joined in repeating this same word. The word recorded by Kotebue could be the Tahitian word for 'thank you', *mauruuru roa*, brought to Tonga by the Europeans. We have already noted that most of the visitors who came to Western Polynesia stopped first in Tahiti. The LMS missionaries followed this path five years later, extending their action to the west from their base in Tahiti, and using the Tahitian and Rarotongan languages.

8. Last exchanges

Off Savai'i, Kotzebue also made a brief stop, noting only one incident among the exchanges that took place. One man, from his canoe, seemed to offer a pig. A bag was handed down to him containing European gifts. When the bag was hauled up, there was no pig inside but a dog instead. Kotzebue thought he was being cheated. But here again, it is possible that the man thought it wiser to use a Tahitian form of gift (dog meat was considered a delicacy in Tahiti, but not in Samoa). Or indeed, as on the first day, this may have been a *fale aitu* kind of joke. The evidence is too scanty to allow us to draw any firm conclusions.

So ended the last visit to Samoa of a round-the-world scientific expedition of 'discovery'. The next expeditions to call at Samoa, although still pursuing scientific studies, would also have a military aspect, in whole or in part (Dumont d'Urville, Wilkes). Besides these organised and heavily armed expeditions, another kind of visit was to become frequent and would have a lasting impact: the commercial vessels of the merchants and the whalers had already begun penetrating Samoan waters.

Chapter 6

Commercial vessels. Another French visit: Lafond de Lurcy

1. Whalers and merchants of the 1820s-1830s

Besides the scientific expeditions in the Pacific, which were under way by the 1760s, issuing mainly from England and France, and the military-diplomatic expeditions, which began in the late 1830s, a whole fleet of whalers and trading vessels invaded Pacific waters from the end of the 18th century and during the first half of the 19th century. The whalers extracted oil from the harpooned whales by heating. The merchants were searching for sandalwood and bêche-de-mer (and furs in the North Pacific), which they took to Manila and Canton, and returned with tea. Soon after, the trade for coconut oil, first transported in its liquid form, later as copra (dried flesh of the nut), greatly increased shipping traffic. The Pacific thus suffered an invasion by these ships beginning in the late 1790s. But as we have seen, the Samoan archipelago remained relatively isolated for some time. Until the late 1820s and early 1830s, ships looked elsewhere for provisions of water and food during their whaling campaigns or their search for sandalwood. Kotzebue's narrative of his visit in the mid-1820s, published in English only in 1830, was the first 'discoverer's' narrative to inform captains that the contact could be pacific. Although Kotzebue still described the Samoans as the 'most ferocious people', he himself had never been attacked by them.

But even before the publication of Kotzebue's account, tales from whalers had begun to change the reputation of Samoa. Thanks to the detailed study of Rhys Richards (1992), we know for certain that the traffic within Samoan waters remained very low until the mid-1830s. In the previous ten years there were less than a dozen visits. But those returning on these ships told that the reputation of Samoa was perhaps inaccurate and that, in any case, the islands there had much to offer in terms of provisions of wood, water and fresh food. In 1834 and 1835, the number of recorded visits suddenly jumped to forty-two . The first permanent establishment of missionaries in Samoa also occurred in the year 1836. This followed on from short visits by Methodists from Tonga in the late 1820s and the pioneering visit of John Williams for the London Missionary Society in 1830 and 1832, not to mention the presence of the small group of Tahitian and Rarotongan 'teachers' left in Samoa by the same Williams from 1830.

Ships brought beachcombers (seamen quitting their job or escaped convicts from Botany Bay); and the news that established adventurers were present brought new ships, because captains knew that they would find people who could act as interpreters and intermediaries with the local inhabitants. Beachcombers made their profit in two ways: by offering their services to captains of incoming ships; and living off the backs of the islanders by exploiting the prestige that accrued to them from their specialised knowledge (iron instruments, firearms) and activity (military adviser and firing man in local wars, blacksmith, carpenter) (Ralston 1977, Campbell 1998).

In Samoa, from 1836, missionaries posed a challenge to these adventurers, as they now themselves assumed the role of intermediaries and interpreters. From 1839, newly established 'consuls' from Great Britain or the United States also began to play their part. Britain initiated the trend in Samoa with a 'vice-consul', W.C. Cunningham, while the 'consul' (and former missionary) George Pritchard was based in Tahiti. Later, when Pritchard was expelled by the newly French colonial administration, he took up the position in Samoa.[1] From 1839, regular trading was active. Commercial exports from Samoa were taking place in 1842: J. C. Williams, the son of John Williams, the pioneer missionary, established himself as a trader and began to export coconut oil. The German firm Godeffroy and Son arrived in the late 1850s and started the copra-drying process. The commercial plantation system was established in the mid-1860s.

But let us return to the 1820s. The first commercial ship was a whaler, which apparently came in 1824 but no documentation is available (Richards 1992: 20). The second or third visit would have been in 1827. It was made by Captain Benjamin Vanderford on the *Clay*.

2. 1827: Vanderford

Barter was conducted with the Samoans, at sea, off Tutuila and Upolu, by the crew of the *Clay*. Captain Vanderford's account remained within the tradition of reporting inaugurated by Bougainville and reinforced by Lapérouse. Vanderford accordingly found the Samoans more 'savage' than the Tahitians and lacking any physical beauty. He even quotes Bougainville to that effect. His conclusion was brief regarding Tutuila: 'The natives were very distant and shy. Never a woman with them. At 4 p.m. a person of some note among them came on board, the first that would venture'.

This man appeared to have been 'kissing the Captain's feet'. If this really happened, we may see in his gesture a sign that, for the Samoans, the *Papālagi* had now become a closer kind of creature to themselves. The 'kiss' signifies a relationship between humans—keeping in mind that throughout Polynesia what was often called a 'kiss' by Westerners was in fact contact between the nose of the person saluting, and either the nose, or the hand, or the feet of the person

---

[1] And was briefly succeeded by his son William, the author of *Polynesian Reminiscences*, to whom we owe the second earliest first-person account of a Samoan marriage (see chapter 3, section 5).

saluted, according to equality (nose to nose), or inequality, of rank. The Samoan then proceeded to tell a long story. By picking out some words, the captain had the impression that the story told of men killed on the other side of the island (the violent encounter with the French in 1787?). The captain, of course, found in this man all the signs of extreme 'savagery', even thinking that he heard his story make reference to cannibalistic meals. And so, 'not liking our new friend, we sent him away'.

Captain Vanderford noted that the canoes around his ship were filled with armed men. He has something to say about the 'ugliness' of the men, and adds for the women:

> The women were tolerable. Two of them those of Oupora and Oyolava [Upolu and Tutuila] had crooked hair. It is true that many of them and some of them [sic] looked very savage. At first sight (recollecting Bougainville's misfortune together with many wonderous [sic] sailor's tales [Vanderford is probably confusing Bougainville and Lapérouse]) one is led to look at them with a sort of horror (Richards 1992: 21).

The 'crooked' hair of two of the women could mean that two virgins were presented as brides-to-be—as with Kotzebue—although the vagueness of the term used by the captain does not allow any certitude.

3. 1827: Plasket

In 1827, the whaling ship *Independence* also came to Samoan waters. The Captain, William Plasket, noted in his log-book:

> 3 January. Began trading… We have now on board the greatest chief of these islands, his name is Matta-tow-ata, and about 26 girls of the first quality. Canoes all around the ship trading.
>
> 4 January. Off the island of Otogga. Employed in boiling breadfruit, Off west end of Surva-ya. Commenced trading as usual.
>
> 8 January. Employed in discharging the ladies and sent them ashore. Also the head chief of these islands. Took our departure (Richards 1992: 22).

The Chief apparently came with a whole *aualuma* (the ceremonial group of unmarried girls of his village), as was customary when receiving visitors from another village or another island. The captain does not mention any sexual proposals, which is not surprising because no instance of a collective sexual offering to visitors by an *aualuma* has ever been mentioned by any source. And if we were to suppose that the puritan attitude of these captains—indeed a number of them were Quakers—would prevent them from mentioning any such happening, we would then have to ask why in this case the Captain mentioned the presence of these '26 girls of the first quality' at all instead of omitting the whole episode.

4. April 1831: Gabriel Lafond de Lurcy

It is not unexpected that it was again a French captain who would explicitly recall Bougainville's scenes of the 'New Cythera' in relation to Samoa, but it comes as a surprise that his conclusion bears on the stark difference between the two places. Lafond insists that the need for him to make a factual report obliged him to admit that Samoa presented none of the opportunities that greeted Bougainville's men in Tahiti:

> The women were the joyous children of nature described with such charm by Bougainville and Lapérouse. All seemed to suggest that they would be found with little virtue, but my task as a historian forces me to add that the only favours they accorded our seductive lovelaces on board were inconsequential frustrations.

An unexpected visit

Lafond de Lurcy lost his ship in a storm in Tongan waters and embarked on the *Lloyd*, a whaler bound for Guam. In April 1831, the boat called at Apia for provisions of water and food (Lafond de Lurcy 1845: 5). The visits of foreign ships had by then become common enough for a system of piloting to be in place. A man came up in his canoe to meet the *Lloyd* and to guide her through the reef. He spoke in Tongan (using the words '*lélé/covi*' ['right/wrong'], to correct the direction taken by the whaling boat; *ibid.*: 6). Was he Tongan, or did he think that speaking Tongan would make him better understood? Numerous canoes approached the ship and the Samoans seemed quite self-assured.

Lafond disembarked and met two British men who 'had been residing in the place for long time'. These men pretended that they had been taken by force by the Samoans of Tutuila when their boat had called there. Lafond suspected that this was a pretext to hide what could have been a desertion, and he refers to rumours about a British whaling ship that had lost seventeen men in Apia a few months before. We can see that in 1830-1831 Samoa was already an appealing place for beachcombers.

Descriptions

Lafond visited the houses (*ibid.*: 10, 16); noted the tattooing of the men (from the navel to halfway down the thigh, *depuis le nombril jusqu'à la moitié des cuisses*, p. 17) and the hair style (long for men, very short for women); wrote down estimates of population, as given to him by his European informants (in thousands: '*Sevaï*' twenty-five, '*Opouzou*' twenty-two, '*Tou-Tou-ila*' twelve, '*Manona*' nine, '*Apolima*' five, '*le groupe seul de Manoua*' twenty-five); and established a short list of words. His text also contains a description of such items as canoes and tools.

5. Beads and girls. 'Grandeur et décadence' of the gift of beads

Lafond and the captain, a man named How, went on to visit the village of Faleata. Lafond observed the canoes with sails and outriggers, the beautiful canoe of the Chief, '35 *pieds*' long, the fishing gear, the wooden kava bowls (*ibid.*: 15-18). They were received with great hospitality and gave the Chief some metal objects. The Chief was pleased, made the formal gesture of thanks by bowing slightly and lifting the gifts above his head, and then asked for blue beads: 'the chief asked us for Souma-mea-Houni, that is, blue glass beads, about as big as a fingertip, which were very much in demand in these islands'.[2]

Lafond and How then saw that six or eight beads were enough to acquire a large hog, and they bartered in this way for several of them. They made the Chief understand that they had more of these beads on board. As soon as the people assembled there understood what was being conveyed, all the men sent their children to go and take all kinds of provisions to the ship. Lafond adds:

> The chief went even so far—I will confess his shameful act—that he offered us two of his daughters, and he added that, in return for some of these beads, there wouldn't be a single mariner among us who couldn't find a wife for himself on the island (*ibid.*: 16).[3]

This is the only other passage in Lafond's description where the question of sexual contacts is mentioned.

It is important, of course, to note the second sentence before trying to interpret the first one. This was not an offer of sexual hospitality for one night. It was an offer of marriage, in the sense that in Samoa in those days it signified that the girl's family was trying their best to have her marry a man of superior rank. Between Samoans, the young girl would be offered to a chief, the family hoping to beget progeny that would link them to the chief's name. The family would also receive a large share of those marriage gifts that came from the male side: cooked food, implements for house building, canoe building and so on. This scheme had been applied by Samoans to the *Papālagi* and to the *Papālagi*'s riches (*'oloa*), which included food (salted beef, tins of biscuit), implements (metal

---

[2] *Le chef nous demanda des Souma-mea-Houni, c'est à dire des grains de verre d'un bleu porcelaine, gros comme le bout du doigt, qui étaient alors très recherchés dans ces îles.* (As there is no Samoan word referring to beads that resembles the awkward 'Souma-mea-Houni', Lafond's transcription could indicate that he heard the Samoan chief say: *se aumai mea uma!* 'would you bring all of it!'; 'mea-Houni' could have been *mea umi* 'long things', referring to the beads 'about as big as a fingertip', in which case the whole expression could have been *se uma mea umi* '[bring] all the long things!'.)

[3] *Le chef alla même, je l'avouerai à sa honte, jusqu'à nous offrir deux de ses filles, et il ajouta que, moyennant quelques-uns de ces grains de verre, il n'était pas un de nos matelots qui ne pût prendre femme dans l'île.*

tools and European cloth) and also those famous beads. I have already hypothesised that this was the context of the scene described by Lapérouse.

It is my contention that these beads had long been famous, possibly since 1616 as a life-giving gift, when the Dutch killed a number of Tongans and then gave gifts of beads to the survivors. In fact, Lafond noted that when they went on and called at the Samoan island of Savai'i two British residents ('escaped, I think, from Botany Bay') told him that 'Samoan chiefs immensely value these beads, and prisoners in wars can purchase their freedom with a necklace of about twenty of these beads' (*ibid.*: 24).[4]

This comment by Lafond is arguably the most important observation about the social importance of these beads in Samoan history. It also turns out to be the last time that these beads are mentioned at all. Soon after, the two-century-long story of the blue beads will come to an end. It is not clear exactly how long the high value of these beads lasted, but sources indicate that in Samoa, by the mid-1840s, it was European cloth and rolls of material which were most valued, certainly under missionary pressure and the new rules of dress for church services. Not only did beads lose their prominent role in the exchanges with visitors, but they were no longer even mentioned.[5] A new era was beginning. By that time, according to what the missionary Mills said to Captain Home, who visited in 1844, there were sixteen missionaries in Samoa (they were highly concentrated: there were ten just for the island of Upolu), and there were also some sixty 'Englishmen deserters, all of bad character' (Home 1850). The same year saw the opening of the Malua Theological College, near Apia, where all the Samoan 'teachers' were to be educated.

6. Last days of Lafond's visit

In Savai'i, Lafond and his party again met with a Tongan, who introduced himself as 'Tangata Tonga' and told them he was a member of a crew that navigated regularly between Tonga and Samoa. Lafond mentions this *'grande pirogue double'*, the same, he says, as one he had seen previously in Tonga, and which, according to his memory, had been coming from Fiji with 'about thirty people' on board (*ibid.*: 25-6). He also mentions that the Tongan had his two little fingers cut at the first joint. This is a common occurrence in Tonga, Lafond adds, and is practised as a sign of grief when one loses one's parents or one's chief.[6]

---

[4] *Les chefs samoens attachaient une importance immense à ces grains de verre, et [que] les prisonniers faits dans les guerres pouvaient racheter leur liberté avec un collier d'une vingtaine de grains.*
[5] See Home (1850: 220, 223; his observations of 1844) and Worth (1852: 542; his observations of March-May 1846).
[6] Lafond provides specific details about the man they met: '*les petits doigts étaient coupés à la première phalange*'; and then generalises: '*Vous savez messieurs que la plupart des habitants de Tonga ont les deux premières phalanges des petits doigts de chaque main enlevées. Ils se les coupent en signe de douleur lorsqu'ils perdent leurs chefs, leurs parents, et les mères ont même la barbarie, à la mort d'un chef vénéré, de faire à leurs enfants cette cruelle opération avec leurs dents, la blessure étant ensuite cicatrisée avec des charbons*

Lafond's description of their landing in Savai'i is also worth noting (*ibid.*: 20-3). The ship was left out at sea and they embarked on two small boats. Immediately, 'two hundred young and old women swam towards us'. The only comment made by Lafond is that the women manifested a great 'curiosity' and that it was difficult to prevent an invasion by these 'sirens'.[7]

Men also surrounded them, sitting in canoes or swimming. Lafond allowed the 'Chief', escorted by a young man, to climb on board; both were swimming among the others because the force of the waves had prevented them from sitting on their canoe. Food was offered to the Chief. Soon after, other Samoans managed to climb onto the ship. But when the food left by their Chief was presented to them, they refused to eat it and did not even want to drink from the coconut which 'the *arii*', as Lafond says, had in his hand.[8] Showing great curiosity, the Samoans seemed to discover a number of things, including mirrors, as if for the first time.

The young man accompanying him hid from the Chief for a time and gave Lafond and How to understand that he wanted to stay on board and to depart with them. How refused and Lafond felt that the young man seemed to express an immense sorrow:

> The savage was very vexed at the lack of success of his request; for he seemed to want to hide from the old chief when he was asking this of me, and tears glinted in his eyes, when he left with his venerable companion, proving to me that in the Samoas, as everywhere, there are men who instinctively have a burning desire to travel (p. 23).[9]

We will never know the name of this Samoan who had wanted to emulate the fate of 'O-mai' and 'Aotourou', the two Tahitians who, sixty years earlier, had convinced Cook and Bougainville respectively to accept them as passengers on the trip back to Europe. Indeed, in all these Polynesian-European first contacts, there were Polynesians who wanted to make a 'voyage of discovery' and to

---

ardents' (pp. 25-6). In 1791, the surgeon Hamilton, who was with Edwards on the *Pandora*, saw this operation performed on the young Tongan virgins who were forcibly presented to the crew of the *Pandora* (Tcherkézoff in press-1).

[7] *Nous eûmes toutes les peines du monde à nous défendre contre l'invasion de ces sirènes qui manifestaient à notre égard la curiosité la plus vive. Les hommes ne tardèrent pas aussi à nous entourer ...*

[8] Lafond is using the Tahitian word *arii*, or transcribes in Tahitian fashion the Samoan word for 'chief', *ali'i*. We have here a clear instance of the rule relating to the well-known Polynesian taboo regarding sacred chiefs: no one could touch them or anything they had touched (out of fear of sickness and ensuing death). They were 'untouchable', *tapu* (in Samoa: *sā*), because of the *mana*-type powers that were incorporated in them.

[9] *Le sauvage fut vivement contrarié du peu de succès de sa requête; car il avait paru vouloir se cacher du vieux chef lorsqu'il me faisait cette demande, et quelques larmes que je vis briller dans ses yeux, lorsqu'il nous quitta avec son vénérable compagnon, me prouvèrent qu'aux Samoas, comme partout, il est des hommes que tourmente un instinct voyageur.*

discover the *Papālagi... Comme partout, il est des hommes que tourmente un instinct voyageur.*

7. Conclusion on Lafond's visit

Lafond's various descriptions and notations, such as on the life-saving use of blue beads, indicates to us that he had time to make some inquiries and to converse with the people, at least with the newly-established European residents mentioned in his narrative. If these Westerners had really seen in Samoa a generalised free-sex pre-marital life, they would have undoubtedly talked about it with Lafond de Lurcy. He himself must have asked questions of this kind, since he tells us that he had in mind Bougainville's description of Tahiti and that he had been surprised to find such a difference in Samoa.

Lafond's account will be confirmed by Dumont d'Urville's own surprise in 1838. But Dumont d'Urville will account for this difference as being entirely due to missionary influence (exercised permanently since 1836). Yet, Lafond's account—based on his observations of 1831, before any discernible missionary influence[10] —bears testimony that Dumont d'Urville's explanation of this difference in 1838 cannot be sustained.

8. 1832: John Stevens

A young surgeon on a whaler, John Stevens quit his ship when it called at Manono (one of the two small Samoan islands situated between Upolu and Savai'i). The missionary Williams met him on his arrival in 1832 (during Williams's second visit) and saw in him 'a respectable young man'. In his journals, Williams tells us how Stevens described to him his own arrival in Samoa:

> When he first went on shore among them, the females gathered around him in great numbers, and some took their mats off before him, exposing their persons as much as possible to his view. Perceiving him bashful, the whole of women [sic], old and young, did the same and began dancing in that state before him desiring him not to be bashful or angry as it was Fa'aSamoa, or Samoan Fashion (Moyle ed., 1984: 232).

In order to understand what happened, one must read Williams's description of the Samoan dances of the time, when a village group welcomed visitors from another village. It was the 'most obscene' dance, says Williams, that the Samoans practised at that time. But his description, far from mentioning any sexual offers and sexual hospitality, shows how groups of adolescents did indeed strip off during the final moments of the dance and had a competition to produce the most outrageous and hilarious display in their telling of sexual jokes and their

---

[10] There was no missionary on the islands, only the few 'teachers' left by Williams *less than a year* before.

sexually suggestive movements. But all of this took place under the surveillance of the old people, who were in charge of the whole performance. The only girls involved in this final performance were the village virgins. After the dances by older women, the young 'virgins' of the village (as explicitly stated by Williams), who always played the main role in receiving the visitors from another village, presented themselves in a state of nudity. But this presentation was not the prelude to anything more (Tcherkézoff 2003b: 384-98).[11]

As to an explanation of the girls' nakedness in such performances, it lends itself to three possible interpretations each of which is in fact a variant of the same fundamental hypothesis about the sacredness of the unmarried female. The first, following Sahlins's analysis for Hawaii, would see in it a theatrical display deriving from a mythology in which male fertility gods were attracted by mortal females. A second hypothesis would refer to how, throughout Polynesia, a very formal manner of greeting a visitor was for high-ranking females to undo the fine mat or barkcloth that enveloped their body and then offer it to the visitors (see chapter 10). A third explanation would look to the typical battle formation of pre-Christian Samoa in which the virgins stood in the front line of the army (see chapter 4, section 7).

---

[11] Williams's account is in his journals (Moyle ed. 1984: 246-7) and in Moyle's study of the Samoan music and dances (Moyle 1988: 208-9, 222). Richards (1992: 29) gives some details about Stevens's life.

Chapter 7

The late 1830s: Dumont d'Urville and Wilkes; Jackson and Erskine

1. August 1838: J.-S.-C. Dumont d'Urville, an overview

Jules-Sebastien-César Dumont d'Urville is the second and only other witness about Samoan sexual freedom to be called upon by both Williamson and Côté (see Introduction). 'D'Urville says that girls were entirely free to dispose of their persons till married', they tell us. And indeed, Dumont d'Urville's general comments on the customs of Samoa do include this statement. But both authors fail to mention that the French captain was merely summarising the view of a local beachcomber whom he had met. They conveniently ignore the fact that even then the man was only referring to a supposed distant past which he had no experience of whatsoever. And they make no mention of the fact that Dumont d'Urville's own experience on land was that, 'contrary to Tahiti', Samoan females in Apia 'constantly refused' to grant their favours to the French; although he adds—and this is his only other reference to the subject—that he had been 'told' that, in another village further away from the newly established missionary post, things were different. Contrary to Bougainville's and Lapérouse's accounts, Dumont d'Urville's narrative of his voyage has never been translated into English;[1] hence, as is the case for Lafond de Lurcy's account, many scholars have not scrutinised the original text.

From 1837 to 1840, Dumont d'Urville was given command, by the King of France, of two ships, the corvettes *Astrolabe* and *Zélée*, for a voyage to Oceania and the South Pole. It was his second opportunity to command an expedition to the Pacific, after his voyage in 1826-1829 that included Australia, New Zealand, Tonga, Fiji, the New Hebrides, New Ireland and New Britain. It was as a result of this first Pacific voyage that the French captain proposed his ideas on 'races' in the Pacific and, in December 1831, coined the name 'Melanesia' to describe a whole geographical and racial region in contradistinction to Polynesia. The second voyage took the French to Antarctica, Australia and Fiji and, in Polynesia, to the Marquesas, Tahiti, Samoa, Tonga and New Zealand. Ten volumes recording the history of the voyage and thirteen volumes on various scientific materials were published between 1841 and 1854. Dumont d'Urville died near Paris in 1842. He had the time to edit the first four volumes (Guillon 1986, Rosenman 1992). The Samoan episode is found in volume 4 (Dumont d'Urville 1842: 91-128).

---

[1] Only excerpts are available (Rosenman 1992).

In September 1838, the French expedition called at Nuku-Hiva (in the Marquesas) and at Tahiti. It is important to note, in relation to the 'very young girls' mentioned by Lapérouse's officer Vaujuas, that Dumont d'Urville was surprised, in Nuku-Hiva, to see how many females were offered to the sailors (*ibid.*: 6). All were young, he said, 'from 12 to 18 years of age' and 'some much younger, no more than 8 to 10 years' (*ibid.*). There were no missionaries there. In Matavai Bay (Tahiti), in his view the situation was much worse even than in Nuku-Hiva: there was a generalised 'prostitution' for European goods, and it was occurring even with the presence in Tahiti of the Protestant missionaries (*ibid.*: 40-90; Rosenman 1992: 147).

Following these two landings, the French arrived that same month in Samoa, and were thus inclined to make a comparison with their two previous ports of call. We shall see that Dumont d'Urville developed the comparison. He had expected to find the same situation in Samoa and this provoked two reactions: (i) he was surprised, from what he *observed*, to find great differences, and (ii) he was quite ready to *believe* that this was only due to recent missionary influence and that, 'before the introduction of Christianity', native 'girls were entirely free to dispose of their persons…'.

In this examination of Dumont d'Urville's visit, I shall merely note how the sentence chosen by Williamson and Côté cannot be considered as valid ethnographic information and must be left out of any discussion on the topic. Later in this chapter, in my analysis of Commodore Wilkes's visit, which took place the same year, I shall explain why the question of the missionary presence in 1838 is irrelevant to the debate (1836 was the date of the first establishment). Furthermore, Lafond's account of 1831 has already precluded any explanation of that kind. And John Jackson's observations made in 1840, on the remote island of Ta'ū (where missionary influence was just beginning), will robustly confirm this conclusion.

2. Arrival in Samoa: meeting with a 'Mr Frazior'

First the French arrived in the Manu'a group. They were heading for Apia, on Upolu, and were not interested in landing there. Dumont d'Urville noted only that, on arriving to the west of Ta'ū, he saw 'some natives gathered on the Western point' (*quelques naturels réunis sur la pointe de l'Ouest*), at the same place that, fifty years before, Lapérouse had sighted the Samoans for the first time. In the channel between the three islands, 'two small canoes' (*deux petites pirogues*) each carrying 'three natives' (*trois naturels*) came near, but no contact was made. He passed Tutuila, saw inhabitants from far away, and on 25 September arrived at the bay of Apia, where he made a six-day visit (*ibid.*: 92-3).

A whaler came to meet him at sea and its captain told the French that 'the islanders of Samoa (the real name of the archipelago) were easy to deal with' (*les insulaires de Samoa (véritable nom de l'archipel) étaient fort traitables*) and that pigs and all kinds of food supplies were plentiful. The whaler introduced to Dumont d'Urville a British local resident by the name of Frazior, who had arrived, he said, six years earlier and who could pilot the French ships into the bay. Frazior went on board the *Astrolabe* with Dumont d'Urville. A Samoan canoe arrived, carrying another Englishman who also offered his services as a pilot. The latter was placed on the *Zélée* (*ibid*.: 94-6). So from the start Dumont d'Urville was guided by Frazior. We shall see that Frazior accompanied the French captain everywhere on land and was the main—indeed the sole—informant of the French.

On disembarking, Dumont d'Urville noted that the attitude of the Samoans made them 'seem very shy in comparison with Nuku-Hiva and Tahiti' (*paraissent bien plus réservés qu'à Nouka-Hiva et à Taiti*). We can thus see that from the first day he explicitly compared his observations in Samoa with his two previous ports of call (in Tahiti sexual relations between indigenous females and European visitors had turned into a sexual trade—the time of the first contacts was now remote and nearly forgotten). 'Slowly', the Samoans 'brought some objects to exchange' (no details are given) (*peu à peu... quelques objets à échanger*) (*ibid*.: 97-8).

A Samoan chief came to greet the French. Frazior explained that his name was 'Pea-Pongui' and that he was the chief of the Apia district. This chief then presented to the French a board on which some words were inscribed, and uttered several times in English the word 'dollars' (at least this is what the French understood). The inscription was actually the first commercial treaty in Samoan history, devised by the missionaries and signed by a Captain Drinkwater of the *Conway* who had visited Samoa shortly before. Its effect was that visiting ships were now supposed to pay a fee. Dumont d'Urville refused immediately and on seeing that Pea did not seem happy he showed him the ship's cannons. According to the French narrative Pea immediately dropped his demand.

Dumont d'Urville and some of his officers, together with Frazior and Pea, walked to Apia, and the French captain admired the 'Fare-tete or public house, a masterpiece of native industry' (*chef-d'œuvre d'industrie sauvage*). As in Lapérouse's case, his

> description of the outside and the inside corresponds to the *fale tele* we know from later sources (*ibid*.: 100).

The group went to see the local missionary, William Mills, and the French expressed their displeasure regarding the port regulations. Mills, who seemed embarrassed (according to the French narrative), seems to have been quick-witted enough to invent an amendment to the treaty: it was a misunderstanding, he said, because the regulations were intended for commercial vessels and not for warships such as those of the French expedition (*ibid*.: 101-2). Mills probably already knew, from his fellow missionary and 'consul' George Pritchard in Tahiti, about the military presence of Captain (later Rear-Admiral) Dupetit-Thouars in Tahiti (from 29 August 1838) and the anger of the French at the London Missionary Society's influence in Tahiti.

A brief summary may be useful. The point at issue had arisen two years before, when Pritchard influenced Queen Pomare to order the expulsion of the French Catholic priests who had just arrived. These priests were from the Mission of the Sacred Heart and had received authority from the Vatican to evangelise Eastern Oceania, while the Marists were created at the same time to do the same in Western Oceania. Established in Mangareva, they disembarked in Tahiti in 1836—this was the first appearance of Catholicism in Tahiti—and told Pomare that they would like to stay and begin their missionary work. Pritchard could not accept this challenge and gave an official response requesting that they be asked to leave the country immediately. But they tried to stay on and found shelter in the house of the United States Consul, J.A. Moerenhout. After a few days, the unruly priests were seized by the Tahitians sent by Pomare, thrown into their vessel, and ordered to leave the country. After an abortive attempt in 1837, the Marists did not return until 1841 (and arrived in Samoa in 1846, as we know from Father Padel's letter).

If Mills had no knowledge of the events in Tahiti, then Dumont d'Urville must soon have set him straight. We can be sure about this because his narrative tells us that when he himself was in Tahiti in early September, just before arriving in Samoa, he had immediately planned to use military violence to retaliate for Pomare's mistreatment of the French priests. But on finding that Dupetit-Thouars had already been there since the end of August, and was dealing with the matter, he left it to him. (The 'Protectorate' was imposed by Dupetit-Thouars in 1842, and signed by the French king in 1843; Pritchard was expelled from Tahiti and the Catholic mission eventually flourished).

3. Observations on the trees, the birds… and the women: internal analysis of the text

Coming out of Mills's house, the group walked around 'in the nearby bush' (*dans la forêt voisine*) which may in fact have been gardens and plantations. Pea took them to a waterfall. Dumont d'Urville wrote an enthusiastic page describing the richness of the vegetation and the variety of birds and concluded that these islands ought to be better known. He then went on directly to the topic of sexual encounters. We should not be surprised: dating from the publication of Bougainville's account, descriptions of lush vegetation would conjure up, in the mind of every French visitor to the South Seas, visions of women offering themselves in the midst of luxuriant tropical greenery. Such images persisted until the 20th century. Then, with the new Western taste for sea shores, swimming and later for tanned bodies as well, coral beaches and lagoons would gradually replace the dense tropical forest as the perfect location for depicting, in narratives and films, 'natural' scenes of the 'free love' which was to be found among the 'South Seas islanders'.

At the end of this passage from Dumont d'Urville's narrative we shall come to the particular sentence that Williamson chose to quote from the original, but the passage preceding it is certainly not to be omitted. This is the relevant passage (*ibid.*: 102-6):

> ...[we were] strolling in the nearby forest ... I have never seen more beautiful trees, not even in New Zealand or in New Guinea ... beautiful pigeons, parakeets darting about in these great woods where they carry the movement of life. Ordered Nature there already appears much richer than in Tahiti ... All my companions and especially Captain Jacquinot seem enchanted to find themselves on these little-known islands. This port of call promises us a thousand benefits both for the health of our crew and for the accumulation of the treasures for Messrs. the naturalists. Today the surface of the globe has been so explored that one needs to congratulate oneself for having found some corner that has been missed by the research of voyagers. The Samoan islands fit this case, unless the companions of Captain Drink-Water have made observations in this regard, for only they have preceded us on this land.
>
> Our Frenchmen, used to the easy beauties of Nouka-Hiva and Tahiti, have wanted here to resume their philandering, but to their great surprise, they are disappointed. The women who at first seemed disposed to accept our sailors' advances, have constantly refused the serious propositions, and they seem to have submitted with sincerity to the prohibitions of their new religion. But they willingly indicate to our men the path to a neighbouring tribe, where the people, holding to their original beliefs, are still completely disposed to barter the favours of their women, and since that moment this path has been frequently and daily travelled by the corvettes' crews.
>
> Frazior, who appears to know the country and the archipelago of Samoa fairly well, has also given me the real names of the islands... (p 102-4).[2]

---

[2] ...*promenade dans la forêt voisine... Jamais je n'ai vu de plus beaux arbres, pas même à la Nouvelle-Zélande ou à la Nouvelle-Guinée... de beaux pigeons... des perruches... voltigent dans ces grands bois où ils portent le mouvement de la vie. La nature organisée s'y montre déjà bien plus riche qu'à Taïti... Tous mes compagnons et surtout le capitaine Jacquinot paraissent enchantés de se trouver sur ces îles encore si peu connues. Cette relâche nous promet mille avantages et pour la santé de nos équipages et pour l'accroissement des richesses de MM. les naturalistes. Aujourd'hui la surface du globe a été tellement explorée, qu'il faut se féliciter d'avoir trouvé quelque coin qui ait échappé aux recherches des voyageurs. Les îles Samoa sont dans ce cas, à moins que les compagnons du capitaine Drink-Water n'aient recueilli des observations à cet égard, car ils nous avaient seuls précédés sur ce terrain.* [pp. 102-3]

Nos Français habitués aux beautés faciles de Nouka-Hiva et de Taïti, ont voulu ici renouveler leurs galanteries, mais à leur grande surprise, ils sont désappointés. Les femmes qui d'abord avaient semblé disposer à accepter

'First Contacts' in Polynesia

The information contained in the preceding paragraphs—on the lush 'forest'; the 'surprising' and 'constant refusal' that the Samoan women opposed to the French sailors' advances; and the story about this other village where women would be more hospitable—is all presented by Dumont d'Urville as his own observations or as something he heard from his men. We can therefore take the sentence about 'the women who have constantly refused' as a *description* and not an interpretation. We cannot know what sort of welcome the 'neighbouring tribe' gave to the French, as clearly Dumont d'Urville did not go there. Apparently he heard from his men that the 'favours of their women' were granted. In the absence of any further information, we cannot know if the reception was of the sort described by Lapérouse or something different.

But from now on, in Dumont d'Urville's account, everything is presented as information given to him by Frazior.

> Frazior, who appears to know the country and the archipelago of Samoa fairly well, has also given me the real names of the islands [there follows a long list and discussion of the names].

> Frazior estimates the population of this group to be 80,000 souls allocated thus: Sevai and Opoulou with 25,000; Tou-tou-ila, 10,000; Manono, 7,000; Apolima, 3,000; the Manoua group being the least inhabited.

> There are already today three missionaries on the island of Opoulou, two on Sevai, two on Tou-tou-ila, and two on Manono. It is only three or four years since the English sought to establish themselves on these islands, but previously they had the way prepared for them by the Tahitians sent under the name of Teachers. (pp. 104-5).[3]

The following passage is a reconstruction of the supposed former religion: there were 'no cult, no temples, no prayers', and this would explain, Dumont d'Urville added, why the Samoans accepted Christianity without any difficulty. Also, 'they had the tabou under the name of Sa, the Kava was known under the

---

les provocations de nos marins, ont refusé constamment les propositions sérieuses, et elles paraissent se soumettre avec sincérité aux défenses de leur nouvelle religion. Mais elles indiquent volontiers à nos hommes le chemin d'une tribu voisine, où ces peuplades conservant leurs premières croyances, sont encore toutes disposées à trafiquer des faveurs de leurs femmes, et dès ce moment cette route est chaque jour souvent parcourue par les habitants des corvettes. [pp. 103-4]

Frazior qui paraît assez bien connaître le pays et l'archipel des Samoa, me donne aussi les véritables noms des îles.
[3] *Frazior qui paraît assez bien connaître le pays et l'archipel des Samoa, me donne aussi les véritables noms des îles...* [long list and discussion of the names].

Frazior estime la population de ce groupe à 80,000 âmes, ainsi réparties: Sevai et Opoulou en contiendraient 25,000, Tou-tou-ila 10,000, Manono 7,000, Apolima 3,000, le groupe de Manoua serait le moins habité.

On compte aujourd'hui déjà trois missionnaires sur l'île d'Opoulou, deux sur Sevai, deux sur Tou-tou-ila et deux sur Manono. Il n'y a que 3 ou 4 ans que les Anglais ont cherché à s'établir sur ces îles, mais auparavant ils avaient fait préparer les voies par des Taïtiens envoyés sous le titre de Teachers. [pp. 104-5]

name of Ava'. Then comes a description of arms used in war, and the final sentence: 'Everything leads one to think that they have never been cannibals' (*Tout fait présumer qu'ils n'ont jamais été cannibales*) (p. 105).

It is clear that this naïve reconstruction of an old religion quite without ritual was not Dumont d'Urville's own hypothesis but was described to him in this way by Frazior. The evidence for this is that (i) the preceding paragraphs begin with 'Frazior gives me the names' and 'Frazior evaluates the size of the population', and (ii) the next paragraph, which touches on Lapérouse's visit, ends with Dumont d'Urville's statement that he has obtained all these details from Frazior.

Right after that comes the passage in which we find the sentence about the girls:

> The massacre of Captain de Langle and his companions was committed by strangers aboard two canoes who wanted to seize the Frenchmen's goods ... [Dumont d'Urville adds that there would have been survivors and that one of them would still be alive but] ...Frazior by whom I am informed of these details seems to have never seen him.
>
> The territories of the archipelago are divided into districts, each governed by a single chief (Arii). They are each independent of the other. There was a time when the entire archipelago recognised a supreme chief, but today that is no longer the case.
>
> Before the introduction of Christianity, the young girls enjoyed complete liberty and disposed of their charms as they liked, but once married, they were obliged to be faithful to their husbands, and there was the threat of death for the adulterous wife. The men had as many wives as they could support, and Pea, although a self-proclaimed Christian, even today has two very young wives, only he keeps them in separate houses. (pp. 105-6).[4]

This is the passage from which Williamson took his other key sentence!

---

[4] *Le massacre du capitaine de Langle et de ses compagnons fut commis par deux pirogues montées par des étrangers qui voulurent s'approprier les objets des Français... et Frazior de qui je tiens ces détails paraît ne l'avoir jamais vu.*

Les terres de l'archipel sont divisées en districts, gouvernés chacun par un seul chef (Arii). Ils sont tous indépendants les uns des autres. Il y a eu une époque où l'archipel entier reconnaissait un chef suprême, mais aujourd'hui cela n'a plus lieu.

Avant l'introduction du christianisme, les jeunes filles jouissaient d'une entière liberté et disposaient de leurs charmes suivant leurs caprices, mais une fois mariées elles étaient obligées à la fidélité envers leurs maris, et il y avait peine de mort pour la femme adultère. Les hommes avaient autant de femmes qu'ils pouvaient en nourrir, et Pea, quoique se disant chrétien, en a encore aujourd'hui deux très jeunes, seulement il les tient dans des cases séparées. [pp. 105-6]

We can see, then, *the source* of Dumont d'Urville's supposition that 'girls were entirely free…': a resident of a mere six years, who claimed to know everything about Old Samoa (he claimed, for instance, to be able to reconstruct the ancient religion) but who appears to have been a naïve and ignorant man, thus prone to repeating the familiar clichés (as can be judged from the content of his reconstruction).[5] Thus, the second quotation cited by Williamson and reiterated by Côté is just as worthless as the first, selected from Lapérouse's narrative.

4. The first perspective of colonisation

The French account does not present the series of events as they happened day by day, and the following pages in Dumont d'Urville's account continue to mix observations and hypothetical reconstructions, as in the pages that we have already examined.

The paragraph following the interpretation made about the freedom of girls in pre-Christian times mentions that about thirty English and American whalers came every year to Samoa, either to 'Apia' or to 'Pango-Pango'. Then the narrative remarks on the existence of a recent sectarian Christian movement in Samoa, founded by 'two natives who had been to Sydney on a whaler and had seen there the religious ceremonies observed by the English' (p. 106).

According to the missionaries, the Samoan religion enjoyed the notion of a 'unique Supreme Being'. The 'pagans' still have their 'chapel', 'which is no further than 300 yards (*300 pas*) from the place where the Christians gather' (p. 107). A short description follows (p. 108). Dumont d'Urville, who is again guided by Frazior, once more describes the scenery and admires the vegetation. Then, with Frazior and Pea, the expedition group leaves this pagan village and goes on to '*Fale-Ata*'. The French are welcomed and given food inside the houses. Dumont d'Urville notes the circular arrangement of the village (p. 111).

He again admires the vegetation, raises the possibility of establishing 'plantations of sugar and coffee', and dreams of a full-fledged colonisation of these

> nearly uninhabited lands (*dans ces solitudes*) [for the benefit of] our old Europe where millions of men usually argue about a few square metres … Our surplus population [should be brought to] these happy islands of Oceania; and the white race will quickly take the place of the primitive race (p. 112).

---

[5] Another remark should be made in relation to the last passage. We have here a comment about the kind of 'polygamy' practised by Samoan chiefs of the time: the wives were kept 'in separate houses'. In this case the two wives are 'very young'. It is probably once again a case where a young virgin has been presented to a chief for marriage and impregnation (see Tcherkézoff 2003b: 378-83 for the limited data about polygamy for the years 1830-1860).

These lines remind us that here, in 1838, we stand at the beginning of a new era impelled by colonial, and racist, vision that would last well into the next century. The years of 'discovery' between 1760 and 1780 are already well behind us. Gone is the discourse of a Bougainville or a Lapérouse. The question is no longer that of deciding whether the Savage is Noble or Ignoble, but of ascertaining whether the land is large enough to accommodate Europe's 'surplus population' and fertile enough to accommodate the establishment of the 'white race'.

The next pages describe a specific incident: a soldier is led by a Samoan into the bush and then, threatened with a club, is divested of his clothing. Dumont d'Urville sends Frazior to the chief of the man's village ('*Sava-lelo*') with a simple message: deliver the culprit, or pay a fine of twenty-five hogs, otherwise the village will be torched, and anyone resisting will be shot. Finally, an agreement is sealed with the provision of ten hogs and the restitution of the stolen garments (pp. 115-20).

This episode, together with the initial threat delivered to Pea when Dumont d'Urville refused to pay any port fees, is also a landmark in the history of contacts between Samoans and *Papālagi*. It was the first time in Samoan history—but certainly not the last—that foreign ships imposed a policy under threat of using cannons or burning a village to the ground. And again, as with European intrusion on Polynesian land, the first expedition to do so in the Samoan case was a French expedition. It is indeed appropriate to remember that Lapérouse and Dumont d'Urville played a key role in the history of the first contacts in Samoa, but certainly not for the reasons invoked by Côté.

On the other side of Apia, two other villages were mentioned by the French. Again the houses were said to be arranged around a central area (p. 121). The final part summarised observations about the physical appearance and characteristics of the men and women. In the last lines, Dumont d'Urville again noted the 'reserved' attitude of the Samoans. This was 'in contrast' with what he read in 'Lapérouse and Kotzebue', where there were 'hundreds of canoes surrounding the ships'. Indeed, in 1838, the *Papālagi* were no longer a novelty for the Samoans. It tells us that the period of the first contacts has ended, at least on the larger islands of Upolu and Tutuila.

We are therefore nearing the end of this inquiry. But one visit remains to be examined, that of the U.S. exploring expedition of 1839, which marks, together with Dumont d'Urville's visit, the turning point between the voyages of 'discovery' and the new era of military and colonial enterprises.

5. 1839: the Wilkes Expedition in Tutuila

This U.S. expedition, comprising several ships, manned with soldiers as well as scientists (naturalists and philologists), cruised for four years and twice visited the Samoan islands. Having studied the various vocabularies collected by travellers in Polynesia (the short lists composed by the Dutch in the 17th century and the long and accurate lists of words for Eastern Polynesian languages recorded during Cook's expeditions), some of the scientists were able to have considerably more meaningful interactions with the inhabitants than before. One of them was the philologist Horatio Hale who made the first systematic comparisons and who, forty years later, would oversee the first modern ethnographic enquiries (directing Franz Boas's field studies among American Indians). Wilkes's comment (relative to Tutuila) was the following:

> The women are far from being good-looking, with the exception of some of the younger ones. They are remarkably domestic and virtuous, exhibiting a strange contrast to those of Tahiti. Here, there is no indiscriminate intercourse, the marriage tie is respected, and parents are extremely fond of their offspring [this last remark is still intended to contrast with the 'Tahiti' of Cook where the infanticide practised by the Arioi had so shocked British readers] ... They are betrothed, without regard to age, the girl being *saa*, or tabooed, until of marriageable age. During the intervening time, all kinds of native property are accumulated, such as mats, etc., for the bridal day (Wilkes 1845, vol. 2, quoted in Richards 1992: 83, 89).

As we can see, in comparisons Tahiti remains the norm, so that in matters of physical attractiveness, Samoan women are still judged unfavourably. In relation to sexual practices, Wilkes also makes the comparison with Tahiti and confirms the impressions of Lafond de Lurcy. Samoa seems to stand in 'strange contrast' to Tahiti—in strange contrast to what the travellers thought that the 'Tahitian custom' was.

Of course, Wilkes mentions the hard work of the missionary Murray who was in charge of Tutuila from 1836. But it can be readily admitted that three years would not be long enough to establish a general, and entirely new, ideology and custom of declaring all girls '*saa*' until marriage (the word *sā*, with a long 'a', is still today the Samoan word for 'forbidden, tabooed, untouchable'). For many other practices condemned by the missionaries, such as tattooing, polygamy and night dances, it took some fifteen to twenty-five years to impose a more or less complete control over the behaviour. It is thus impossible to imagine that the major and complete transformation constituted by the change from a generalised sexual freedom in adolescence to a situation in which all girls were 'untouchable' before marriage could have taken place in just three years. Moreover, the kind of contrast Wilkes is stressing in relation to Tahiti implies that he is speaking about what seemed to him to be a Samoan 'custom' and not some very recent transformation due entirely to the missionaries' presence.

The same remark applies to the observations of his companions. Wilkes is not the only one to make such comments. Joseph Clark (1848: 79) wrote that:

The females are very reserved in their manners. I was struck with admiration and astonishment at the conduct of these females on all occasions. They never suffer any liberties to be taken with them, and seem particularly cautious in their intercourse with foreigners. Salaciousness does not exist here, with the females, in such a high degree as at many other islands which we have visited, and particularly Otaheite.

Of course Clark was an admirer of the civilising work of the missionaries, as he noted several times in his account. This is why he condemned the Tahitian custom—again according to what he thought that the Tahitian habits were—and praised the Samoan one. But this does not explain why he found such a contrast in Samoa. We can also quote another companion of Wilkes, the Lieutenant Colvocoresses (1852: 86): 'The girls are pretty and quite modest' (no other details are given).

Our study of pre-missionary accounts must stop here in relation to the larger islands of Savai'i, Upolu and Tutuila, where missionary work started in 1836, even though it would take another fifteen years for the handful of missionaries there to train enough Samoan 'teachers' to spread the Christian message to most of the villages. But we can make a last visit to the tiny and rocky island of Ta'ū, in the Manu'a group, which did not receive the flux of visitors that had been arriving in the larger islands since the mid-1830s. There, in 1840, the highest chief, Tu'i Manu'a, had adopted a young British mariner.

6. 1840: John Jackson in Ta'ū

The kidnapping of a Papālagi

We learn from his own account that this twenty-year old man was kidnapped by the Samoans in Ta'ū, and kept in the compound of the great chief Tu'i Manu'a for three months (Jackson 1853). When his companions bartered for pigs and cooked them on the beach before re-embarking on their whaling ship, Jackson went walking a little further. He was immediately seized and hidden. His companions looked in vain for him and departed.

This incident reminds us that, in the first half of the 19th century, every Samoan or Tongan chief wanted to have near him 'his *Papālagi*'. The chiefs looked to take advantage of these men's technical knowledge in war and to learn from them the secrets of the *Papālagi*. They would also use them as interpreters and as intermediaries with incoming vessels.[6]

---

[6] See the remarks made by several visitors: a Salem trader, on the *Emerald* who called at Upolu in 1835 (Richards 1992: 45) or the missionary Turner who remembers from the 1840s that 'A chief thought it added vastly to his importance to have a white man in his train' (*ibid.*: 35). For comparative examples throughout Polynesia, see Campbell (1998: 111 *ff*).

Jackson managed to escape and to jump on board another boat. Opportunistically using his role as intermediary, he persuaded the Chief to let him go on board one of the passing ships to explain to the visitors how many pigs they could get in exchange for their goods. He helped with the transaction and managed to return to the ship delivering the load of pigs, but this time he was careful to stay on board! As the captain 'had his full complement of men', he agreed only to take Jackson as far as Tutuila. Later on, Jackson told his story to Captain John Erskine, who asked him to write it down, and who published it as an appendix to the narrative of his own journey (Jackson 1853; Campbell 1998: 74-80).[7]

Jackson knew of three boats that called into Ta'ū in the three months that he found himself on the island. The first one brought him there; the third took him away (Jackson had tried to board the second one but failed). The number of European residents must have been very few. Jackson mentions only 'one New Zealander' whom he met briefly (but does not describe) and reported that 'some time previous to my being taken', a missionary vessel had landed two Rarotongan 'teachers' who 'soon mustered many converts'. The consecration of the first church occasioned a great feast, with hundreds of pigs slaughtered, and the gift of 'most valuable presents to the teachers, consisting chiefly of fine mats'. But mass conversion was only just beginning, as Jackson notes that on Ta'ū there were still Samoans who held to their ancient customs as well as those who had been converted: 'I was equally well treated both by the Tevolo and Lotu parties' (the 'Devil' side and the 'Church' side). The virtual absence of Europeans can also be deduced from Jackson's description of the oil lamps (a half coconut, containing some coconut meat to which coconut oil had been added) and of the way the Samoans lit them with two wooden sticks.

Fifteen or twenty virgins

Jackson was treated at first like a child of the house. He was washed, anointed with oil, his hair was combed, 'which they said was *lelei* ['good'] and *faa Samoa* ['customary in Samoa']' [Jackson 1853: 412]). Then he was treated as a guest of honour. This is indicated by his sitting-place in the house and by the fact that he drank the kava just after the Chief did. His description of the main house ('fale-tele') corresponds with what we know for the *fale tele* throughout the 19th century. He mentioned the meetings in the house. The Chief was seated between his two 'fula fela' (*tulafale*, the orators). In the middle of the house there were three kava bowls. Jackson noted that these bowls were 'surrounded by fifteen or twenty virgins, who were chewing the root'.

---

[7] The real name of our adventurer was William Diaper, but he used the name of Jackson while in Samoa and in Fiji (Legge 1966, Campbell *ibid.*).

Thus we find that, in 1840, on Ta'ū (the very island which Mead was to visit in 1925), the ceremonial status of virgins was clearly attested to by our witness. These twenty girls could not all have been 'taupou' (ceremonial virgins)—the only kind of virginity recognised by Côté and other defenders of Mead's version as highly valued.[8] For there was normally only one *taupou* per village, and two or three at the most. The other girls obviously constituted the *aualuma* of the place—the village group of unmarried girls. Nevertheless Jackson called all of them 'virgins'; and we may judge from what follows that he knew what he was talking about.

An intercultural dialogue

One particular episode is revealing about the way Samoans related to the *Papālagi* at that time. Nothing in their behaviour could give the impression that the *Papālagi* were still seen as some kind of extraordinary beings whereas, when he was in Fiji, Jackson noted a dual attitude: in some villages he was treated as an ordinary person; in others he was called a *kalou*, 'spirit, ghost, god', which implied a link to the super-human world.

Disgusted by a piece of pork which was given to him but which seemed rotten, Jackson threw it away. This was, in fact, a serious offence, since cooked food was and always is a ceremonial offering in Samoa. For instance, early sources already show that it was by accepting the cooked food brought by the party of a boy from another village, that a girl (and her family) signified that the talks for a potential marriage could be initiated. Eating is an act performed only when 'sitting' (*nofo*), and that attitude is a ceremonial one, in distinct opposition to profane activities which are performed while standing. It was wholly to be expected that the Chief would shout at Jackson. Indeed he told him: 'pua alo!' [*pua'a elo*] 'stinking pig!' Jackson, whose hot temper erupted many times in his future peregrinations in Fiji, responded very violently: 'I slapped him on his face in my passion'. The Chief, perceiving that the young boy did not realise that he had suddenly condemned himself to certain death, immediately tore off a piece of the barkcloth that he was wearing and put it on Jackson's neck, saying '*faa saa*' ('forbidden', that is: 'he has become untouchable') (*ibid*.: 413).

A quite remarkable episode in a number of ways. It was the Tu'i Manu'a who did the anthropological work of interpretation in perceiving that Jackson did not properly understand the rules and the situation in which he found himself. We learn too that the *Papālagi* could be cursed, and of course killed (Jackson tells us that after he had slapped the Chief, 'all the natives immediately rushed up with their clubs'). We also see evidence of a particular practice characteristic of the High Chiefs of the time: the placing of temporary taboos on objects, on

---

[8] 'Taupou' in the sense it had in the European literature (see the discussion in the following section).

land, on sea, and on individuals as well (the word *fa'asā* is still the term used today for the announcement that something is forbidden by a village law or a State law). This episode also provides one of the earliest descriptions we have of the *ifoga* gesture by which one covers oneself with a sacred cloth (barkcloth *siapo* or a fine mat) in order to avoid the bloody revenge of another party. And finally, the Chief's protective gesture is one of the early indications that the barkcloth did not just have a practical use as clothing (kilts made with strong leaves were often used for that purpose) but it was also a sacred item (see chapter 10).

On women as 'wife' (ava)

Jackson stayed only three months but we can see how intimately he was integrated into the islander community. We are then justified in assuming that what he has to tell us about the access to women is accurate. At no time does he report any form of sexual hospitality for visitors or sexual freedom for unmarried people. Of course, as an adopted young man, the Chief proposed to him that he should marry: 'he frequently asked me to point out the prettiest girl, and then asked me if I would like her for my "avaa" (wife), but at the same time telling me I was too young for a wife' (*ibid*.: 413). We note that the word used by the Chief is *avā*, which is indeed the word for 'wife' and never for 'girl' (*teine*, 'girl' in a general sense and, in the parlance of young males, in the sense of potential sexual prey). And Jackson does not suggest that the Chief ever proposed that he could share his wives, but he does mention such offers when he lives with Fijian chiefs.

When Jackson managed to leave Ta'ū, he was disembarked at Leone on Tutuila. He thought for a time that he might stay in Tutuila and establish himself as a trader, 'as the natives were all Christians in this place' (nominally that is: mission work had begun four years ago). He tells us: 'I found a young girl to my liking, and then took her to the Missionary and asked him if he would marry us'. The missionary refused, arguing that Jackson would not stay long and would leave his wife behind. Our young man then decided to leave for Fiji and took the first boat which called at Pago-Pago.[9]

None of this bears any correspondence at all to the Samoa which Côté would like us to imagine, one in keeping with the scenario invented by Mead—on this very island of Ta'ū—and which elaborates to an even greater degree the idea of an 'institutionalised' sexual freedom prevailing in pre-missionary times. If Jackson had been a young man looking for girls and had easily been able to find them, then he would have told us about it. And if, on the other hand, he was

---

[9] Eight years later, a traveller noted that missionaries in Samoa tried to proscribe such marriages between European men and Samoan women for the same reasons, but that many Samoan females were determined to have a *Papālagi* husband (Walpole 1849: 354).

someone whose religious upbringing made him eager to abide by the Church's rules about marriage, he would hardly have failed to describe the sexual freedom among the adolescents—had it existed—that would have been obvious everywhere and would have shocked him.

There is no reason to think that his surroundings (the household of the Tu'i Manu'a) had been already transformed through Christian influence, because Jackson also describes one of the 'marriages' of the Chief. It was performed entirely in the pre-Christian way (public defloration of the bride) and explicitly contradicted the rules enacted by the missionaries and their 'teachers'.[10] Finally, when Jackson describes, in one page, how he spent his days in Ta'ū, he only discusses three topics and gives each of them equal importance: meals, fishing, and the evening dances (unfortunately these are not described). Thus, although they are both talking about the same small island, Jackson provides nothing approaching the 'Day in Samoa' which Mead depicts in the first chapter of *Coming of Age in Samoa*, and where she constantly evokes lush images of adolescent sexual encounters (Tcherkézoff 2001a: 57-8).

7. 1848: John Elphinstone Erskine

John Erskine, the Captain who met Jackson in 1850 and who, struck by what he heard from him, asked him to write down his story, had himself called at Samoa in 1848. That date is already outside the historical frame of this study. By the mid-1840s, the missionary influence was beginning to be quite noticeable. Although these historical processes are continuous, a useful endpoint can be placed at 1844, the year that saw the opening of the Malua theological college, which produced all the Samoan 'teachers' (and later the 'pastors'). We have already noted that 1844 was also the year that, for the first time, glass beads were no longer mentioned in the description of exchanges with a European ship.

But one of Erskine's observations undoubtedly reveals an aspect of the pre-Christian era and should be noted. Erskine narrates that, after anchoring, he saw 'several young ladies of the district' coming towards him and his crew. One of these young ladies seemed to be about fifteen years old and was presented as the daughter of a High Chief. She wore around her waist a ceremonial white mat made of hibiscus fibres. There can be no doubt that this was the *'ie sina*, which could be worn *only by a girl who was a virgin who was presented as a bride-to-be*—for this ceremonial mat was supposed to receive the stain of the blood from her deflowering.[11] Indeed, Erskine notes that 'her hair was cut short, which, our informant told us, intimated she was ready for a husband'. Erskine

---

[10] The narrative is given in my description of marriage ceremonies of the 19th century (Tcherkézoff 2003b: 354).
[11] As it is attested in early descriptions of marriage ceremonies (Tcherkézoff 2003b: 351, 354, 361, 365); see also Te Rangi Hiroa (1930: index *''ie sina'*).

goes on, apparently summarising what his 'informant' (not named or detailed) explained to him:

> Although associating familiarly with the other young women, she is looked upon as of a higher grade, being under the special care of the Chief, who, with the consent of the council (or 'fono'), will probably provide a suitable match for her. When visits of ceremony from other tribes take place, she is called upon to play the part of the 'te mai-tai', or great lady, and is then dressed in her smartest garments, and gives directions to the other women. Should she misconduct herself, however, or make a marriage without the consent of the authorities, she would certainly lose this position – one, probably, not much coveted; indeed, she was said to have lately narrowly escaped from the wiles of a Tutuilan dandy, who had almost persuaded her to elope with him (Erskine 1853: 50-1).

The narrative then switches to another topic.

We find here the word *tama'ita'i*, which is a confirmation of the high status and the virginity of the girl (probably, the full expression given to Erskine had been: *sa'o tama'ita'i*). Clearly, this 'great lady under the special care of the Chief' is what subsequent literature will call a 'taupou'. It is interesting to note that this word 'taupou' has not appeared yet; at least it is not the first word used to define such a girl, since Erskine did not note it but only heard '*tama'ita'i*'. It confirms an hypothesis suggested to me in the early 1980s by Professor Aiono Dr Fanaafi Le Tagaloa (personal communication) who said that, in the European literature and, to some extent, in Samoan discourse, 'taupou' possibly came to designate the village ceremonial virgins only in the last third of the 19th century. 'Before that, the word was *augafa'apae*', she added, without further explanation. It seems to me that the explanation for this linguistic change relates to significant social change: the end of the 19th century was the time when a certain levelling of the hierarchies of titles and ranks began throughout Samoa (Tcherkézoff 2000a, 2000b). This levelling had as a consequence that the status of ceremonial virgin which was formerly restricted to certain high-ranking names, the *sa'otama'ita'i*, became diluted, now expressing the general idea of 'virgin daughter'; consequently, the specialised terms such as *augafa'apae* and *sa'otama'ita* nearly disappeared and the word *taupou* which was formerly used as the general 'polite' term (formal vocabulary) for 'virgin'[12] now began to be applied to the specialised status of village ceremonial virgin as well. Soon its meaning became restricted to this status, and the only general term for 'virgin' which remained was the non-formal expression (*teine muli*).

---

[12] A linguistic discussion confirms this view if we consider that the etymology (*taupou* 'still new' [*tau-pou<*fou*] [Pawley 1982]) corresponds exactly to the expression for 'virgin girl' used in the non-formal vocabulary: *teine muli* 'girl still behind, still not ripe'.

No other part of Erskine's narrative contains any allusion to an upbringing and environment that permitted or encouraged a generalised free expression in pre-marital sexual behaviour.

Chapter 8

Conclusion

1. Early Western misconceptions about Samoan adolescence

We can see that, from 1722 up until the 1830s to 1840s, the contacts between Samoans and Europeans all followed the same pattern of mutual defiance. This tendency increased markedly on the European side after 1787. For the Samoans, it had probably been there almost from the very beginning, following the spread of the stories about the Dutch cannons, which were reinforced after they had experienced the firepower of the French in 1787 (Lapérouse) and of the British in 1791 (the crew of the tender of Edwards's expedition).

The only significant change in the overall pattern was that, after 1771, the Tahitian interlude described in Bougainville's narrative became part of every European captain's mental landscape. The first to express it was Lapérouse in 1787, in the wake of Bougainville himself who used Tahiti as a benchmark when he met the Samoans. Two things followed from this constant reference to Tahiti. The Samoans in general became 'less' attractive, 'more savage' than the Tahitians; and their women's and girls' sexual attitude came to be systematically compared to the Tahitian scene. Samoan sexual behaviour was invoked either to be rapidly assimilated to its Tahitian counterpart, albeit through supposition rather than observation (mainly Lapérouse and Dumont d'Urville, and Hamilton to some extent), or to be contrasted with it based on more accurate observations (Lafond de Lurcy, Wilkes and his companions).

As for the question of sexual freedom in adolescence, we are now in a position to reach a conclusion that can leave no room for doubt. If we discard the moral judgements and the overinterpreted conclusions of Lapérouse and Dumont d'Urville who reiterated the stereotyped formulas from Bougainville's account for Tahiti, these two French captains being the only witnesses called upon today by Côté, there is no evidence left for the thesis of customary pre-marital sexual freedom. When we consider only the daily events as recorded by each voyager, including the descriptions of Lapérouse and Dumont d'Urville, we cannot in any way view pre-Christian Samoan custom in the terms set down by Williamson and Côté. From 1722 to the 1840s there is not a single observation that could lead to the view that 'girls were entirely free to dispose of their persons till married' and that 'girls were, before marriage, mistresses of their own favours'. The Old Samoa imagined by Côté via Williamson has never been observed by any traveller.

2. The Western myth of sexual hospitality

In the Samoan case, just as for the first contacts in Tahiti, European interpreters have made a double error. Firstly, the presentation of young girls to early European visitors has been mistaken for sexual hospitality offered by 'women', when it was in fact a ritual presentation of '(very) young girls' who were (always or often?) virgins. For Samoa, the sources only give us a description of the ritual presentation of young girls and, later, proposals of marriage as well as explicit 'refusals' to grant favours according to a European commercial notion of payment for sexual acts. The presentations of young girls may have been part of a strategy of theogamy and an *atua* or 'divine' pregnancy. This last explanation remains here a suggestive hypothesis.

Secondly, it has been erroneously inferred that these presentations of girls were an indication that an attitude promoting sexual freedom prevailed within the indigenous society. Such reasoning, which equates the relationship between Samoans and the first Europeans with the daily relationship between Samoans themselves, supposes that the newcomers had been viewed by the Samoans as ordinary men coming from some other neighbouring island. But this appears to be a total absurdity: it is contradicted by all the evidence we have about Polynesian attitudes to the *Papālagi*. The 18th-century encounters in Samoa show clearly that the *Papālagi* had by no means been viewed as ordinary men, and we shall see in Part Two that much comparative data, as well as the linguistic discussion of the word *Papālagi*, confirms this.

The European voyagers of the 18th century thought that they had been welcomed as ordinary human foreign visitors. Later, in the 19th century, and to an even greater extent in the 20th century, European visitors and scholars developed the mistaken idea that the Polynesians had viewed the first Europeans as 'gods'. Recent academic critiques of this late European invention of an 'apotheosis' have led some scholars to reject any inquiry about the Polynesian interpretation of the *other-than-merely-human* nature of the first Europeans. Some have denounced as victims of a 'Western-inspired myth' anyone interested in understanding why the Polynesians had—hesitantly, and with many queries—expressed the notion that the nature of the newcomers had something to do with the 'sky' and with the 'sun'. In Part Two, I shall try to clarify these academic misunderstandings and to give more evidence in relation to the interpretations that Polynesians made about Europeans in those earlier times.

PART TWO

Methodological comparisons

Chapter 9

'On the boat of Tangaroa'. Humanity and divinity in Polynesian-European first contacts: a reconsideration

For Marshall Sahlins

> 'The sheer impossibility of thinking that!' In anticipation of his readers' incredulous reactions to the marvels he described on Cook's first voyage, Sir Joseph Banks quoted an old Joe Miller quip to the effect of: 'Since you say so, I have to believe you; but I daresay if I had seen it myself, I would have doubted it exceedingly.' But the point once more is that 'objectivity' is culturally constituted. It is always a distinctive ontology. Nor is it then some sort of hypothesis or 'belief' that is likely to be shaken by this or that person's skepticism or experimental attitude. It is not a simple sensory epistemology but a *total cultural cosmology* that is precipitated in Hawaiian empirical judgments of divinity (Sahlins 1995: 169).

1. Who has the right to speak about what?

Anthropology: a study of the Others' Other

The story of the first encounters between Polynesians and Europeans has, until now, only been told by Europeans, or more generally by Westerners. That is why, too often, it is subject to two main qualifications. First of all the perspective from which the encounters are viewed is one-sided. The 'discovery' in question is made by voyagers who set sail one day from the Thames, or from the coast of Brittany, for the Pacific. But what was the other significant discovery that resulted from these voyages, the discovery that the Polynesians were forced to make at the same time? Samoan voices from this time cannot speak to us now, but in Part One I have tried to provide some answers to the question of the nature of the Samoan response to first contacts using an ethnohistorical methodology. This involves critically re-reading the European narratives and looking at both the early and the contemporary ethnographic accounts for clarification and confirmation.

But there is a second qualification. Too often the objective or analytical viewpoint is just as one-sided. The analytical grid applied to the observations contained in the accounts from this period, whether these come from Polynesians or Europeans, is based on the assumption that all the protagonists had exactly the same thought processes as those of Westerners of the modern period (1750-1970) when they conceived possible relationships to the Other, namely as a relationship of either exclusion or assimilation. What risks being overlooked here is that the Polynesians at that time had adopted a different model of alterity and identity which allowed the integration of every sort of difference into the social structure as a whole by assigning each one to a particular hierarchical level of the same encompassing whole.

For the Westerner, everything comes down to mutually exclusive alternatives, the binary logic of 'either/or': man or beast; divine or human; civilised or savage; pristine 'state of nature' (the Noble Savage, typical example: the Polynesians) or fallen humanity living in a state of misery (typical example: the Patagonians in Tierra del Fuego, the 'Hottentots' in southern Africa, or the 'New-Hollanders' [Australians] in the 18th-century versions of Dampier, Buffon, de Brosses, Bougainville or Forster). But for the Polynesians everything was a question of integration and of the relationship between a whole and its different parts, as contradictory as the relationship of identity might seem. A god was an invisible whole and every visible manifestation of this god was a partial form of that whole. A chief was thus a partial form of a god. A new creature could just as easily be a visible form of the divine or meaningless and virtually non-existent.

Which of these two poles did the Polynesian interpretation of the European Others tend towards? It turns out that when the Europeans appeared on the scene particular attention was paid to the colour of their skin. The 'whiteness' of their skin seemed to take its luminosity from the light of the sun. And there were all the things that came with that whiteness: their boats, their weapons, their tools and, last but not least, their clothes. Therefore the place that the Europeans were assigned was with the gods rather than with the meaningless creatures. Western Polynesia provides a particularly good example. In Samoa, if the newcomers, whose whiteness of skin seemed to have something of the nature of the sunlight, were considered as partial forms of the 'luminous' superhuman world, men whose skin was black (inhabitants of the Solomon Islands for example) who appeared much later (they were brought to Samoa during the 19th century by German colonisers to work on the plantations) were described as 'black living things', where the term 'living things' (*mea ola*) applies to the whole of the biosphere and, significantly, makes no distinction between men and animals.[2] The two kinds of strangers were each designated as 'other'

---

[2] The word 'thing', *mea*, conveying here the idea of 'living thing', *mea ola*, a category which unites men and animals under the sign of the vital bodily principle with no hierarchical ordering of the diverse cosmological origins of those included in it. It signifies life in an almost biological sense, food that is still raw, body without soul, where the only differentiating principle is that of sex (male/female)–and not that of kinship, or chieftainship, or any other kind of social ranking; for a summary of Samoan classification, see Tcherkézoff (2001a: chapter 1 and 2003b: chapters 7 and 8).

in relation to Samoan identity, but differently other, occupying quite different places in the Samoan conception of alterity.

In these first contacts, there were indeed two discoveries operating simultaneously, as we saw in Part One. But we must also understand that the looks and perceptions that intersected during these first contacts each stemmed from a very different vision of the Other. On one side—for the Polynesians—it was a question of the level of integration into one encompassing whole (the cosmos). I shall give a number of different examples in the following pages where I concentrate on the Polynesian perspective. On the other side—for the Europeans—everything was black or white, the same or different, good or bad, from their 'world' or from 'another world'. Thus Europeans were most likely to assimilate Polynesians whom they judged 'good' (before 1787) and 'almost as white as Europeans', and to deny similar human status to Melanesians, 'black as Negroes', and thought to be incapable of establishing 'civilised' societies. But that is another story, the whole misconception by which Western scientists misconstrued 'Oceania' as peopled by 'two races' (Tcherkézoff 2003a). What also needs to be recovered is the nature of the Polynesian construction—as well as misconstruing—of Europeans.

Valid ethnohistorical questions versus spurious academic debates

One thing is certain: the islanders did not simply take the newcomers for 'men', *ta(n)gata*, and nothing more. At least, they did not use this word. They used words that were applicable to gods, spirits, and ritual objects (*atua, tupua; kalou* in the Fijian archipelago) or alternatively, when they spoke of 'men', they added 'men who belong to, or come from, the *Papālagi*' (Tongan words collected by Cook in 1777; see chapter 11 for discussion of the meaning of the term *Papālagi*). This was because the Polynesians only knew men like themselves (those who inhabited all the Polynesian archipelagos and the Fijian islands as well as part of Micronesia). Something else is certain as well: in most cases, the islanders did not see the newcomers as monsters who needed to be cast out or destroyed as quickly as possible. There was in fact a desire to integrate them and to capture some of their powers, since the predominant interpretation placed these new arrivals on the side of the 'sun', as we shall see. In a civilisation where, for the pre-Christian period, we can talk about a sun cult (Tcherkézoff 2003b: chapter 1), such a desire was quite understandable.

Neither just 'men', nor meaningless creatures, nor monsters: this was the taxonomic dilemma posed by the newcomers. The only possibility, therefore, was to make use of the other categories that already existed: gods who created the world, local gods, ancestors, spirits like ghosts, sprites and goblins, and so on. But there was no category that corresponded exactly to what the Polynesians had before their very eyes. Integration therefore involved a simultaneous process of intellectual *inquiry* and taxonomic *innovation*.

One famous case has been studied in great detail, that of the arrival of Captain Cook in Hawaii in 1778. Marshall Sahlins has shown how James Cook was taken for a manifestation, but one that was partial and new, of the Hawaiian god Lono: an 'image of Lono', a 'body' (*kino*) of Lono, a visible aspect of an encompassing principle Lono, a 'refraction of the inclusive Lono' (Sahlins 1981, 1985a, 1989: 384-5). The archival sources make this quite clear: Cook was called 'Lono' on a number of occasions by the Hawaiians and he was manipulated in ceremonies in the same way that certain *images* of Lono were normally manipulated in the rites of the ceremonial cycle devoted to this god. In sum, Cook was taken 'for Lono'. But what we need to understand is this: he was taken for a *visible and therefore partial* manifestation of Lono. No doubt it was a manifestation that was somewhat unexpected, but the logic of the whole to its parts that regulates the relationship between the divine encompassing principle as invisible and its *visible* forms allows, by definition, for the possibility of an infinite variety of visible manifestations.

To say that Cook was taken for a god can be confusing to those who are not aware of the fluidity of the Polynesian pantheon. Every 'god' in the pantheon is a partial form of the beginning of the world and of the great demiurge, at the same time as it already contains the seeds of all human forms to come. Furthermore, these gods become manifest in the form of images. Lono would traverse the main island each year at exactly the same time in the guise of a large white barkcloth decorated in a special way. Sahlins has shown that Captain Cook was another of these images of Lono: 'Cook indeed became the image of Lono, a duplicate of the crosspiece icon (constructed of wood staves) which is the appearance of the god' (1985a: 105). When the rite was over the image was destroyed. And when Cook returned to the island outside this ritual period, he too was destroyed. But 'Lono' is immortal, by definition, and each year he would reappear in a new form. And so it was that having killed Captain Cook-image-of-Lono the Hawaiians asked the English to tell them the date that Cook would come back to visit them.

Sahlins's book *Historical Metaphors and Mythical Realities* (1981), whose title is rich in layers of meaning, was published some years ago now. There, and in other texts that had appeared earlier, and subsequently, Sahlins has developed his exposition of this particular case (1979, 1985a: chapters 1, 3, 4, 5). This Hawaiian assimilation of Captain Cook was a 'historical metaphor'. It had serious consequences. Sahlins explained the ritual acts performed on Cook by the Hawaiians after they had led him into a temple, and the fate that they had in store for him when he and his expedition, having left the archipelago as Lono did each year after the ceremonies of the New Year, returned unexpectedly (to repair a mast). This return of Lono at a date when, in the normal course of events, he would have retired again to the island of the dead, leaving the main ceremonial role to the king, servant of the god Kū, amounted to a provocation in relation to Kū. It caused a battle in which Cook died. But this metaphor Cook=Lono, with the historical consequences that ensued, namely the death of Cook, immediately became a 'mythical reality'. The Hawaiians hoped that Cook 'would return soon' and put this question of his return to the Europeans who landed there after him. At the same time, Cook's incorporation into the Hawaiian superhuman realm set up the interpretive framework that Hawaiians built around the newcomers and their objects during the visits of the other European expeditions which were not slow in following. A new reality modified the whole of the Hawaiian interpretative structure, even if that structure remained 'mythical'.

Discussion about the various convergences between Cook's stay in Hawaii and the ritual cycle built around the god Lono is a matter for those with specialist knowledge of the Hawaiian sources (Sahlins 1989, 1991). A number of significant issues are open for discussion here. A more general but nonetheless quite spurious debate has arisen in relation to a purportedly radical critique of Sahlins's position. According to this critique, to claim that the Hawaiians were unintelligent enough to believe that a group of men, albeit of quite different appearance, were their gods who were returning to them and for once were appearing before them in flesh and blood, is the kind of proposition revealing yet again that the social sciences are nothing but a Western ethnocentric discourse. Because, as the argument goes, this amounts to affirming once again that non-Westerners are just overgrown children who, driven by pre-logical thinking that is mystical and irrational, will, at the drop of a hat, jump to conclusions that are patently absurd. Only a Westerner could demonstrate such contempt, thereby prolonging the economic and ideological imperialism of the past two centuries.

An anthropologist of Sri Lankan origin, Gananath Obeyesekere, who teaches in the United States but has never done work in Oceania or written about this field of research, has become the champion of this position by claiming that his status as a non-Westerner has allowed him to perceive and reveal this Western manner of 'mythifying' other cultures. In 1992 he published *The Apotheosis of Captain Cook: European mythmaking in the Pacific*. For Obeyesekere, Sahlins's theory about a deification of Cook by the Hawaiians is yet another example of the countless fantasies that Europeans have conceived about Pacific peoples and all such exotic 'natives'. Sahlins's analysis is just an extension of the manner in which Westerners have always condescendingly interpreted the cultural representations of exotic peoples. Moreover, the critic, on the grounds that he is of Asian origin, claims to be in a better position to analyse Polynesian history than a Westerner.[3]

It is clear that we have to reject the notion that Obeyesekere could have, *a priori*, a point of view closer to the 'native' one just because he is not a Westerner. Have we reached the point where it is birth certificates that confer or withhold the right to talk about cultures other than our own? How starkly Obeyesekere's treatment of this episode of Polynesian history represents a new version of Orientalism! Indeed, Obeyesekere invokes the history of India and Southeast Asia to define his position in relation to the Polynesian case. To support his argument he calls upon the absence of facts similar to the situation as Sahlins reconstructed it—or, that is, as Obeyesekere (over)interprets Sahlins's reconstruction. No Eastern history source indicates, he says, that men mistook other men for gods:

> When Sahlins expounded his thesis ... I was completely taken aback at his assertion that when Cook arrived in Hawai'i the natives believed that he was their god Lono and called him Lono. Why so? Naturally my mind went back to my Sri Lankan and South Asian experience. I could not think of any parallel example in the long history of contact between foreigners and Sri Lankans or, for that matter, Indians (Obeyesekere 1992: 8).

This position has nothing to do with the historical anthropology of Polynesia. Rather it relates solely to the concerns of the members of certain Western intellectual milieux[4] who, as in Obeyesekere's case, demonstrate their inability to conceive of cultural difference without wanting to assimilate and reduce that difference. Because of course the notion of 'divinity' they have in mind is that of the Christian West—or of a certain Orientalism in which 'Eastern religions' are redefined and forced into the mould of Western binary logic (human *or* divine). How can one seriously mount an argument by making a comparison of this sort? For several millennia the history of this South Asian region of the world has been one of migrations, conquests, and the appearance of peoples speaking an unknown language. The idea of the existence of different peoples had long been a familiar one throughout the region. But, at the same time, the Hawaiians, like all the inhabitants of Eastern Polynesia, had only seen and known

---

[3] See Sahlins's response (1995) and commentaries criticising Obeyesekere (Borofsky 1997, Zimmermann 1998). Sahlins (*ibid*.) provides a comprehensive bibliography of his numerous previous works about Captain Cook. And he mentions (p. 3) critiques similar to Obeyesekere's but published earlier to which he had immediately replied (Sahlins 1989). In the preface Sahlins (1995) suggests that, if the lengthy titles of 18th-century texts were still in vogue, the title of his book could have been: 'How Gananath Obeyesekere Turned the Hawaiians into Bourgeois Realists on the Grounds That They Were "Natives" Just Like Sri Lankans, in Opposition to Anthropologists and Other Prisoners of Western Mythical Thinking'.

[4] It needs to be emphasised that Obeyesekere is an American professor, even if he originally came from Sri Lanka. It is in the United States that his book has been given prominence by different associations.

men like themselves, neighbouring peoples whose languages were closely related, since the settlement of their islands by the Eastern Polynesians a thousand years ago, and after the Western Polynesians (and the Eastern Fijians) had colonised the previously uninhabited western islands one or two thousand years earlier. It is therefore necessary to accept the hypothesis that, in the Polynesian case, the appearance of creatures who were totally different has given rise to particular interpretations and responses that were drawn from the non-human world.

We must also inquire into the way in which the Polynesians conceived the non-human. The logic operating here was not necessarily based on that of *distinctive opposition*. We can see Obeyesekere's sleight of hand in placing on the same level of equivalence a fact reported by Sahlins and attested to in the relevant documents—'they called him Lono'—and an abrupt summary of Sahlins's analysis—'he was their god Lono'—, as if this latter statement of identity were self-evident and did not demand precisely that the Polynesian relationship to the divine ('to be a god') be differentiated from other similar relationships in other cultures. Obeyesekere is unaware that in this broad Polynesian terrain the notion of *atua*—which signifies 'god' but also, if I may offer a definition, 'every person or thing presenting a mysterious aspect and to which one attributes the productive power of *mana*'—has no more to do with the Western-Christian notion of 'divine' than it has to do with the gods of India or Southeast Asia. But we still need to use the word 'god' for Lono, Kū, Tangaroa, and so on as there is not another more appropriate term. Furthermore, Obeyesekere does not seem to realise that the Hawaiians, like all the peoples of the earth, only knew their gods through the 'images' that they themselves made of them for their rituals. The interpretation of Cook's arrival was subject to this same way of thinking. Thus the sails of the European boats bore a strong resemblance to the image of the god Lono which was carried around to be displayed throughout the island during the ritual (the white barkcloth fixed to a wooden frame).

There is no point in devoting any more attention to this critique of Obeyesekere's. But it does serve to remind us once again of the extent to which Western scientific thought falls so easily into the trap of dichotomous thinking: exclusion/assimilation (Tcherkézoff 1987). Some exclude: in Obeyesekere's view that would be Sahlins's attitude. Others assimilate: that is in fact Obeyesekere's attitude when he forcibly assimilates Polynesian cosmology to a Western (or 'Oriental') one in which the divine is irrevocably cut off from the human world, as it is for Westerners or in what Westerners call 'Oriental' thought (this category being itself constructed by Westerners in what is a mixture of straightforward oppositions and naive assimilations to a Western model).

Let us leave all of this aside and try to rediscover what happened in that last third of the 18th century when this scenario was being played out. I am going

'First Contacts' in Polynesia

to refer here to other cases than the Hawaiian one and use as supporting evidence what we already know from the Samoan example.

These cases reveal that the Polynesians asked themselves more *questions* than they formulated answers, just as the Amerindians did two and a half centuries earlier when facing the Spanish conquest. Sometimes the answer that was given to these questions was ambiguous. When we look more closely at the linguistic forms used at the time to formulate ideas about the newcomers, we can see that the Europeans were indeed taken for superhuman beings—there is no doubt about it—but as envoys and representatives, in a rather new form, of the great creator (often the god in question was Tangaroa). The newness of the form was no obstacle: Tangaroa (literally 'the Unlimited') had unlimited powers of innovation. The newcomers were neither gods nor ancestors properly speaking, then, but a partial form of these higher powers.

2. The hierarchy of 'light'

The idea of an assimilation to the divine is obviously troubling if one makes the mistake of interpreting it in the Christian manner. For the moment, let us simply say that the Polynesians considered the strange nature of the Europeans in the light of divinity rather than of barbarism (at least in the beginning). Or, more simply still, let us accept the notion that the newcomers were seen as superhuman, not subhuman, beings. What was the reason for this? A number of factors were operating here: the way the Europeans looked to the Polynesians, as well as the objects they brought with them. These objects were terrifying (firearms) or amazing (items made of linen, metal and glass).

'Luminous' appearance

There is no doubt that the look of their skin played a part in the way that the Europeans were viewed by the Polynesians. The word used in Western Polynesia since the 17th century to designate the Europeans (*Papāla(n)gi*), and still used today (see chapter 11), continues to be applied only to light-skinned foreigners. It is not used for a 'Melanesian' or African visitor. The paleness of the visitors became incorporated into a pan-Polynesian cosmology in which light, clarity and whiteness were and still are highly valued as beneficent signs of the divine, and stand in opposition to the obscurity of night, where death reigns supreme. The world was first of all the Night-darkness, *Po*. The primordial gods and the source of the powers of life are found there in perpetuity. But there would have been no life if, subsequently, Night had not left a place for the appearance of Day-light, *Ao*.[5] Since then, the work of ritual which guarantees social life consists of extracting from the Night certain powers which, once brought into the Day,

---

[5] See Sahlins (1985a: 110; 1985b; 1989: 373) and Babadzan (1982, 1993). For Samoa and Tahiti, Tcherkézoff (2003b: chapter 1) provides several examples and some cosmogonic narratives; for Tahiti, see Babadzan (1993).

can be domesticated and used to reproduce life. Agriculture and fishing—with their complementary stage of cooking—as well as producing children, are based on this dynamic. The reference to the 'sky' and to the 'light' is therefore fundamental.

The appearance of superhuman beings of 'luminous' appearance was the promise that the (re)production of life would be guaranteed through this ritual activity. The missionaries who came much later on were not to know the extent to which this religious interpretation of first contact with Europeans had already established frameworks that would make their integration into Polynesian society much easier. It may be that certain legends were born at this time, legends that would be invoked by the chiefs much later, in the 19th century, about a power that the sky had been promising them for a long time (Ma'ia'i 1960).

Throughout Polynesia much attention was paid to the fairness of the skin. It was never a question of 'skin colour' as Europeans said and still say. On the contrary, in places where, as in Samoa, age-old conceptions concerning the high value placed on the fairness of the skin are still current, modern experience has produced a notion now thought to be of great merit, a notion that defines anti-racism. When talking about American or South African history, Samoans (young people, not just teachers) condemn the racism that has been rife in those countries and say, 'one should not be *fa'ailogalanu*', 'one should not attribute any meaning to [skin] colour'. The fairness of the skin (Samoans say 'the whiteness') relates to the cosmological and cosmogonic value of the sun's 'light', *ao*—which, for Samoans is not a question of skin 'colour'.

Persons of high status stayed inside their houses in order to avoid the fairness of the skin darkening under the rays of the sun. Those who were deeply tanned thus showed that they worked for others, in the plantations or at sea. In Samoa, this imperative to keep the skin as fair as it had been at birth applied particularly to women who were not married and who were said still to be virgins. In Tahiti, women of high rank would often withdraw from their normal outdoor activities with this aim.[6] In the Cook Islands when it was decided to hold a great feast, the participants allowed themselves a year of preparation not only to rehearse new dance movements and prepare a mountain of yams, but also to give the main actors time to become whiter and fatter since, at the feast, there would be competition over who would 'be the fairest and the fattest of all present'.[7] Obesity was doubly significant: the abundance of food meant an abundance of 'services' offered by dependants and, too, a tauter skin more easily regained the fairness of skin that everyone loved to see in the newborn child. In Samoa the

---

[6] For Samoa, my field notes; for Tahiti, see Oliver (1974: 157, 435).
[7] Account given to the missionary William Wyatt Gill at Mangaia for the period at the end of the 18th century and the beginning of the 19th. The words are Gill's who gives a summary without quoting (1880: 181).

chiefs avidly sought the young girls with the lightest hair. When a girl fitted this requirement, she was forbidden to cut her hair because, once it was long enough, it was used for making ceremonial headdresses after it had been bleached with different preparations to produce a reddish colour.

Polynesian notions about chieftainship and hierarchy also illustrate the high prestige accorded to sunlight and its brightness, as Sahlins has already noted for Hawaii. The Hawaiian chief is currently referred to as 'the heavenly one' (*ka lani*). More generally, says Sahlins,

> The specific quality of aristocratic beauty is a brilliance and luminosity that Hawaiians do not fail to connect, in myth, rite, and chant, with the sun. Such beauty is properly called divine, for like the gods themselves, *it causes things to be seen* (1985a:18, my emphasis).

The objects of the Europeans also fitted with the premium placed on light and brilliance: the fire from cannons and muskets, the gleaming of objects made of metal and glass, and of course the reflective power of mirrors. We might add that if all this cosmic sociology remained opaque to the Europeans, they knew perfectly well what could be of use to them. They managed to conduct a rather profitable trade in glass (we have seen the extraordinary fate of glass beads in Samoa) and then, quite rapidly, they made huge profits selling coloured materials (after their initial success with red fabrics at the time of the earliest contacts, as we have seen too). Today the sale of printed fabrics with floral designs in the brightest colours has made Southeast Asia the supplier of the shirts that are described as 'Hawaiian' for the whole of Polynesia. And the demand is not about to dry up. Everyone can compete easily enough when the competition for 'brilliance and luminosity' is limited to garments. A shirt with a new design can be acquired more easily than the power of old (often called *mana*) which called for wars and sacrifices.

Let me say something more about this basic notion of visibility. Sahlins also quotes a warrior legend (*ibid.*). The hero gets ready to join battle. When he appears, the crowd shouts out, praising his beauty. Even the animals sing his praises. The pebbles on the beach clash and clang. The thunder rumbles, the dead come back to life and the spirits suddenly become visible. The grass goes yellow, smoke descends towards the ground. This legend provides a particularly good illustration of the power of visibility. The brightness of the chief is cosmic: men, animals and things are affected by it. Like every manifestation of the divine it is also simultaneously an act of wonder, 'beautiful' and luminous, and immensely dangerous: the world could easily turn upside down. Indeed, the smoke descends and the spirits, who by definition are invisible and dangerous, become visible. But here too there is ambivalence. If the spirits are made visible, do they not then become more controllable? Or at least one can avoid them more easily. Night becomes *visible*—hence controllable—and that is thanks to the *luminous source* that the person of the chief embodies.

Sahlins also mentions the importance of the gaze in old Hawaiian ritual. 'To respect'—or 'to desire sexually'—someone was expressed by 'to set one's eyes on' *kau ka maka*. He adds: '"to see" (*ike*) in Hawaiian (as in French or English) is "to understand", but it is also "to know sexually"' (*ibid.*: 18-19). 'To see' is 'to understand' (similarly in Samoan). In human sacrifice, where the victim was generally a man guilty of transgressing, his eyes were dealt with first (gouged out; the left eye was given first to the god to 'eat'). Indeed, through his transgression, the victim, it was said, was 'he whose eyes were "cooked" *makawela*'.[8] In the same vein, you could not look at a chief: to do so would have broken a taboo.[9]

The Polynesian hierarchy

'Such beauty is properly called divine, for ... it causes things to be seen.' Sahlins is not generalising, but we have here, with these notions about the source of light and visibility, *the best illustration possible of the functioning of the Polynesian hierarchy*, both in the east (Tahiti, Hawaii etc.) and in the west (Samoa, Tonga etc.), at the time of contact and still today in some cases, particularly in the west. This hierarchical logic relating chiefs to dependants explains the continuity between gods and men. This continuity characterises the whole set of Polynesian social representations which were called into play in early contacts, as in the context of Cook's arrival in Hawaii.

In Polynesia, before the introduction of Western commerce, the relationship superior/inferior was always a question of status, within an inclusive hierarchy (holism), and not of stratification where difference arises from quantitative comparisons between individuals of their relative amounts of power, wealth and so on.[10] The hierarchical relationship implies two aspects which are not incompatible despite appearances: mutuality and unilaterality. The relationship is one of interdependence, and this interdependence is oriented in one direction

---

[8] Sahlins says only 'burnt eyes' for *makawela* (p. 19).

[9] In the Polynesian conception of taboo, *tapu*, which acts to maintain social distance, contrary to the Indian logic of the *varna* and the caste system of avoidance, it is not the superior who is contaminated, but the inferior. Of course, as the transgressor who had dared to look at a chief was cooked (in a real sacrifice) before he could become fully contaminated and 'burned' by the brilliance emanating from the chief, the burning power of the chief's gaze could never actually be put to the test. The pan-Polynesian manifestations of respect by lowering oneself in front of a superior took various forms: bowing the head and thus avoiding looking into the eyes of the superior, sitting down, getting out of one's canoe and swimming beside it when passing (at sea) in front of a chief's house, and also, as we shall see in chapter 10, undressing the upper part of one's body.

[10] I have explored elsewhere the pertinence of this distinction between two forms of inequality: in relation to categories of social differentiation in Samoa (Tcherkézoff 1995a, 2003b: chapters 5 and 6) and, from a trans-cultural point of view, in the area of dual classifications (Tcherkézoff 1987, 1994a, 1994b).

only. Interdependence exists because each of the two poles in this dual relationship is meaningless without the other. But there is a hierarchical orientation to the relationship since one of the poles is everything for the other but the inverse never holds true.

Indeed, when the value which is the point of reference is something like 'light' rather than, for example, the production of metal tools, that value *implies interdependence*. What is a source of light if this source finds nothing to illuminate? What is a god without a world that he has created? One would not even know that there was a light. A light is not *seen* unless it rests on some being or on some object. In the same way a Polynesian chief without dependants has no existence. But the relationship is directional: one of the participants is the source of light and the other becomes visible because he is illuminated. The dependant finds a way to participate in life (the world of 'light' *Ao*) solely through his relationship to the chief: he is then illuminated. For him, the chief is therefore *a source of life*. The same goes for the chief in relation to the gods. In Western Polynesia, this relationship has continued into the present (Samoa, Tonga), even if the divine point of reference is now that of the Bible.

That is why, in the Polynesian hierarchical system, social differentiation is always conceptualised as the local replication of a divine/human relationship. In this sense, every person who is superior to me is an ancestor-god to me, a source of light, a source of life. But this does not imply any kind of mysticism or theory about a superhuman substance found in the body of the chiefs. On the contrary, it is a very down-to-earth form of reasoning which stems from the physical nature of light.

According to this way of thinking, the gods are ancestor-gods: the first ancestors are always 'children' of the gods and they acquire their powers; the chiefs personify these gods and ancestors, they are said to 'incarnate' them (see below). In the same way, the gods are already human and by definition they possess the character weaknesses of men (therefore one could cajole them in the rituals with offerings, or take them unawares by seizing their wealth in ritual raids).

The reasoning behind ownership is quite different. With a principle of superiority based on the possession of metal tools, each person can establish an independent productive capacity (using these tools to produce carved goods) and enter into competition with other producers in selling these goods. In fact, since contact, this notion of stratification, which is differentiation through ownership, has been added on to the concept of hierarchy, in order to increase an actor's prestige very rapidly. In some cases, it has nearly eliminated the traditional hierarchy. The new political powers and the new markets that arose in 19th-century Polynesia illustrate this socio-economic transformation. In Hawaii today the way in which it developed could not even be guessed at without consulting the archival sources. In some other places, as in Samoa, this transformative process is being completed right now, and a wealth of information applicable to the whole of Polynesia can be gained from observing the way in which it is happening.[11]

The example of land, a crucial issue in contemporary Samoa, also provides one of the clearest illustrations of this process. As long as land is not an individual good that can be bought and sold, as long as it remains 'customary', that is a good whose sole owner is the founding ancestor, rivalry between clans is expressed by claims relating to the length of time that has elapsed since the founding of their respective territories. Length of settlement is shown by the seating positions around the ceremonial 'circle' at gatherings that bring together all the families of the village. Rivalry thus presupposes a minimal level of agreement about the rules of belonging to this 'circle'. This is still the situation in eighty per cent of Samoan territory. Competition is played out within the hierarchy. But, on the island of Oahu in Hawaii where the capital Honolulu is situated, rivalry is played out on the foreign exchange market between the dollar and the yen, because most of the land (we need to talk rather of buildings and building sites) belongs to foreign firms. There is no common belonging that needs to be reaffirmed at each gathering. Membership here no longer depends upon local landowners but on a global notion: the foreign exchange market.

To summarise, when we talk about a 'chief' in relation to Polynesia, we need always to ask what is the system of social differentiation by which this 'chief' has established his status: stratification or hierarchy? At the time of contact, there is no doubt that it was the second system that held sway. That fact is important to this discussion, because hierarchy, by contrast with stratification, involves a continuous gradation which includes within it the social body *in toto*. There is a continuum stretching from the greatest gods to the humblest of men.

Every human being is therefore a part of the divine. According to this logic, every individual exists solely because a source of light illuminates them. This source of light is referred to by the idea of 'god' and of 'ancestor'; it is personified on earth by the 'chiefs'. The Europeans arrived in this context: a hierarchy of light. By their appearance and their objects, they seemed to be situated on the side of the light, and they even appeared more luminous than some of the 'chiefs'. They were therefore asked, quite reasonably, if, during their voyage, they had 'passed through the sun' (see below).

3. Weapons, tools, glass jewellery and fabrics

A basic element of the Polynesian perspective relating to contact was to observe the mastery of lightning by the Europeans, from within their muskets and

---

[11] For concrete examples, in the Samoan case, see Tcherkézoff (1997a: second part; 2003b: chapters 3, issues about land, and 6, issues about the political system).

cannons. Thunder and lightning, besides their intrinsic power, are 'celestial' elements, attributes of the demiurge Ta'aroa-Tagaloa-Tangaroa and/or of the other primordial gods.[12] There is a tendency in the ethnohistory of early contacts to overlook the presence of firearms, but all the first contacts brought with them scenes of violence and death. As soon as the Europeans believed that they were being attacked because the canoes which were coming to meet them were too numerous or because the men who climbed on board, sometimes without being invited, began seizing or just touching what they could, sometimes throwing the strange objects that they saw on the deck towards their canoes, they would use their muskets and then their cannons. I have already discussed, in relation to the visit of Lapérouse, how we might understand these 'thefts'.

The story should be told of how, at the first salvo that killed a Tahitian in a canoe, the man's companions tried to sit him up again in his seat, and were a long time in accepting that this body which made no response to any entreaty was quite lifeless, even though it had been struck neither by spear nor club. And then there is the terror of a group of Tahitians who, standing on the beach watching the first skirmish between the warriors of the island and Wallis's soldiers, suddenly found cannon balls fired first on to the sand and then into the forest when women and old men tried to take refuge there in their fright.

The guns and cannons were not the only new objects which seemed to be superhuman. The Polynesians also admired the metal tools (in a number of cases, but not in Samoa, as we know) and glass jewellery. The hardest wood, the finest basalt blade, the most highly honed bone and the sharpest cutting shell were no match for the axe and the knife, as well as for the nails that could be made into gimlets and fish hooks (at that time the European nails used at sea were the size of a small dagger). Cutting tools were already highly revered since they made it possible to build houses and boats, which were always dedicated to the ancestors and whose size was a clear sign of status. These tools were themselves subject to rites of consecration. So the new metal tools were a great boon because they were classified as part of the class of tools that were already 'taboo', while at the same time they increased tenfold the effectiveness of these taboo implements in cutting pieces of wood.[13] The hooks were no less sacred. They

---

[12] Clearly we need to make a precise interpretation for each particular case. In Tonga, for example, Tangaloa was the great god of the sky at Tongatapu, the southern part, but only the god of the craftsmen in the northern part of the archipelago. Elsewhere he was only one of the four creator gods. Generally speaking, the gods normally lived at Pulotu (an invisible island, situated in the west), and when thunder was heard, it was, some Tongans say, the sound of the heated discussions between the gods which reached human ears (Ferdon 1987: 70-1).

[13] This relationship of one to ten was attested to by the Tahitians in 1797, by which time stone adzes were already a thing of the past, thirty years after Wallis's arrival (Baré 1985: 180, and see p. 178 for the incantation for the consecration rite of the adze).

featured in the ceremonial exchange of precious goods.[14] It is therefore not at all surprising to see that the first nails that were obtained from the Europeans were not even made into tools but were kept as sacred objects in the ritual basket of a chief or priest.[15]

Furthermore, the Europeans did not only come with prefabricated metal tools but they also brought their forge which was needed for doing repairs in the course of a voyage. The Polynesians saw these newcomers gain control over an element which was first of all malleable, reddish in colour, and gave off the kind of heat that only lava flows can produce, but which then turned hard as stone. So it is no surprise to learn that in Western Polynesia the term chosen to designate iron is a word which was used for volcanic lava.[16] This association with subterranean forces must have strongly influenced the Polynesians' interpretation of the kind of being that the newcomers were in the direction of a certain form of divinity-superhumanity, especially since, on occasions, heavenly fire and earthly (volcanic) fire are associated. In Hawaii, thunder and lightning depended upon the god Lono, volcanoes on the goddess Pele. Now Lono was the uncle of Pele, and it was he who made sure that Pele's fire never went out. Volcanic activity could be directly associated with storms. And the rain clouds were manifestations of Lono.[17]

The topic of mirrors[18] and glass jewellery (the Samoan case of the blue beads is enough to show the importance of this category) would need to be taken up again if we wanted to provide a fuller discussion of this topic. And we also need to mention fabrics: we have seen how they have featured in all the first contacts in Samoa and we shall see them again in the first contacts in Tahiti (chapter 10). The quantity of fabric with which the body was swathed was a sign of status in Eastern and Western Polynesia. We shall meet this again at the end of this discussion when Captain Cook, and then, after his death, his portrait, which was carried by a local chief, were offered ceremonial fabrics. The Polynesians

---

[14] For instance in Tikopia where, in 1928, Raymond Firth was able to observe the social life of Polynesians who had only been acquainted with white men for a very short time, as well as in Samoa where hooks have been a category of objects conferred at marriage by the man's side.

[15] As Firth found when he arrived in Tikopia, a small Polynesian island situated in Melanesian territory and where contact occurred very late. See Firth (1936: 33) for iron objects, obtained in Vanuatu, that came from Lapérouse's shipwreck, and were kept in a temple; for the sacred basket holding the nails, see Firth (1967).

[16] In Tongan *ukamea*, in Samoan *u'amea*, from *uka*, meaning a state that is viscous but still hard (mud for example), and *mea*, reddish. These two basic words derive from proto-Polynesian. This note about metal has benefited from a comment made by Françoise Douaire-Marsaudon (1993: 795, 799 note 15) about a Tongan creation myth concerning a stone referred to by this word that is linked to a volcanic eruption.

[17] These mythological connections, pointed out by specialists such as Pukui, Beckwith and others, are revisited by Sahlins (1989: 379-80).

[18] In Samoa, the mother-of-pearl fixed to the great ceremonial headdresses, the *tuiga*, was replaced by little mirrors. Today these mirrored headdresses—which are still used on grand occasions—are considered as being made according to 'tradition' (*aganuu*).

desperately wanted to get the sheets, shirts and jackets of the newcomers, especially as these fabrics were water-resistant, whereas barkcloth, the material used in making Polynesian ceremonial attire, came from bark that had to be beaten out for a long time (the resulting pieces then being stuck together along their edges) and it disintegrated in the rain. The coats and jackets of the captains had great appeal: several layers enclosed the body, and red and gold braid shone brightly along the edges. Now the use of red braid to envelop the body was already a central ritual element in the great Tongan ceremony of the first fruits (yams symbolised the body and were entirely swathed in red bindings made from the tender part of the pandanus leaf) (Douaire-Marsaudon 1998). The large Hawaiian and Tahitian ceremonial capes were made of red and yellow feathers. The supreme Tahitian insignia, the *maro'ura*, was an ornament of red feathers, and the gift cycle in which it figured was of fundamental importance in the society (Babadzan 1993). I have already mentioned how, on the fine Samoan mats, rows of red feathers along the edges were, and still are, the most sought-after decoration. It should also be noted that, in pan-Polynesian mythology, the gods were supposed not to have hair (which appeared with men), but feathers.

4. The 'gods of here below' and the notion of *atua*

To summarise the situation, all of these perceived similarities placed the Europeans in the category of 'celestial' beings. But there is no need to see in this a new or extraordinary category. The creator god is celestial and the first chiefs are always the product of unions between the celestial beings and a mortal woman; so begin the genealogies of the great chiefs' names.[19] The legends are full of comings and goings between heaven and earth, involving the gods and the heroes as well as mere mortals. It is simply the case that sacredness is on the side of heaven. And the Europeans were very logically placed in this classification. Here again the idea of a hierarchy contrasted with that of stratification is relevant. The category of heaven is not a supernatural world, another 'stratum' of a stratification, but it is an ideal for humanity, the best that there can be along a continuum.

Therefore, to reject Sahlins's proposition that Cook was seen as a 'god', *akua*, by the Hawaiians and to overlook other sources that are equally clear on this point, is to refuse to accept that the Polynesians saw their chiefs as the descendants of divine unions or of unions that were half-divine and half-human. But this is exactly what the genealogists in these Polynesian societies related. It is quite undeniable that the Polynesians took the Europeans for '*atua*' (*akua* and so on), for '*aitu*', or for '*kalou*' (in Fijian). They actually used these words. For example, in the Marquesas Islands several sources from the end of the 18th

---

[19] Krämer (1995) has a number of Samoan examples.

century show quite unambiguously that the word *atua* was applied to the Europeans (Sahlins 1995: 174; Dening 1974: 73-4). In Tahiti, certain diviners or prophets in a state of trance were similarly called *atua*, where, too, the word also applied to the gods (Baré 1985: 115). We shall meet the Fijian example of *kalou* again. But we should keep in mind that the Hawaiian word *akua* applied at the same time to the gods (the entities of the Hawaiian world which seem to correspond to a Western notion of divinity) and to any supernatural entity, to any cult object, as well as to any strange and frightening object like the different instruments of the first voyagers (Sahlins 1995: 173). In short, there was no 'divine' form (*atua*) that was, by itself, (all of) god.[20]

This same logic operated when the Polynesians called the Europeans—or at least the captains—'chiefs', *ari'i*, since in this period chiefs were always manifestations of the gods and ancestors: manifestations, that is to say images. In 1788 the Tahitians mentioned Cook's name to Bligh as being 'the *ari'i* of Tahiti' (Baré 1985:160). We shall come across this expression again in the prayer that the Tahitians addressed to a portrait of Cook in 1790. Already in 1774, when the exchanges that were taking place between Cook and the Tahitian chiefs had become frequent, the Tahitians made an explicit comparison between their own social hierarchy and that which they observed on board the European ships: Cook was already an *ari'i* in the simple sense when his behaviour showed that he was the chief of his own people; it was the same thing in the case of Vancouver, and for the officers of the first missionary ship, the *Duff*, in 1797 (Baré 1985: 159, 162). The Samoan case presents a significant particularity. There, little by little, all the Europeans came to be called *ali'i* 'out of politeness' (*fa'aaloalo*), so that in Samoan the word took on the sense of the English 'Sir', and *ali'i* thus gained an additional meaning to that of 'chief'. Today, in the contemporary language, in verbal exchanges between Samoans, there are really two words *ali'i*, one of which means 'chief' and the other simply 'Mister, Sir'. But we should not forget that, at the time of contact, the chiefs (*ari'i*, *ali'i*) were themselves a manifestation of the divine.

The Europeans were therefore both *atua* and *ari'i*. Does that mean that they were untouchable in the way that the most prominent manifestations of the sacred would be untouchable in any religion? Not at all. When we examine the archival sources we see that the Polynesians of that period had great respect for what the European represented, but at the same time had no hesitation in treating this or that European familiarly, or harshly, or even abusively if he did not respect the local customs. The Tahitians had no hesitation in striking or even killing one of their European guests if, for example, he had conducted himself

---

[20] The remarkable study of the Hawaiian pantheon by Valeri (1985) shows this as well. The same logic was recognised by Durkheim who made use of it in constructing a model of the relationship, operating in the religious conceptions of numerous societies, between the concept of the individual soul and the collective sacred (Tcherkézoff 1995b).

improperly with a woman, or if he had killed another European adventurer whom they had adopted (Morrison 1989: 66, 72; Baré 1985: 162). We have already encountered a very good Samoan example in the adventurer Jackson's 1840 sojourn when he was residing with the Tu'i Manu'a, the chief, and was almost killed for having struck his host.

We should not be surprised at this. Even today we can observe how Samoans treat their own 'chiefs' (*matai ali'i* / *matai tulāfale*) and what they say about them. A *matai* is chosen to be the receptacle for the name of the founding ancestor. Every insult made to the 'title-name' and thereby passed down from generation to generation is avenged by death. But if the man himself shows that he is unworthy of representing this 'title', there will be no hesitation in abusing and even deposing him. The chief is a temporary 'body' of the founding ancestor, as the Samoans and the Tongans used to say and still do today: the category of the Tongan high chiefs is called the category of the 'chiefs-who-have-incarnated', *sino'eiki* ('body' is *tino*, *sino*). A chief has 'incarnated' the original sacred principle represented by the name of the ancestor and the corresponding land. All of this is *atua*.[21]

That is why still today the Samoan chief can be called, in a ceremonial way, 'an *atua* from here below'. In contemporary Samoan the chiefs are ceremonially referred to as *o atua o lalonei* (*atua*, 'god'; *lalo*, 'below'; *nei*, 'here'). The chief is 'an *atua* from here below', while God (previously the pre-Christian gods, now 'The Father', *O le Tamā*) 'is the God', *O le Atua*, with no other specification. The chief is a divine manifestation: a visible form here below of the sources of light-and-of-life situated in the sky. And even then it is only the 'title-name' that this chief bears (the name of the founding ancestor). We are not talking about the actual person that one has before one's eyes; he is a man like any other.

Here is a case where contemporary ethnographic observation notes that 'the Samoans can call their *matai* chiefs "*atua*"' in ceremonial forms of address. And yet, as anyone who has spent any length of time in Samoa will know, no Samoan sees his *matai* chief as 'god' (*O le Atua*, the name of the god of present-day Samoan Christianity). What is the '*atua*' dimension of this *matai* chief? Quite simply it is that title-name with which he is invested, the name of the founding

---

[21] I have pointed out that Father Padel would have gathered from the Samoans that they took the Europeans for '*aitu*'. The word *aitu* is post-missionary terminology for everything that is supernatural and which is not God. But, in the pre-contact era, and for some time after, all the *atua* (the spiritual forces that were behind or above, that were celestial) and all the *aitu* (the spiritual forces far on the horizon or down below, hidden in the forest, beneath the earth and in the sea) formed a continuum, as far as we can ascertain (from Cain's analysis, 1979, and the fact that missionaries like Stair or Turner had the greatest difficulty in coming to grips with the cosmology and were unable to provide coherent tables of classification which could discriminate between *atua* and *aitu*). It is only after Christianisation that a clear dichotomy was set up between an *Atua* as unique, sheer heavenly light, and the numerous *aitu* reduced to the status of nocturnal and malevolent spirits; in the case of the Australs, see Babadzan (1982).

ancestor. From the moment that he is invested as *matai*, at the death or deposition of the preceding *matai*, he incorporates the name of the founding ancestor and the group's genealogical memory. He becomes the *visible proof* that all the members of the family are 'the children of this land' where the founding ancestor settled.

What different behaviour can be observed among the members of the family to show that, after his investiture, this man has become an *'atua* from here below'? Firstly, there is the way of addressing him. He had a birth name. From the day of his investiture, it is the family name that he now takes as his name: the name of the founding ancestor replaces his birth name. And it can be seen that everyone, including his own, even his very young, children, suddenly changes their way of addressing him, even in private. They no longer call him by his birth name but by his '*matai* name' and in so doing address themselves as much to him as to all the *matai* who have borne this name, beginning with the founding ancestor. This, then, is what it means to be an '*atua*' man in Polynesia in the 1990s.[22] I do not think that things were very different in 1770, in Samoa or in Hawaii.

The Polynesians took the Europeans for '*atua*' entities. This translates, admittedly a little too rapidly, as: 'they took them for gods'. But to say that the Polynesians took men for gods is a summary expression used to indicate the *hierarchical continuity* that links the creator of the world, passing through the chiefs, and the lowliest little worm. The Polynesian chiefs were gods metonymically, because a Polynesian god, as a total being, always and only ever manifested itself in an infinity of partial forms. We have seen that this idea was often expressed in Polynesia by the word 'body' (*tino, kino, sino*), or 'image' (*ata, aka*). For, even today, in the case of the Samoan chiefs one can say that in a certain way the body of the individual who has been invested as chief in each generation is only the image of the title-name (the family name).

As soon as we recall these ideas, we realise that Obeyesekere's recent critique is completely inadequate, despite the bestseller status that it seems to have enjoyed. It is our vocabulary ('god' versus 'man') that creates a false impression of discontinuity where there is in fact none at all, as well as a false impression of identity in the notion of 'god', since Polynesians did and do discriminate the invisible *atua* and all its visible and partial bodies and images.

5. The boat-islands and images

It is the same linguistic trap that blinds us when it stops us from seeing that 'boats could be islands'. In his study of the way in which the Tahitians perceived

---

[22] For information about the whole of the contemporary *matai* system and its evolution since 1850, see the analysis in Tcherkézoff (1997a, 2003b: chapters 5 and 6) and, in English, but more briefly, Tcherkézoff (1998a, 2000a, 2000b).

the boats of Wallis, Bougainville and Cook, Baré (1985: 113-17) cites the 19th-century observers who collected local traditions and he draws on them to make an appropriate critique of all the readings that he terms 'positivist'. According to the missionary William Ellis, the European boats were described as 'islands inhabited by beings of a superior nature, upon whose orders lightning flashed and thunder rumbled' (the muskets and cannons). According to the trader and consul J.A. Moerenhout, 'the O-Tahitians mistook Wallis's ship for a floating island, seeing the masts as trees, the pumps as streams'. Teuira Henry, who assembled the notes of her grandfather, one of the first missionaries, adds that the stern or the prow of Wallis's ship 'was compared to a rock'. Baré notes that Sahlins finds the same traditions in Hawaii.

For the idea of a 'floating island', Baré recalls the presence of this metaphor in Tahitian myths that certainly seem to pre-date contact. These relate how the islands such as Tahiti arrived where they are 'like a ship' (the big Polynesian canoes which could carry scores of people, even as many as two hundred, and which were to disappear in the 19th century),[23] how the cliffs in the east of Tahiti were compared to the sculpture on the prow, how the political structure of each territory was called a 'canoe', the relative status of the dignitaries being shown by places occupied 'at the prow', 'on the mast', 'on the rigging' and so forth.

It is in this light that we might be able to understand an account from 1840 relating how a Tongan chief would have interpreted the arrival of Cook seventy years earlier.

> ... the old Chief gave me the following account of Captain Cook's visit: 'I was a little boy when Captain Cook and Captain Clark came. I went onboard ship, and took up a nail. Man called me "teef" (thief); me no teef. At first we went with our canoe, yams, and pigs, and seeing the fine figure-head on the vessel, thought *that* [emphasis in original] Captain Cook. We called to it a long time, and it would not speak or buy yams. We continued crying, "Will you buy yams, hogs, &c."; but there was no answer. So we stood gazing and wondering, till at last the Captain appeared, and then we found out our mistake. They sent up sky-rockets, and we were greatly alarmed, They went [up] to the sky, and then burst. We all thought them gods, and were much afraid.'[24]

---

[23] In Henry there can also be found myths comparing the island of Tahiti to a 'fish' that has arrived there and that the civilising hero has carved, which has immobilised it and produced the particular shape of the island (two islands linked by a narrow plain). See the myth cited by Danielsson (1981: 51).
[24] 'John Waterhouse, Journal of a Second Voyage from Hobart-town, Van-Diemen's Land, to the Polynesian Islands, commenced Wednesday, October 29th, 1840', entry for 22 March 1841 – Tongatapu, pp. 18-19': the text and the reference were given to me by Fergus Clunie (personal communication, February 2003).

Overlooking this translation from 1840 ('buy' etc), and assuming that, quite obviously, the word 'god' here translates *atua*, we should take note of how the prow of these ships might appear to Polynesian eyes. They would not have suddenly worked out a specific representation for the European boats, still less would they have had recourse to animism. But, quite simply, they saw the Europeans in the way that they did because the sculpture on the prow of a big ocean-going vessel often represented the *image* of the ancestor or the clan.

Our modern scruples are therefore unwarranted. In a sense, the *Dolphin* (Wallis's boat, the first European ship to come to Tahiti) was like a boat and the Europeans were like men. In another sense, the *Dolphin* was not a boat from the Polynesian perspective. For if the largest Polynesian craft could carry as many men as the *Dolphin*, or even more, such a craft nonetheless had two small keels instead of one large, deep keel. Moreover, it was a lot lower, it had no decks, hull, cabins, or iron anchors, it had only one sail—and, most significantly, it did not carry cannons. And these men were not men: they had mastery over lightning, they could forge the lava flow, and, as certain Hawaiians expressed it, they pulled from their bodies (their pockets) unknown riches, like iron and glass.[25] In summary, if the islands could be ships to the Tahitians, then ships larger than their ships could easily 'be' floating islands. And if the Tahitian or Hawaiian chiefs 'were' gods, then men who were more than men could easily be 'chiefs' (*ari'i*, *ali'i*, etc.) and 'gods' (*atua*, *akua*).[26] The two sets of terms were used to refer to the Europeans.

The image of the Hawaiian god Lono was a white barkcloth, which was stretched over a wooden framework for display as it was carried around. The sails of the Europeans ships resembled this image. *The European captains and sailors, swathed in layers of material, also resembled this image.* Indeed we need to be aware that the barkcloth was used as ceremonial dress and as the covering for the *tiki* (wooden or stone images representing the gods).[27] The European captains, who were covered in even more material, were more similar still to the image of the god: *a likeness running from image to image*. And in the example of the Tongan narrative from 1840, we should bear in mind that the prow firstly, and then James Cook in person, were both taken in turn for the image of the invisible principle that was supposed to guide these strange creatures, *Papālagi*,

---

[25] In Hawaii it was said that the Europeans thrust their hands into their bodies to take out riches (see the references in Baré 1985: 135). No Polynesian item of clothing had a pocket. (Clothing was made of leaves, or from mats of leaf strips, or of barkcloth, beaten out bark. All of these were wound around the body. No part of the mat or barkcloth would be in exactly the same place when the wearer put the garment on again. The technique of fine sewing was unknown.)

[26] The reader who is not familiar with Polynesia might be very surprised that a boat could be mistaken for a sacred place. It needs to be made clear that certain Polynesian boats were double canoes with a deck and carried a shrine on the deck: most reasonably, one departed with one's family, one's warriors *and one's gods* (as well as pets).

[27] In the case of Hawaii, see Valeri (1985) and for Tahiti, see Babadzan (1993, 2003).

on their boat. The Tongan's mistake is therefore understandable. He did not mistake a piece of wood for a man, but he wanted to know what these images stood for or represented. An *atua* image could as easily be inanimate, like the cult images that the Tongans and the other Polynesians possessed, or animate, as in the case of the 'chiefs-who-have-incarnated'—and in the case of James Cook as well, when he sailed in Tongan and Hawaiian water.

6. The sun as the point of reference, the canopy of heaven and Polynesian space-time

Sun, clouds and sky

As we have seen in the preceding section, the partial and particular character of the Polynesian attribution of 'divinity' (*atua*) to Captain Cook and other European visitors is shown by the fact that some European objects were just as 'divine' as their owners. It is also shown in a logic which unified geographical space and genealogical time.

The time the scientists on Cook's third voyage spent in looking at the sky and the instruments they used to do so was all observed with the utmost attention. The Hawaiians had numerous questions that they tried to articulate about what they saw. They came to the conclusion that the Europeans were intimately connected with the sun. John Ledyard, a member of Cook's expedition, wrote:

> [The Hawaiians thought that we] had so much to do with the sun and the rest of the planets ... [that] we must either have come from thence, or by some other way [be] particularly connected with these objects. ... to strengthen this inference they observed that the colour of our skins partook of the red from the sun (cited by Sahlins 1995: 173).

Another of Cook's companions relates how the Hawaiians seemed to assume that the route followed by the Europeans passed through the sun and that the flash from the fire of their muskets came from this same source.[28] An Australian newspaper published an article in 1804 on 'The Manners and Customs of the Inhabitants of Tongataboo', based on the recollections of a European resident, the wife of a Tongan chief:

> ...they adopt by common consent the strange and ludicrous supposition that such European visitors as have in too many instances unfortunately touched at their inhospitable spot have fallen in a state of exile from the clouds, and still retain the power of exciting *thunder*. Devoid of every idea that could be productive of a probable inference, they regard a

---

[28] John Rickman (Cook's third voyage), cited by Sahlins (1995: 174).

European with a jealous eye, because his difference of complexion implies something preternatural.[29]

In 1798, Captain Edmund Fanning, when he was at anchor in the Washington Islands (now the Marquesas), was given to understand by the missionary William Pascoe Crook (who was translating) that the inhabitants said of the ship that it

> must certainly have come from the clouds, and very soon after paddled off to a more respectful distance, but did not, however, cease their shouting or blowing their war conks [*sic:* conchae]. When some of the nearest chiefs beheld the bright blade of a broad-sword glittering in the sun's rays, they declared, one to another, that that battle axe must have come from the sun, it was so dazzling.

Later on, at Nukuhiva, an 'old chief' came on board to present 'a green branch' and 'a small pig'. The chief, in an 'uneasy state of mind', 'presented in the first place the green branch, accompanying this act with a short address; after which, doing in like manner with the pig'. The chief then bowed or touched the deck with his head:

> when on deck he insisted upon paying homage, but such I informed him, while raising him from his posture, and handing him to a seat on the quarter-deck, was not the manner of salutation when friends meet friends in my country, and as such I hoped we had now come together, adding that I myself was but a chief like himself: yet, said he, as I was given to understand through the interpretation of Mr Crook, there is this difference, you come from the thunder in the clouds, and are therefore more powerful than even my king.[30]

In the same period, in the Marquesas, Edward Robarts had noted in his journal, on arriving at Hivaoa:

> Great numbers of the inhabitants came to see me, my being the first white man that ever came to that part. In fact some was [*sic*] afraid to come near me, said I was a ghost. Others said I was from the sky. I endeavoured to undeceive them. Some of the fair sex would come and feel my hands, arms and feet. Others more rude would pinch me to see if I had feeling.[31]

A visitor to Fiji in 1808 noted that some of the women had told him where they thought he had come from. They pointed to the sun and said: 'peppa langa

---

[29] 'Said person was Elizabeth Morey, ex-ship 'Portland'- wife of Tongatapu chief Tukava' (Fergus Clunie, personal communication, February 2003). The emphasis is in the original text.
[30] 'Edmund Fanning's *Voyages and Discoveries in the South Seas 1792-1832* (1989: 103, 113)' (Clunie, personal communication, February 2003).
[31] See Dening (1974: 76-7). I am grateful to Fergus Clunie and Marshall Sahlins for drawing this reference to my attention.

tooranga martinasinger' [*papalagi turaga matanisiga*], which means 'the Papalagi are chiefs from the sun'.[32]

The world 'under the sky'

The reference to the sun might suggest that the Polynesians placed the Europeans in the remotest possible realm of their cosmos.[33] But, in the worldview of the Polynesians, the reference to the sun in fact helped to *narrow the genealogical distance* between them and the Europeans. A major source of intercultural misunderstanding between Europeans and Polynesians arose from the inability of Europeans to conceptualise space in the way that Polynesians did and still do in some contexts: where space is indissolubly linked to time.[34] The very idea which underpinned the European voyages after 1760, the idea of a geographical and cultural other world which had to be discovered, limited Europeans to a frame of vision that was solely spatial. How could it have been otherwise? These men were sailors, whose constant preoccupation from day to day was to determine their position on the ocean as accurately as possible, and they did this using maps and charts, the very navigational tools whose efficacy would be considerably enhanced in this second half of the 18th century.

But the Polynesians did not voyage in the European way, either in their mythical memories or along their trade routes. Their islands were ships that had once arrived in Polynesian waters. This metaphor was obviously linked to the history of their migrations. The elsewhere whence the island boat came was the place of origin, and therefore the place-time of Polynesian genealogical beginnings. Territories on these islands were hierarchically organised according to the length of the occupation of the land by each clan, so that the social organisation of space was also an historical image of elapsed time. In this geographical-and-chronological view of the world, the island that was most distant *in space* was always that which could be closest *in time* to the point of origin when the world of 'light' began.

Even the geometry of the cosmos conformed to this view. The world was a flat circle of islands and surrounding sea, overlooked and bounded by the canopy

---

[32] Marshall Sahlins (personal communication, February 2003), with reference to 'Patterson (1808: 106)'. Geraghty and Tent (2001: 174) also quote this. See *ibid*. for the bibliographical reference to Patterson 1817.

[33] This is how, later, certain European analysts (from missionaries to modern scholars) devised the erroneous idea that 1) Polynesians had deified the Europeans (in the Christian sense) and/or 2) that the Polynesians had believed that the Europeans came from another world (see chapter 11).

[34] The problem is a general one and is being felt keenly today when it resurfaces in discussions between Tahitian intellectuals about the 'right' way to use terms like *mua* ('before, in front of') and *muri* ('after, behind'), and about the fact that the 'right' way, because it is authentic ('traditional'), was, and must continue to be, fundamentally different from the logic underlying Western categories of thought, and, therefore, of the French language. The real problem is overlooked: the fundamental opposition is the Tahitian socio-centric way of evaluating the position of Ego in space and time *versus* the French universalistic-individualistic one (Tcherkézoff, 1998).

of heaven which formed a sort of bell on the surface of the land and the sea.³⁵ That is why, in the past as in the present, Samoans describe the 'whole world' by the expression 'what is under the sky', *'o le lalolagi*. At the end of the horizon, the sky and the land-sea meet. But this most distant point is also the oldest. At the very beginning, before the appearance of man, the sky lay flat upon the earth-sea, leaving no space for life to exist. But a civilising hero-god came and pushed back the sky by bending it, and then there was light. So he who would venture to the end of the horizon would rediscover the conditions that existed at the beginning of the world. In essence, he who is the most distant in space *and* in the relationship of *identity*, that is, he who is most different, still might prove to be the most original as well, the closest to the very inception of the world.

So it was that the more the Europeans who arrived appeared other—while being placed in the right category, that of the 'light'—the more they were seen as being a manifestation of the origin. There were not two possible origins, because there were not two 'worlds' (something which the first missionaries did not understand; see chapter 11). The Tahitians or the Hawaiians at the time could not conceive that there was another world and other human beings beyond the space which they habitually travelled over by land or sea and which was bounded by the canopy of heaven.

Nevertheless, this space was very big. For the Tahitians, it included all of Eastern Polynesia and perhaps even a part of Western Polynesia, maybe even as far as Rotuma, as shown on the famous 'map of Tupaia' which was dictated to Cook and was able to name so many distant islands. It was the same with the Maori (New Zealand) who remembered that they had come from elsewhere. This left room for various questions: the newcomers 'are spirits, but perhaps not the spirits of our ancestors'. They are creatures who are undoubtedly under the supervision of the creator of the world, Tangaroa, but they must have come from other islands, far, far away...

Here again the Western critique can sometimes go off the rails. Some would maintain that it is a reductive Western view to credit the Polynesians with a conception of their pre-Christian cosmos that is as closed in on itself as this (Geraghty and Tent 2001: 183, 185). The critics see this as an invention of the missionaries, especially of the missionary J.B. Stair who lived in Samoa in the

---

³⁵ For Tahiti, see Babadzan (1993) and the cosmogonic narrative in Tcherkézoff (2003b: chapter 1). For Samoa, see Stair (1897). The same thing was found in Tonga, Fiji and other islands. According to the journal of George T. Sinclair (1838-1842), who was Acting Master aboard the *Relief*, the *Porpoise* and the *Flying Fish*, Fijians thought their islands 'are in the centre of the world, which is a plain; the sky reaching it on all sides, tho' the sky they think ther [sic] is an outlet to other countrys [sic]. They think that the white men or Papylangys live beyond the sky and when they first saw them they thought they were spirits, hence their name Papilange or people of the sky'. It may be that his informant was a Tongan, Tupou Toutai, who was in the company of the Fijian chief with whom Sinclair was residing (text, reference and commentaries provided by Sahlins and Clunie).

1840s. On this analysis, proof that it is a Western misconception to represent the Polynesian cosmos as strictly circumscribed by the canopy of heaven would be the fact that the Polynesians would often travel from one archipelago to the other (*ibid*.). And they certainly did so, but where is the contradiction in that? Polynesian cosmology conceived of a world in the form of a bell: why doubt this idea given the large number of archival sources to support it? But even so, the canopy of heaven over the earth was not and is not static. *The canopy can expand as much as one likes to incorporate anything new*. The 'world under the sky', *lalolagi,* as Samoans say, is subject to an almost infinite extension because other islands are always able to be imagined. An example was given to me in 1981 by an old Samoan man. Several times he had heard reports, on the national radio of Western Samoa, about the people who were holding Tahiti 'hostage' by colonial rule and by conducting their 'terrifying tests which were polluting the Pacific'. When he learnt that I was French he said to me (in English): 'Ah yes, you come from that island near Tahiti which looks after it'. France, as the colonial power that governs Tahiti, was thought of as a Pacific island. 'The sea of islands'—as the Pacific is viewed by Polynesians (Hau'ofa *et al.*, 1993)—can always incorporate new 'islands' while remaining the same 'world'.

7. First conclusion: men/chiefs/gods

The misunderstanding propagated by Obeyesekere and others is very revealing about the typical Eurocentric intellectual conceptualisation of otherness. In the first place it is a kind of displaced paternalism: 'the Polynesians could not be unintelligent enough to mistake men for gods'. It is also a functionalist interpretation of political behaviour, something which we need to examine more closely.

Obeyesekere takes up arguments that had already been put forward by other researchers: Cook was perceived as the chief of his crew and so he was received as a 'chief', *ari'i*. Now, honorifically, Polynesian chiefs were often referred to, and treated, as gods. If Cook was compared to a god, it was only a matter of the Hawaiians using a form of politeness to refer to him. It is only later, during the 19th century, with the European reinterpretation of these early contacts, particularly among missionaries, that the hypothesis of Cook's deification came about.[36]

---

[36] The critique mounted in 1988 by several colleagues from Copenhagen (Bergendorff *et al.* 1988, and see bibliography in Sahlins 1989) contended that the Hawaiian deification of Cook as 'Lono' was just a hypothesis which emanated from Hawaiian students of the American mission in Hawaii in the 1830s (some of whom were to write treatises on ancient Hawaii). Thus it is a 'Western representation—one made from within a Christian paradigm'. In 1778 Cook was simply assimilated to a general Hawaiian category of a more or less deified chief, a category which would only be split in two (men/gods) later on in the context of the European Christian interpretation of the Hawaiian pantheon. We can see how Obeyesekere took up the same erroneous idea, namely that in order to examine the Hawaiian equation 'Cook=Lono' we must keep in mind the absolute distinction between the categories 'men' and 'gods'—and how he then concluded that in Hawaii in 1778 Cook was never viewed as Lono. Both Obeyesekere and

In response to this argument about Cook's divinity amounting to no more than an honorific term of address, Sahlins, calling on Valerio Valeri, replied that, in pre-1820 Hawaii, a chief was called by the name of a god because he was perceived as a real 'manifestation' of the divine among men:

> Valeri (1985:143-53) gives another textual example. The very notion of 'godly blood' (*waiakua*) signifies the categorical assimilation of god and chief in Polynesian terms, inasmuch as the ancestor is to his descendants as a general class is to particular instances. Valeri argues that naming a chief after a god again means the same: a chief designated Lono would be a manifestation of Lono (Sahlins 1995: 128-9).

To deny this second version would be to deny that the Polynesians of that time possessed, like any other society, a theory of ritual efficacy. But every society, 'exotic' or Western, past or present, prides itself on having a theory of this kind (even if 'we', meaning contemporary Westerners, reserve the epithet 'ritual' for people other than us and invest our own theory of efficacy in 'science'): a particular method for handling ritual (or 'scientific') objects allows life-giving powers to be made present and domesticated for a brief time, these powers always being represented as exterior to the social group. In each case a category of beings or objects serves to bring about this domestication. In Polynesia it was the 'chief'. The Polynesian notion of 'chief' consisted—and sometimes still consists—of making a man, through ritual, become the receptacle of a portion of these powers.

In Samoa, on the day-to-day level, this seems to happen as simply as through a process of naming. As soon as the rite of investiture for the chief of the extended family (*matai*) is over, the new office-holder is no longer called by the name by which he has been known since his birth, but by the title-name (the name of the ancestor or of a god) assigned to him, as I have already described. Is this just a simple honorific practice? In that case how would we explain that still today, in Samoa, such a man's own children, even the very youngest ones, immediately

---

the proponents of the earlier critique fail to see the difference between a hierarchical-encompassing type of opposition and a purely *distinctive* opposition of the phonological type (Tcherkézoff 1994a, 1994b).

Furthermore, in both cases there is the misplaced belief that a critical reading of the European misconceptions produced during the 19th century by itself can provide a sufficient basis for understanding what happened in Pacific societies in pre-contact and early contact times. If such a reading tells us what did *not* happen, it does not tell us anything about what actually *did* happen. Only the appraisal of detailed ethnographic accounts written by those who worked in the local language (men such as Morrison for Tahiti or Krämer for Samoa) can provide us with the information we need to make reliable ethnohistorical judgements about the beliefs and practices of Pacific societies of the pre-contact and early contact era. Significantly, Obeyesekere is now extending his method to another topic—'Cannibal talk in the South Seas'— in order to create another artificial controversy, this time about the supposed European invention of cannibalistic practices as a feature of numerous pre-contact Pacific societies (see Obeyesekere 1998, 2003, and the critique by Sahlins 2003; see web pages ('Topical issues': 1. 'Cannibal talk...' at <http://www.pacific-credo.net>).

begin calling him by this new name in the most ordinary interactions of daily life? In Samoa and elsewhere in Polynesia, the terminology of address, even in the most private contexts, uses only proper names. Thus, in the family circle, the way of saying 'dad' can be seen to change abruptly: the birth name is replaced by the title-name acquired in the rite of investiture to the headship of the extended family. It is quite unnecessary that these children have some kind of representation of a mystical principle or of an ancestral substance that has entered their father's body. Firstly, they are too young to fully understand this kind of representation. Secondly, in contemporary Samoa, there is no theory of this kind that holds sway even among adults. However, verbal intercourse shows that it is not a matter of honorific formality but of a whole new identity.[37]

The critique addressed to Sahlins reveals a naïve assumption: the members of the Polynesian social group have put in place a social contract between themselves—'we choose you as "chief"'—and have bestowed an 'honour' upon the person in question (calling him 'god') to make him more visible…but in relation to whom? If the conferring of the name of a god or an ancestor is merely honorific, for whose benefit is this staged? We fall back inevitably upon the kind of explanation in which elites of chief-priests are manipulating the masses. But in contemporary Samoa it takes no more than a few days spent in the company of a group who has just elected its chief to see the absurdity of this model. When the chief of a Samoan family is called 'an *atua* on earth', a 'god of here-below'—but with all the ambiguities of the word *atua* (*akua*) that we have already seen in the Hawaiian, Marquesan, Tahitian and Maori examples—this term of address, while ceremonial, is not on that account just metaphorical. The chiefs, once invested, make the reality of ancestral origins visible. I have emphasised the importance of this notion of 'visibility': to make something visible is to unveil it. It is also to make it understood: the word 'understand' is formed by reduplicating the word 'light' in Samoan or the word 'image' in Hawaiian.

At the time of early contact, Polynesian ontology was *holistic* in the following sense. The individual is always the partial and visible aspect of another encompassing reality (gods, founding ancestor of a title-name); he is an imperfect and incomplete replica like all re-presentations. But Western observers have difficulty in understanding this. For them, this other reality must be analysed as a 'religious' or 'political' supplement added on to the individual. In short, it comes down to a question of belief and of function. These beliefs are instantly and resolutely confined within the boundaries of a healthy Western Christian rationality where men and God cannot be confused.

---

[37] This does not prevent the same 'chief' who has been invested in this way from being stripped of this title-name if he shows himself to be 'unworthy' in acts that he may subsequently commit. He will lose the title-name and it will be given to another man according to ritual. The particular individual is not confused with what he represents of the ancestral origins of his group.

Our Western observers ask themselves: 'human *or* divine?' But this question was meaningless in pre-Christian Polynesia and often it still is meaningless. We talk about 'descending' from our ancestors, but, for us, the ancestor is like his descendant: he is, was, an individual. But the Polynesian view was completely different: the Polynesians considered that the god is to the chief (and to all men), and the ancestor is to his descendants, what a class is to its elements, according to the formula already quoted from Sahlins. Here again it is the same relationship that needs to be conceived between Lono as concept and his various 'manifestations' in ritual, those assembled on the spot (the barkcloth stretched over a wooden frame) and those which have occasionally presented themselves to the Hawaiians, as with James Cook in person:

> In any event it is good to keep in mind this Hawaiian principle that gods called 'Lono' are so many bodies (*kino*) or specific refractions of the inclusive Lono when reading the tortuous argument of Bergendorff *et al.* about why the Hawaiians could not have assimilated Captain Cook to the god Lono (Sahlins 1989: 384-5).[38]

We shall encounter this 'principle' again at the end of this discussion in relation to the treatment of the image-of-Cook by the Tahitians.

8. The questions on the lips of the islanders at the time of the first contacts: 'perhaps not like our goblins', 'perhaps on a boat sent by Tangaroa'

A Hawaiian tradition tells of how the chief of an island was warned of the arrival of the Europeans who had already made a stay at another island: their speech was incomprehensible, their boat was 'like a temple', their clothes were stuck on to their skin, smoke came out of their mouths (from their pipes), and so on.[39] When we come across descriptions such as these, we can see how the conclusions drawn by the inhabitants of different islands might have varied. For the Hawaiians the chief of these never-before-encountered people must have been a form of the god Lono. But elsewhere in Polynesia these people were simply taken for a kind of 'spirit': *aitu* in Samoa, as we know, or *tupua* among the Maori.

---

[38] See also Sahlins (1985a: 146-51) for a discussion of this aspect in terms of a 'hierarchy of logical types in the structure of the discourse'. He points out very simply that: 'the English (or French) distinction between 'god' and 'man' is not the same as the apparent Hawaiian parallel of *akua* and *kanaka*, because *kanaka* as designating '(ordinary) men' thus stands in definitional contrast as well to *ali'i* or 'chief'. In the Hawaiian, 'chief' and 'god' are transitively alike by opposition to men; nor would the difference of gods and men correspond to that between spirits and mortals, since some mortals (chiefs) are also gods. There is no necessary starting point for any such cultural scheme in "reality"...' (ibid.: 147).

[39] Kamakau, cited by Sahlins (1995:176).

Aotearoa-New Zealand: beings who are 'spirits but perhaps not our spirits'

Certain Maori traditions show that the newcomers were seen as *tupua*. Let us be clear that the Maori *tupua* were 'visible beings of supernatural origin, regarded with a mixture of terror and awe and placated with *karakia* (ritual chants) or offerings'. But the word *atua* was used as well.[40] Thus we are still within the same frame of reference as for the Hawaiian, Tahitian, Tongan use of *akua, atua*. I have referred to the curiosity of the Hawaiians who wondered whether the Europeans who observed the sky with their telescopes came from the sun or whether they only visited this star on their voyages. Concerning the use of *atua* by the Maori, Elsdon Best, one of the reliable ethnographers, had noted that the term, of which one tradition says that it was used to refer to Europeans, meant 'god, demon, supernatural being'. As to the other word used for Europeans, *tupua*, Best gives the meaning: 'anything extraordinary, especially if it be credited with supernatural powers' (Sahlins 1995:179).

Quite clearly the image of the European was ambiguous, generating a plethora of questions that the Polynesians put to themselves and to which they could not find answers. The Europeans could not help them either. Since at the linguistic level mutual understanding had scarcely begun, the Polynesians and the Europeans could barely understand one another. And where they did understand one another, the answer that the Europeans gave (the astronomers on Cook's voyage: 'we are looking at the sun') raised still more questions—or confirmed first impressions about the 'celestial' nature of these beings.

This level of ambiguity—something that Obeyesekere's type of critique is incapable of grasping—is set out in a Maori narrative. When the Europeans were considered to be 'spirits', *tupua*, by the Maori, the nature of the comparison could be formulated more precisely: the Europeans were '*tupua* but perhaps not our *tupua*'. The narrative was recorded in the middle of the 19th century, from the mouth of an old man who, in 1769, happened to be at the spot where Cook's expedition landed:

> We lived at Whitianga, and a vessel came there, and when our old men saw the ship they said it was an *atua*, a god, and the people on board were *tupua*, strange beings or 'goblins'. The ship came to anchor, and the boats pulled on shore. As our old men looked at the manner in which they came on shore, the rowers pulling with their backs to the bows of the boat, the old people said, 'Yes, it is so: these people are goblins; their eyes are at the back of their heads; they pull on shore with their backs to the land to which they are going.' When these goblins came on shore, we (the children and women) took notice of them, but we ran away from

---

[40] Salmond cited in *ibid.*: 179; Best cited in *ibid.*

them into the forest, and the warriors alone stayed in the presence of those goblins; but as the goblins stayed some time, and did not do any evil to our braves, we came back one by one, and gazed at them, and we stroked their garments with our hands, and we were pleased with the whiteness of their skins and the blue of the eyes of some of them.

These goblins began to gather oysters, and we gave some kumara, fish, and fernroot to them. These they accepted, and we (the women and the children) began to roast cockles for them; and as we saw that these goblins were eating kumara, fish, and cockles, we were startled, and said 'Perhaps they are not goblins like the Maori goblins'.[41]

This text is interesting because it establishes several distinctions: between the gods and spirit-sprites on the one hand, and between the latter and the ancestors properly speaking on the other. The extraordinary ship was described as a 'something divine' *atua*, and the people on the ship as 'spirits' or 'sprites' *tupua*. The *tupua*, as Anne Salmond (1991: 88) makes clear, could take on human form but they did not eat; in any event, they did not eat the cooked food eaten by human beings. And so, the fact of seeing the men from the ship eat sweet potatoes and fish, after giving the Maori to understand by gesturing that they wanted these foods cooked, forced the Maori to attach a large question mark to the formulation: 'they are undoubtedly *tupua*, but perhaps not our *tupua*?' Finally, Maori terminology distinguishes between these spirit-imps, *tupua*, and the ancestors properly called *tupuna*.[42]

The newcomers were superhuman, undoubtedly, but they were difficult to classify because they could do more than the ancestors proper, with their boat-islands and their thunder-cannons, but they could not do as much as the gods who had created the world, who had invented thunder and lightning and who had fished the islands up from the bottom of the ocean with their huge fishhooks. When the Polynesians said of the Europeans that they were *atua* or *tupua*, we need to remember that this always involved a questioning of their status as well. These same words when used normally already seemed to imply some measure of uncertainty. What is divine, *atua*, is everything which *seems* to be driven by a divine power, a power *delegated* by a god; *atua* does not just designate *the* god himself. In any case, even at the level of the invisible and the

---

[41] The narrative was published by White in 1888 (see White 1989: vol. 5) and is cited by Salmond (1991: 87-8) whose text I am following here. The author, Horeta Te Taniwha, was a young child who happened to be on the beach that day in November 1769 when Captain Cook's ship landed on the coast of New Zealand and stayed for twelve days. He lived long enough to be able to pass on his memories seventy years later.

[42] I am grateful to Marshall Sahlins who drew my attention to this difference which I had overlooked in an early version of this text (personal communication, November 1997). Williams's dictionary (1971) does indeed make a distinction between *tupua* ('1. goblin, demon, object of terror; 2. one versed in magic arts; 3. foreigner; 4. strange sickness; 5. strange; 6. steal, kidnap'—we can see the common thread in these different instances of *tupua*) and *tupuna* ('ancestor, grand-parent').

mythical, the great gods were constantly splitting themselves into countless partial forms as, for example, in Samoan mythology where there is Tagaloa-the-Creator, who sends Tagaloa-the-Messenger and other Tagaloas to carry out his business on earth, and so on.

In the Cook Islands and in Tonga: envoys from the gods 'on the boat of Tangaroa'

Let us move from New Zealand to the archipelago of the Cook Islands whose inhabitants first heard about Captain Cook from the Tahitians. When, in 1823, the missionary John Williams arrived in Rarotonga where he was the first European to disembark, he recorded a narrative, that of a meeting between the inhabitants of Aitutaki (an island in the north of the Cook archipelago) and two Tahitians whose canoe was brought there by head winds. The Tahitians told the inhabitants of Aitutaki about the visit of Captain Cook; they told them about the deathly power of the guns, but also about the extraordinary properties of the axes and the nails given to them by these beings whom they named Tuti (from the word 'Cook'). The men of Aitutaki would then have made their prayers to the creator Tangaroa: 'O great Tangaroa, send your large ship to our land, let us see the Cookes ... to give us nails and iron and axes ...' (Thomson, 1915: 40-1, n. 2). The 'Tuti' were on a boat *of* Tangaroa the creator of the world, but they were not confused with this creator. They were the representatives, in unknown form, of the god that the Polynesians knew. This was exactly the same as when Cook's crew had been described by the Maori as sprites, *tupua*, who had embarked on a divine-boat, *atua*.

Even when Cook and those who were with him were called 'divine', *atua*, with all the nuances already elicited for this term, they were still envoys *of* Tangaroa. Another example taken from the same archipelago shows this. The missionary William Wyatt Gill was posted at another of the Cook Islands, Mangaia, from 1851. In 1777 Captain Cook had anchored off Mangaia; he had not landed but he had exchanged several objects with an inhabitant who was brave enough to paddle up to the English ship and go on board. Eighty years later Gill recorded a song describing Cook's visit, which told of the 'big boat', and mentioned the Tahitian 'Mai' who was on board and who was such a useful interpreter to Cook. The refrain is pertinent to this discussion: 'It is the boat belonging to/originating from Tangaroa, it has sailed on/from the sky; they are very frightening *akua*' (*No Tangaroa te vaka: kua tere i te aka i te rangi ē! E atua mataku oki*).[43] Certain important points need to be made about these terms:

---

[43] The lines preceding those quoted mention the paleness of the visitors' faces, the strange language that they seemed to speak and the possibility that they came from a 'very distant island'. The above translation is mine and differs from Gill's (1880:183, 185). Gill translates the first line as: 'Tangaroa has sent a ship, Which has burst through the solid blue-vault'. We shall return to this missionary idea of 'bursting through the sky' in chapter 11.

Tangaroa is the great creator god; *te* is 'the', *vaka*, 'canoe'; *no* means 'of' with an important nuance. Buse's dictionary (1995) glosses this *'no'* as: 'belonging to, of (where the possession is, or is conventionally treated as, inherent, inalienable, non-agentive)'. What we have here is one of the two kinds of relationship of ownership as distinguished from each other in most Polynesian languages: non-agentive to agentive, a relationship of belonging to a whole as compared to a relationship where there is only a simple distinction between the possessor and the possessed, or, more concretely, the relationship to the chief, to the land, to the house, to the ancestors, in contrast with, for example, the relationship to a purchased object. In the latter case 'of' is expressed as *nā*. Thus, the presence of *'no'* shows us that the *relationship of the Europeans to Tangaroa was like that of an individual to his chief, to his ancestors, to his clan and to his ancestral origins.*

In some parts of Tonga too, where the great creator was the god Hikuleo, it was said that the Europeans were on a boat from the god Tangaroa, the younger brother of Hikuleo. One of the first Wesleyan missionaries to land there, in 1797, wrote later:

> Tangaloa resides in the sky. He sends forth the thunder and lightning; and when a thunder-storm occurs, it is supposed that he is killing a Chief. Tangaloa is a god of the carpenters, whose business is the most honourable employment in the Friendly Islands. He is supposed to be the god of all the foreigners, whom he has taught to construct such beautiful vessels. Captain Cook and others were supposed to have come from the sky, sent by Tangaloa. The Heathen will sometimes use this plea for not worshipping the God of the foreigners: 'You serve Tangaloa, the saucy younger brother; we serve Hikuleo, the elder: why should we leave the elder to serve the younger brother?'...[44]

In 1777 Cook anchored off Atiu, another island of the archipelago which today bears the name of the English navigator. Lieutenant Gore went ashore in a rowing-boat. During the 1850s Gill recorded there a number of recollections from elderly men whose fathers had witnessed Cook's arrival:

> On Lieutenant Gore's landing, the chiefs asked him, amongst other things, 'Are you one of the glorious sons of Tetumu? Are you a son of the Great Root or Cause, whose children are half divine, half human?' According to their mythology, Tetumu was the father of gods and men, and the maker of all things ... On that memorable day the strangers were the guests of Tiaputa, who ordered the dances and other amusements in honour of the occasion. The *kava*-drinking, the nectar of the Polynesian gods, and the feasting were extravagant. Forty pigs, mostly small, were

---

[44] 'Rev. Walter Lawry, *Friendly and Feejee Islands,* London, Ch. Gilpin, 1847' (Fergus Clunie, personal communication, February 2003).

cooked and presented to their visitors, who were led to the *marae*, where a sort of worship was paid to them as the favoured children of Tetumu (Gill 1880: 187).

'Are you a spirit?' (Fiji)

These were the questions on the lips of the inhabitants, but questions that were already inflected: 'Are you the envoys of the great creator god? Are you his children?'

The case of Fiji can also be cited, as reported by Sahlins in another of his studies. There, too, there were questions:

> For decades after Savage [one of the early beach-combers], White men who were able to repair Fijian muskets were asked if they were not 'spirits' (*kalou*). Perhaps most pertinent was Naulivou's questioning of William Cary to this effect, when Cary had fixed the Bau chief's firearms: 'Are you a spirit?' I told him no, that I was flesh and blood the same as himself. 'Well', he said, 'if you are the same as me, what makes you so white?'
>
> Of the Fijians in those days it might be said that nothing foreign was merely human to them. The *vulagi*, the stranger, was a kind of divine guest, as Hocart observed; the notion could be glossed as 'heavenly god' or 'heavenly ancestor', For the notion of spirit (*kalou*) itself had a spatial dimension: a being from the beyond, outside the bounds. (Sahlins 1994:75)

'Nothing foreign was merely human to them': for the era preceding the beginnings of globalisation in the modern world, this formula expresses the attitude of the Polynesians and all the peoples of the Pacific, and no doubt of the inhabitants of every continent on earth as well, each time that they were confronted with beings who were different enough to make their identification problematic.

9. Super-human and yet human: the 'sexual contacts'

For the Polynesians, then, this problematic identification gave rise to a host of questions and some very ambiguous answers. The incidents that have most caught the attention of Europeans in these early contacts in Polynesia—the presentation of young girls to the visitors—are clear evidence of this.

Once the European interpretation of these sexual encounters is deconstructed in a number of cases, as in the Samoan case examined in Part One and in the Tahitian case examined elsewhere (Tcherkézoff in press-1), we can definitively discount the hypothesis of sexual hospitality offered to the voyagers as well as that of a local custom of adolescent sexual freedom. Furthermore, the description of certain facts (ritual decorum, girls dragged by force, their young age and so on) that were present in these early sexual contacts[45] demands that we look for an interpretation based in ritual. The only conceivable line of research is, following Sahlins's suggestion for Hawaii (1985a: chapter 1), to make a connection between the myths about the impregnation of women and the presentation of women to the ancestor-gods in the dances linked to the cycles of fertility, but with the addition of an unexpected element which seems always, or at least very often, to be at work: young age and virginity (see chapter 3 above). But if the hypothesis leads to the conclusion that the Polynesians carried this mythical structure over to the scene of these early contacts with Europeans, it is still the case that they did their very utmost (this is fully described in the narratives) to persuade their European male visitors to perform—not symbolically but for real—a sexual act on the girls presented to them. This clearly implies that the Polynesians saw in their visitors (i) a form of power attractive enough to them that they tried everything in order to harness it (a form of power, therefore, that went beyond local resources), and, at the same time, (ii) beings of flesh and blood capable of sexually penetrating a woman and giving her their sperm.[46]

There is a perfect example of this with the misadventure of Bougainville's cook in April 1768 on the expedition's arrival at Tahiti. Even before a landing had been made, but after the French crew had seen the local 'Venus' board the ship and, once disrobed by her companions, 'appear as did Venus revealing herself to the Phrygian shepherd', Bougainville's cook, driven to go ashore, took off in a boat to go and meet a 'Venus' for himself. (There were other young girls in canoes surrounding the ship or on the shore.) But as soon as he got there and found himself, as we might imagine, surrounded by a crowd of Tahitians, he was handled in a way he did not expect: he was promptly and forcibly undressed, and everyone felt 'all the parts of his body' (and therefore, as we may assume, the genitals as well). *Once that was done*, the young girl (whom, it seems, the cook had encountered on disembarking or after seeing her in a canoe close to the ship) was presented to him and he was energetically made to understand what was expected of him. The poor cook, absolutely terrified, could not do anything at all and showed by the signs he was making that he wanted to return to the ship. On his return he said to Bougainville that whatever punishment his captain might come up with to punish him for his escape, it would be less frightening than what he had just lived through (Bougainville [1771] 1968: 186-7).

Then when the first officers went ashore, the Tahitians took them into a chief's house and presented them with a young girl. Bougainville drew on this incident in his famous phrase about the sexual hospitality offered in 'every

---

[45] See above concerning Lapérouse's visit to Samoa; the same elements are also found in Fesche's journal of Bougainville's visit to Tahiti.
[46] All the recorded Polynesian representations of procreation recognised the role of the sperm (Tcherkézoff 2003b: 375-6).

house', but Fesche's journal shows that the girl was brought there by the women, that she was crying and that she was a virgin.

10. Polynesia-America: the same 'question'

If we now turn parenthetically to a comparable situation, namely that of America, we see that there, too, how to conceptualise the first Europeans was a matter for constant questioning on the part of the inhabitants.

In Polynesia, there are legends suggesting that the arrival of celestial beings was expected. In Samoa, the chief who greeted the first missionary is also the subject of a legend. The legend tells that a goddess (Nafanua) reigned on earth, carried off victories, established a measure of order, and then, just before she disappeared, announced to this man that he would soon be a great chief and that his 'kingdom would come from the sky' (Ma'ia'i 1960: 46-8). I have already suggested the hypothesis that these legends could have arisen earlier at the time when the inhabitants were trying to comprehend the appearance of the first Europeans in the region (the contacts in Tonga and/or Fiji). Of course these legends could have been in existence at a still earlier period, in relation to the pan-Polynesian Sky/Earth cosmology, but they received a sort of confirmation at the time of contact. Then a kind of semantic intensification occurred in the late 18th and early 19th century with the arrival of more visitors and the missionaries who spoke of 'luminous' and 'celestial' powers.[47] In fact, by placing the missionaries under his protection, the Samoan chief in question, Malietoa Vaiinupo, assured the rapid spread of his control over part of the country. In America, too, the Europeans were incorporated into 'the myth of the civilising god who, after his beneficent reign, disappeared mysteriously promising men that he would one day return' (Wachtel [1971:42] 1977:14).

Whether or not these myths or legends were produced after the event (something that we cannot know as, clearly, the recording of these myths by observers always occurs after first contact), they nonetheless reveal a recurring pattern of thought. But it would be quite naïve to believe that, in Polynesia as in America, this process of matching the newcomers to pre-existing supernatural entities in myth and legend was seen as a statement of empirical fact. If the correspondence between spirits-gods and Europeans was mythically articulated in this way, where supernatural facts were always included in the myths—facts set apart from everyday reality even in the pre-Christian thought of the local inhabitants—it is because *the reason for this articulation was to formulate a question* concerning this correspondence—'are these our gods visiting us?'—and not to make an affirmation.

---

[47] This is the time when, probably, the word '*Papālagi*' was re-analysed by Western Polynesians with the meaning of 'people from the sky' (see chapter 11).

Previous studies about the Polynesian perception of the Europeans have not sufficiently stressed this aspect. The Polynesian formulation was a comparison (with the gods-ancestors-spirits) that was always accompanied by a question. For, indeed, the Polynesians were not blind to the many differences between the Europeans and the superhuman beings as they usually imagined them. At the same time, the space-time logic that I have talked about did not allow them to imagine an 'ancestrality' that could have given rise to another kind of humanity. The remoteness from which the Europeans had come was as such an origin and there could not be two distinct origins since, we may suppose, in Polynesia at that time it was not possible to hold a plural vision of humanity.

The American story told by Nathan Wachtel shows similarly how it was 'questions' and not an affirmation that guided the 'the vision of the vanquished':

> The intrusion of the Europeans into a society which had lived in isolation for centuries, was an interruption in the normal course of events. So we must not be astonished that Moctezuma saw Cortés as the god Quetzalcoalt returning to his people. On the contrary, we must realize that he was trying to rationalize this extraordinary event. Moctezuma was using the mental equipment of his society, the only one at his disposal. He was turning to traditional mythology in order to integrate into his vision of the world something quite beyond any of his previous experiences. This was also the way the Guatemalan Indians and Huascar's partisans reasoned the matter. Yet Atahuallpa, the Mayas of Yucatan and the Cholula Indians reacted differently. Why?
>
> Not all of the Indians took the Spaniards for gods, but all when confronted with their unexpected appearance asked themselves the question: 'Are they gods or men?' All the societies we are concerned with have one thing in common: the invasion of their world by the unknown. All their documents, Aztec, Mayan, Inca, describe the strange attributes (beards, horses) and powers (writing, thunderbolts) of the Spaniards. The whole of Indian mythology implied the *possibility* that the white men might be gods and everywhere this was a source of doubt and anguish. The *answer* to the question 'men or gods?' could be yes or no, depending on the particular circumstances of local history.
>
> This interpretation is confirmed by a remarkable episode. As they approached Cuzco, Pizarro's soldiers captured some Indian messengers. These men, on their way from Callcuchima, one of Atahuallpa's generals, to another general, Quizquiz, were bearers of an important item of news concerning the nature of the invaders: 'Callcuchima had sent them to inform Quizquiz that they [the Spaniards] were mortals'. (Wachtel 1977: 23-4).

'First Contacts' in Polynesia

The power of their cannons certainly gave a divine aspect to the newcomers, but they were white and bearded, which was strange. An attempt was made to give them offerings in the usual way: foods dripping blood (after human sacrifices) but, strangely, these visiting gods were revolted by such offerings. So then there was doubt. At times, the inhabitants attacked the newcomers using sorcery, at times they offered them signs of victory. Gods, chiefs, sorcerers, warriors, the newcomers were all of these at once (Wachtel [1971: 44-5] 1977: 14-16). Some groups made an alliance with the Europeans to fight against other groups.[48]

On both the American continent and in Oceania the spiralling cycle of fighting and the exchange of objects clearly led to a constant modification of their understanding of the newcomers by the local populations. Very rapidly Inca messengers were sent to allied groups to tell them that these strangers seemed to be mortal after all. The Polynesians for their part understood with great alacrity that the terrifying weapons of these 'spirits who are not our spirits' could be acquired and used, and even turned against them.[49]

11. Exchanges of images: image of Lono, image of Cook (Tahiti)

Behind the affirmation 'the Europeans were taken for gods' which seems to cause certain scholars some concern, we can now see more precisely what happened: Cook was assimilated *to the image of Lono*. The whole semantic field of the words *atua, aitu* and so on, and the mythical realities of such things as island-boats and a curved space-time, all point strongly in this direction. There is also another indirect proof: there was no difference in the way the Polynesians treated the flesh-and-blood Captain Cook and Captain Cook's image.

In Hawaii the god Lono was represented in ritual by an image (the white barkcloth carried on a wooden frame) which was made by the priests. After the ritual, the image returned to being a simple piece of material, just as the wooden statues used in other rituals became profane again after they had been used. All of this ritual apparatus was put back again in the cupboard in the temple. If the following year the materials had deteriorated, an image would be rebuilt. When the Europeans arrived, their boats, their sails, their objects and they themselves

---

[48] In the same way as, three centuries later, the Samoan chief Malietoa Vaiinupo used these new powers (and the guns that he thereby acquired) for his wars against other districts.
[49] Throughout Polynesia, the attitude of the chiefs was for each of them to acquire as many white adventurers (deserters etc.) as possible, if need be by kidnapping them on the shore (I have mentioned the case of Jackson at Ta'ū in 1840), so that the Europeans could teach them how to handle weapons and serve as intermediaries in the trade with whaling ships, who sold them guns (and much else besides) in exchange for fresh supplies of food. In America, the same thing has been noted, even if it was much less general because it occurred in the period of armed struggle which did not last for very long: three years after the arrival of the Spaniards, an Inca chief was using harquebuses and had the gunpowder made by European prisoners (Wachtel 1971: 258). In Samoa a trading economy based on guns lasted from 1830 to 1890.

were considered to be images of this kind. The priests manipulated Captain Cook so as to establish this particular quality: an image of Lono. There was one difference though. This time, a particular image of Lono was sent by the gods, perhaps by Lono, made by them and by him, and not by men—since Cook's appearance was a European event and not a device set up by the Hawaiian priests. And this explains the ambivalence surrounding the way in which this image was treated. The usual kind of image can be thrown away, broken, or destroyed when one is no longer in the appropriate phase of the ritual. This is what happened when Cook was murdered having returned to the island out of time (Cook's arrival corresponded to the ritual cycle of Lono, and his departure did too; but, because of damage to his ship a short time after he had left Hawaii, Cook made an about turn and returned to the same island). But because *this* image was a divine, not a human, creation, because it 'was *atua*', the expectation was that *it would return of its own accord*. So, after his murder, the Hawaiians asked other members of the expedition when Cook would return (Sahlins 1989: 377ff; 1995: 85).

That is not the end of the story. The Polynesians thought it logical that fabricated images should reproduce this image sent by the gods. That is why the image of Cook-image of Lono was itself used in the ritual. This actually happened in Tahiti. A picture of Cook, painted by John Webber during Cook's visit to Tahiti in 1777, was left with the local chiefs as a memento. Thirteen years later, the Tahitians, who had learnt of Cook's death, used his portrait as a representation of a sacred power so that offerings could be made to it.

James Morrison and some of the other mutineers from the *Bounty*, among those who had decided to stay in Tahiti, were present at a *heiva* festival. Morrison noted in his journal:

> February 1790. – On the 1st of February our attention was drawn from our Work by a Heiva which according to Custom was performd in our Neighbourhood before the Chief of the District, to see which all the inhabitants of the District were Assembled.
>
> Everything being ready Captain Cooks picture was brought (by an Old Man who has the Charge of it) and placed in front, and the Cloth with which it was covered being removed ... The Master of the Ceremonies then made the Oodoo (or usual offering) making a long speech to the picture, acknowledging Captain Cook to be Chief of Maatavye and placing a Young Plantain tree with a sucking pig tyed to it before the Picture.
>
> The Speech running to this purpose – 'Hail, all hail Cook, Chief of Air Earth & Water, we acknowledge you Chief from the Beach to the Mountains, over Men, Trees and Cattle over the Birds of the Air and Fishes of the Sea &c. &c.'

After which they proceeded to perform their dance, which was done by two young woemen Neatly and elegantly dressd in fine Cloth, and two Men, the whole was conducted with much regularity and exactness, beating drums & playing flutes to which they kept true time for near four Hours.

On a signal being given the Woemen Slip'd off their Dresses and retired, and the whole of the Cloth and Matting which was spread to perform on, was rolld up to the Picture and the old man took possession of it for the use of Captain Cook (Morrison 1935: 85-6).[50]

The practice of giving mats and barkcloth at the end of a dance is well attested to in the narratives of the first voyagers and later on (see next chapter). This offering was typically made to the representatives of the gods: the Arioi during their dance (given the particular character of this Tahitian brotherhood whose role is to make the gods present on earth in certain rituals: they tear off the barkcloth worn by the women), the local and visiting chiefs and, when they began to appear on the scene, the European guests. Cook and Banks were themselves made this offering, with this same ceremonial, when they came to Tahiti, as we shall see in the next chapter. And we have just seen that the offering was made to Captain Cook a second time in Tahiti, in 1790, when the deceased navigator was made present in the form of this image-of-Cook.

12. Political appropriation: Europeans as adopted cousins (Napoleon, the 'Kamehameha' of Europe)

From the very beginning of this work of conceptualisation that the Polynesians were obliged to make in their regard, the Europeans were placed at the outer (but original) limits of the world: they were envoys of the gods, 'spirits' but in a new form, 'celestial' beings but ones not known up until then and for whom it was necessary to coin new terms (like *Papālagi*, see chapter 11). But the Polynesians also called the captains 'chief', *ari'i*. The Tahitian invocation made to the Image-of-Cook ('Chief of Air..., Chief from the Beach to the Mountains...')

---

[50] Morrison notes that, in 1790, the Tahitians still often talked about Cook. In relation to the cows and goats brought by Cook, they remembered that Captain Cook had brought them; he also notes that they took more care of his portrait than of anything else. This portrait was painted by Webber in 1777 (Cook's third voyage) and given to Tu, chief of Matavai. After Cook's departure, Tahiti had no more visits for eleven years. Then in 1788 a ship arrived from Australia, with Lieutenant Watts, a member of the crew on Cook's last voyage, on board. As soon as the boat had anchored, the Tahitians announced the arrival of the chief Tu. Watts, as well as Captain Sever, went ashore. They were received by Tu. Standing next to the king was a man bearing the portrait of Captain Cook. The Tahitians seem to have treated it with the utmost care because it was like new. Watts would learn that chief Tu always kept this portrait at his side (Watts's journal, cited by Scemla 1994: 330). Oliver (1974: 1358 n. 2) takes this passage from Morrison's narrative but does not comment on it except to say that even as early as Wallis's voyage (1767), the flag planted by the latter had become, with some ornaments added to it, the central element of the Tahitian regalia used for the enthronement of the principal chief. This passage from Morrison has not escaped the notice of Sahlins either, but he only quotes the prayer, in a discussion concerning the divine character of the Polynesian chiefs (1995: 128 n. 6).

has just reminded us of this. That in no way negated their primary characteristic as 'super-human', *atua*, since the local chiefs were by definition images of the gods (they were men imbued with a principle which is—or which is 'the life' of—the founding ancestor of the title in question, himself a child or image of the creator gods). But the Western social hierarchy came to be compared with, and integrated into, Polynesian society. That was how it became comprehensible. The sequence could have been the following: 'King George' (the English captains, from 1760 to 1820, in stating the name of their king put the Tahitian word 'chief', *ari'i*, in front of it, and this was memorised by the Polynesian chiefs), then the captains as 'chief-priests', the officers who were similar to the 'orators', and finally the sailors who were like the 'young men who are non-chiefs', *taurearea*. This hierarchy became an issue at the local level over who, among the local chiefs, would have the closest possible relationship with the captain and who, among the highest chiefs, would call himself 'brother or cousin of King George' (Baré 1985: 169-72).

But the chiefs did not call themselves 'cousins' in order to be adopted by these white-skinned-superior-divine beings—something that did not enter into the Polynesians' thinking at all. Rather they used the term 'cousin' *so that these Europeans could be adoptable and adopted*. This was the conceptual framework in which the round of sexual presentations of young girls took place: to adopt the newcomer by making him a son-in-law. It was the same thing when 'King George' was invoked *by the local god-chiefs* in their prayers, as Vancouver noted when he in turn arrived in Hawaii in 1792. And it was the same, too, when the portrait of Cook, manipulated by Tahitian priests in the service of a local chief, began to attract offerings of cloth, following on from a pattern already established when a flag left by Wallis in 1767 became a coveted sign of the supreme chieftainship in Tahiti. Did this signify timorous devotion to the Europeans who were taken for all-powerful magicians? Not at all. *It was a straightforward attempt at political appropriation by the Polynesians of the productive link that they imagined was operating between the gods and the gods' new-found representatives.*

It was the same again not many years later when the Tongan chiefs, hearing about that other great European chief, namely Napoleon Bonaparte, made him one of theirs, as they told the missionary Lorimer Fison in the middle of the 19th century. This narrative has not been missed by Sahlins and I summarise here from his précis of the account given to Fison by a Tongan informant (1994: 78-9).

Napoleon's mother, explained the Tongan, was a very tall American woman who fell pregnant during a call at Tonga when the first American whalers began putting into port in this archipelago. The woman returned to America and gave birth to a child. Some years later, a number of Frenchmen went to America to seek help against their English enemies because their priest had foretold that they would find there a child who would lead them to victory. After different incidents they found the child. He had been motionless and silent from birth. But when the French explained the purpose of their visit he got up and spoke, revealing for the first time his height which was such that it went beyond that of any human being. Sahlins makes a comment in passing about the height of the king of Tonga:

> So was King George Tupou, it might be noted, while the sudden metamorphosis from an abnormal passivity to Herculean action is a common Polynesian theme, a device for revealing the superhuman qualities of the hero. The rousing of the warrior from the stable condition of the autonomous sacred chief is also iconic of the reversal of hierarchy under discussion here. (1994:79)

The Tongan, having related the warrior exploits of Napoleon, finished by saying that, if the French freely admitted that the 'royal clan of Napoleon' came from an island, they were lying about the location of this island: it was not where they came from but in the Tongan archipelago (*ibid.*).

This mythical appropriation is exemplary. It is certainly true that the discourse remains at the level of metaphor, but the same logic is being applied. In speaking of Kamehameha, the great king of Hawaii at the time of contact and the author of unification by conquest, Western visitors said that he was the Napoleon of the Pacific. But, as Sahlins points out with more than a hint of irony, from a Polynesian viewpoint it was Napoleon who was the Kamehameha of Europe (*ibid.*).

It is this, perhaps, that certain Westerners find hardest to understand or admit. The Polynesians, seeing the first voyagers, then the missionaries, then the colonisers, all coming amongst them, have assimilated this alterity all the more effectively by not allowing themselves to drift into accepting the values that the various Europeans wanted to inculcate in them by persuasion or by force. These resistances have clearly set in train a host of internal changes—and the adoption of these European cousin-kings is one of them. A little later, in some cases, there was purely and simply military destruction and massive despoiling of their land.[51] But in any event, the image that the Polynesians have kept of these past encounters, and that which they have formed of recent encounters or those that are ongoing, comes down to a form of 'adoption'. A selective adoption of certain Europeans, certain objects from the West, certain values; but certainly not a complete replacement nor one that has been imposed on them. What we have here is an integration of some of these outside elements

---

[51] The major exception being Western Polynesia where still today between eighty and ninety per cent of the territory of each independent country has remained under customary rule of the extended families: the land is inalienable as the only recognised 'owner' is the founding ancestor.

13. Epilogue: what is the situation today? Exchanges of names and gazes that meet

Assimilation that is very strong but at the same time is kept at a distance is a well-known phenomenon. After the early voyages of the English, the Tahitian, Hawaiian or Tongan chiefs considered themselves to be 'cousins of King George', without on that account forgetting who their ancestors were (Baré 1985: 171-2). George III reigned for the whole of this period, from the 1760s to 1820, his exceptional longevity contributing to this assimilation. The Tahitians and other Polynesians heard Wallis in 1767, Cook from 1769 to 1777, Vancouver in 1791, the first missionaries in 1797, and still others after that forever invoking this same king (clearly using the word 'chief, *ari'i*). There is thus no cause for surprise at what Vancouver heard in 1791: the spirit of his king was invoked together with the gods Oro and Ta'aroa; and in Hawaii several chiefs had chosen the name George for one of their children (*ibid.*).

Fictional images, but ones whose settings were relatively faithful to the Polynesian scene (American films of the 1960s set in Hawaii), and especially documentaries (about the present king of Tonga, often filmed by the BBC when he was one of the most obese men in the world – he has recently been dieting) have shown the extent to which the protocol of the royal court of England was followed to the letter in Polynesia, military regalia, ceremonial swords and ermine robes included. This was true of the Hawaii of the 19th century; it is still true of the Tongan court. More generally, Polynesians today, at least those in the western part where English has remained the first foreign language to be learnt, still exhibit a passionate interest in the lives of the members of the English royal family. Let me give a recent example.

Samoans are in the habit of naming their children after a relative (uncle, aunt, grandparents etc.).[53] Samoans who have emigrated to New Zealand do this just as much as those who have remained in Samoa. In New Zealand, where the Queen of England is still the constitutional Head of State, shock at the news of the car accident which took the life of Princess Diana and her close companion Dodi Al Fayed on 31 August 1997 was as great as it was in London. For two weeks the tragedy was all that was talked about on television. The Samoans, whose relationship to England is very strong and of long standing, dating as it does from the work of evangelisation undertaken by the London Missionary Society in 1830, were very shocked. Those who had emigrated to New Zealand and who

---

[52] For the Samoan case, see Tcherkézoff (1997a: Part 2).
[53] Often the linguistic composition of this first name where the child is named after a relative seems to refer to a founding event, but this event is unknown. Today, the creation of a new first name by naming a child after an event, instead of after a relative, is quite rare.

saw these images every night on television were especially affected. Soon after the fatal accident, on 8 September 1997, a young Samoan mother from Auckland gave birth to a daughter. She already had a boy named Lui (after a cousin of her father's), another named Selega (after her sister's husband), and a third named Siva (after her eldest brother). But in the case of the daughter, born during this time when all anyone talked about was the death of Diana and Dodi, the parents did not hesitate for a moment. The princely couple had to be honoured in the choice of a name. The girl was named 'Dodiana', to bear witness to the fact that the lives of Dodi and Diana had been claimed in a double tragedy, the couple thereby becoming a single being for the purpose of conferring a name.[54]

A new name, 'Dodiana', has in this way been added to the stock of Samoan names. Like all names it will be re-used in another generation. From now on, this English historical event (the accident) has become the element of a Samoan mythical structure (through the naming process whereby the names of 'relatives' are reused). Equally, the mythical structure (English royalty as Polynesian tutelary figure) has become a Samoan event, even if it is only an anecdote: a birth in a family who has emigrated to the suburbs of Auckland, New Zealand. But this modern mythical structure is already the result of an early combination of myth and history when the English captains of the 18th century were ancestralised *cum grano salis*, when their King George became the 'cousin' of the local kings and when these kings called their eldest son Siaosi ('George').[55]

It is quite true that naming a child after an event is a universal practice. But something quite specific applies here: the feeling that anything which touches the *English* royal family is a story which the Polynesians feel close to. And this has been the case since the appearance on their beaches first of Cook and then of the London missionaries, with the veneration which resulted for 'cousin George'.

The Polynesians made 'cousins' of these first Europeans who represented the best *of themselves*. In fact these 'cousins' bore witness to the ancestral origins, they were sent by the gods, they had come from the outer limits where one goes back in the space and time of a world of which they, the Polynesians, 'the children of the earth', are the recognised inheritors. At the same moment in time, the Europeans for their part also believed that they had discovered on these islands bearers of a common origin, in the human, and not divine, sense this time: 'natural' man, the Noble Savage and the dweller in the Garden of Eden, practising a 'sexual freedom' which was forbidden everywhere else after the Fall.

---

[54] Information confirmed by the mother (personal communication, October 1997; my thanks to Ruta E.)

[55] Siaosi is the Samoan transliteration of 'George'; other Polynesian transliterations differ slightly.

Since then, the encounter between Polynesians and Westerners, when it takes place among the Polynesians, takes a form which, I believe, exists nowhere else. Each group sees in the other a mythic value that it tries to appropriate. But for one of these two groups—the Polynesians—appropriation is hierarchical: it is a question of knowing the level on which the powers that one is aiming to integrate should be placed. For the other group—the Westerners—it is an assimilation, or rather a projection of what one constructs in imaginary terms as a desired Same: the cult of a sexuality disencumbered of all social constraints.

The Polynesians, as we have seen, have assimilated Western first names, but not just any names. First of all there were those of the great 'chiefs', beginning with George after the king; and then Napoleon as well, a name that is more common today in the Pacific than in Europe;[56] then of course biblical names; and today as in the past, those that are linked to the British royal family, not only George or Elizabeth, but also, recently, for the reasons that I have explained, Diana, or even in one case, 'Dodiana'. Westerners, too, call their children by Polynesian names. But it is a different thing for them. These are people who have gone to live 'in the islands' and they are drawn to the resonance of certain names or those which somehow evoke the dream that they have followed by going there. Having noted the frequency of requests by Western families ('*Popa'a*') living in Tahiti to adopt a Polynesian child, Bruno Saura adds:

> Failing to adopt a baby, a number of *Popa'a* living in French Polynesia content themselves with giving their own children a Tahitian name... . This practice says much about the regard in which Westerners hold the Tahitians: 'Are there many colonial countries...', wonders Michel Panoff in *Tahiti Métisse*, 'where the coloniser systematically baptises his children with names borrowed from the colonised and which are strictly preserved in their original linguistic form?...' ... (Saura 1998: 46)

Saura nevertheless tempers what we might deduce from this: 'We might still wonder if the parents' who came as civil servants, police, administrators and teachers 'are not shifting on to their children's generation the possibility of bringing about an integration that they are not genuinely seeking for themselves' (*ibid*.: 47).

The Polynesians, having discovered the Europeans and thought that they had seen representatives of the creator gods (and having seen and heard about their chiefs—the captains and kings) are continually assimilating to their own powerful lineages the authority that they attribute to men of power from the West. But the Europeans, believing that Bougainville, one day in the year 1768, had discovered for them the 'garden of Eden' in the form of a 'new Cythera',

---

[56] A Samoan 'Napoleon' (well known in the academic milieu that was interested in Mead's investigation into adolescence) is the teacher who was Mead's special male informant (Tcherkézoff 2001a: chapter 8).

are continually wanting to identify themselves with these imaginary 'Polynesians', in an attempt to go back in time to regain Paradise.

The European approach is a turning back to the past—and to a past that never existed. It often leads to disappointment. The Polynesian approach, however, signifies a turning to the future and has allowed the Polynesian technocrats and rulers of the contemporary nations, States or Territories, to move with great ease in the world of international politics. In relation to the size of the countries in question and in relation to the short span of their post-colonial history, it comes as something of a surprise to see the relaxed assurance of their foreign ambassadors or their ministers abroad. But this sense of surprise goes away as soon as we realise that, in their self-image, the renown of their chiefs has been talked about in the 'world' (the 'world-under-the-sky', *lalolagi*) for centuries if not for millennia—even if the *Papalagi-Popa'a* took some time to get sent by Tangaroa in order to tell them about their 'cousin George', and even if, for us Westerners, this 'world' was only a part of the Pacific and a small part of the 'whole world'.

It is not difficult to foresee a more lasting future for this Polynesian way of apprehending the Other. It brings more satisfaction to those who practise it since it allows them, much more so than in the Western approach, to believe that the results obtained correspond quite closely to the hopes that they have expressed in their quest for power and authority.

Chapter 10

Sacred cloth and sacred women. On cloth, gifts and nudity in Tahitian first contacts: a culture of 'wrapping-in'

For Alfred Gell, in memoriam

1. European misconceptions

The ethnohistory of the early encounters between Samoans and Europeans has shown us the important role played by the offerings of cloth, on both sides on the encounter. This cloth exchange is in no way specific to the Samoan case and was indeed a crucial element of all early Polynesian-European contacts. In order to achieve a certain level of generalisation on this point, I shall now add to this discussion the available data for Tahiti. A study aiming at a pan-Polynesian comparison cannot limit itself to one side of Polynesia and must at least include for comparative purposes a case from the western groups and a case from the central and/or eastern groups.[1]

In cross-cultural encounters it is the things one thinks one has recognised that often turn out to be the most misleading. Analysts of encounters between Polynesians and Europeans will be familiar with the issues of 'power' and 'religion' that are involved here (for Eastern Polynesia, see Baré 1985; Saura 1990, 1993). Further studies have shown that differing conceptions of 'gender' also need to be taken into account (for Western Polynesia, see Tcherkézoff 1993; Douaire-Marsaudon 1998; Suali'i-Sauni 2001). As we have seen in Part One, recent debates and studies about Samoa have even added 'sexuality' to the list as a major source of misinterpretation when considering historical transformations (see also Anae *et al.* 2000). It is nonetheless somewhat surprising to discover that one also needs to consider how a material item like cloth can give rise to serious misunderstandings.

From a European perspective, our surprise stems from the fact that we are used to thinking of cloth as being subject to cultural variation only in terms of design or technique. The social functions of cloth seem to remain the same cross-culturally: cloth provides a supple material, it provides protection and,

---

[1] The following is an enlarged version (particularly section 12) of a text published as chapter 2 of Chloe Colchester (ed.), *Clothing the Pacific*, Oxford, Berg, 2003, the subject of which is the ethnohistorical role of cloth in the Pacific. I would like to thank the Editor and the Publisher for their permission to use that text as the basis for the present chapter.

furthermore, depending upon its formal properties (the material, the colour, the way it is cut etc.), it provides a marker of social status. Again from a European perspective, cloth and clothing are conceptually opposed to nudity, since being dressed is conceptually opposed to being undressed. A body stripped of its clothing is said to be 'nude'. This basic opposition gives rise to all kinds of associations that, given our deeply entrenched Judaeo-Christian tendency to see a direct link between nudity and sexuality, serve to oppose the clothed person, who represents obedience to social rules, to the unclothed person, who represents 'savagery' and/or the open expression of sexual desire.

Given these rather limited notions, it comes as no surprise to discover that, from early contact to contemporary times, European reports and studies entirely misconstrued the significance that Polynesians accorded (and which in certain circumstances they continue to ascribe) to the social uses and handling of cloth, to its presentation as a ceremonial gift, or to simple acts of dressing and undressing. For by focusing upon the functional aspects of cloth (as a form of protection), Europeans overlooked the fact that certain kinds of cloth could be objects of great value and, as such, sacred gifts. By focusing upon the design and the material of clothing as a sign of social status, Europeans overlooked the fact that dressing and undressing could be social acts whose significance owed little to either the kind of material or the style of clothing involved. Last but not least, the conceptual opposition between dressing and undressing trapped them into seeing nakedness as nudity and undressing as stripping in anticipation of sex.

2. Cloth

Throughout Polynesia, 'cloth' was and is, in Western words, 'barkcloth' (or 'tapa' in the French literature), made from beaten strips of bark, or woven material, made from dried strips of leaves or fibres (mats, called 'fine mats' in the literature, and cloaks, sometimes decorated or even covered with tiny feathers). In Eastern Polynesia, the woven items were mostly cloaks, in Western Polynesia mostly fine mats. I shall consider both the Western Polynesian fine mats woven from dried and very fine strips of pandanus leaves and the all-Polynesian barkcloth or 'tapa'.

The expression 'fine mats' used by early visitors to the Pacific is misleading. Although both fine mats and floor mats are made from varieties of pandanus, their uses are different. Fine mats are a kind of ceremonial dress that can be wrapped around the body. In pre-Christian times, fine mats were also wrapped around sacred representations of the gods, such as sacred stones, or were spread on the floor to provide a seat for high chiefs or for the gods.

The French Pacific term 'tapa' originally derives from the Eastern Polynesian term *kapa, tapa*; it rarely occurs in Western Polynesian languages and then it means only the border of a piece of cloth. But like the word 'taboo' (derived from the Polynesian *tapu*) it became part of the Pacific vocabulary of the Europeans, and was used indiscriminately, irrespective of local usage. Nevertheless, I shall retain it for this chapter because the term 'barkcloth', which was used only by English-speaking visitors, is a misleading translation that reduces *tapa* to 'cloth' or 'clothes'. This fails to convey how, throughout Polynesia, the bark (which was often painted) served to wrap people of rank as well as other ritual objects (see, for Tahiti, Babadzan 1993, 2003) or, in Western Polynesia, was placed on top of a pile of other ceremonial gifts, completing a gift-giving prestation (as in Tikopia, Lau, Samoa, etc.).

Other forms of dress, such as leaves tied around the waist, were never presented as gifts, and although introduced cotton fabrics have come to be used either as a substitute for *tapa* in many parts of Eastern Polynesia and in Uvea and Futuna (see Küchler 2003), this is not the case in Samoa, where people make a clear-cut distinction between fine mats (*'ie tōga*) and imported fabrics and clothes. The variety of patterns in the continuity and discontinuity of indigenous cloth usage in Polynesia is wide. Nowadays, Samoan families only use fine mats as gifts; *tapa* is almost no longer used. In neighbouring Tonga and Fiji, however, both *tapa* and fine mats are used in abundance. In Eastern Polynesia, where *tapa* and feather cloaks were once the primary gift objects used in ritual exchange, their usage ceased in the 19th century (Babadzan *ibid.*, Küchler *ibid.*, Valeri 1985).

In Samoa and elsewhere in Polynesia the only garments to have a purely functional role were leaf skirts. They protected the midriff and served to conceal the lower part of the body. We must remember, in light of what will be discussed later, that the obligation to cover this part of the body pre-dated missionary arrival, as Morrison had witnessed, and was not the result of Christian puritanism.[2] Leaf skirts were used for this purpose because such clothing does not dissolve in water while *tapa* disintegrates if it gets wet. (We can understand why, as soon as Polynesians discovered materials on the European ships which looked like unpainted *tapa*, namely white linen, and like painted *tapa*, namely velvets and silks of all colours, but which did not dissolve when wet, there began an extraordinary demand for European fabrics.) The functional leaf skirt was only worn outdoors, for in Samoa and elsewhere in Polynesia formal dress was/is largely worn inside the house; in common with Polynesian tradition, in Samoa the interior of the house is still largely regarded as a formal public space, not as a place of intimacy (Tcherkézoff 1997a; 2003b: chapter 2). In the past the

---

[2] Morrison, who stayed in Tahiti in the end of the 1780s, before any missionary influence, had observed that 'The Single Young Men also had dances wherein they shew many indecent Gestures which would be reproachable among themselves at any other time but at the dance, it being deem'd shameful for either Sex to expose themselves Naked even to each other and they are more remarkable for hiding their Nakedness in Bathing than many Europeans, always supplying the place of Cloaths with leaves at going and coming out of the Water.' (Morrison 1935: 225 cited in Oliver 1974: I:153).

formal dress that was worn inside was *tapa*; today it is a length of spotless, vibrantly coloured printed cotton or, for very formal occasions (Church or political meetings), a dark fabric without any printed patterns.

In fact, there are no Polynesian words meaning 'cloth', 'fabric' or 'garment'. In Samoan, the notion of 'fabric' is denoted by the word *'ie* (from the Samoan term for the kind of pandanus species used for fine mats) followed by a secondary term. The word for 'clothes' is *'ofu*, which is also followed by a second, specifying term. This term *'ofu* conveys the idea of wrapping, and it can also be used to describe the wrapping of food, for example. The secondary term will specify whether the clothes are a pair of trousers or a shirt. What *tapa* and fine mats shared in common, then, was not so much that they were kinds of cloth as that both of these materials were made from plants that were seen as being integral to the group's identity. Both pandanus and paper mulberry were/are grown close to the house, rather than further afield in the plantations. The bark of the mulberry was beaten and then printed with designs. In Samoa, fine mats showed—and still show—how lineages became interwoven, while their feather borders were once an indication of the rank of the family. (Now, they all tend to be alike.)

In what follows, the term 'cloth' will be restricted to the sacred cloths that could serve as a sacred gift or in ritual procedures: *tapa* and fine mats, but not cotton fabrics or leaf and fibre skirts.

3. Ceremonial gifts of cloth

A number of different cultures, apart from Polynesian ones, have based the acquisition of power and prestige on the act of giving. Anyone who has given a great deal may at any point activate the network of connections made up of all those people who have been on the receiving end of a gift. By giving constantly one accumulates relationships. In Polynesia, two broad categories of gifts were, and indeed remain, prominent: food and (sacred) cloth. Both items are ceremonially prepared and formally presented. Food is presented wrapped in leaves. Cloth is initially presented rolled up and is then spread out in front of the recipients (and then refolded or divided and cut up, as the case may be). It is important to note that cloth and food are presented in tandem; somehow each plays its own and necessary part. The following discussion will focus on the part played by cloth.

It is mandatory to give cloth in Polynesia (and eastern Melanesia). Although the way in which cloth is presented may suggest it is a gift that the giver was in no way obliged to make, everyone present is well aware of the truth, which is clear to the outside observer as well. In contemporary Samoa, if a household does not make any contributions to ceremonies involving the extended family or village (for births, marriages, funerals, the consecration of a house or a church, the installation of a new family or village leader, etc.) this is taken as a sign of their withdrawal from the family or village circle. The threat is actually an eviction order. Here lies the answer to the apparent enigma of the obligation to give that puzzled Marcel Mauss, the founder of the French school of social and cultural anthropology, and which led him to publish his famous essay, *The Gift* (*Essai sur le don*), in 1925. In this essay Mauss showed that a common feature of these practices was the sacred nature of the objects presented. Here the term sacredness should be interpreted in the Maussian-Durkheimian sense as the object that symbolises the larger group, be it society as a whole or one of its subgroups. Such objects are opposed (in Maussian terms) to 'individual' possessions. Only cloth of this kind was, or is, an object of gift exchange in Polynesia. Fine mats or *tapa* are never owned by an individual (while previously leaf skirts and now printed fabric are); they always represent the identity of a group.

The first example discussed by Mauss in the opening chapter of *The Gift* relates to Samoa. Quoting several missionary sources, Mauss noted that gifts could be of two kinds in Samoa: food and household implements, on the one hand, and 'emblazoned mats' (*nattes blasonnées*) on the other hand (mats bearing the history—invisible but proclaimed in the oratory accompanying the gift—and thus comparable to the coat of arms of a noble European family). Quite remarkably Mauss immediately intuited that only the second kind of gifts—the mats—were relevant to what he was looking for as they were the symbol of a group (a family, clan, or similar) and were inherited, whereas the objects in the other category seemed to be attached to an individual. This enabled him to link his Samoan example to other instances in which the objects given had the same character of 'totality' as he identified it; that is, in which they symbolised a social unit (as in the case of the Maori sacred gifts, *taonga*, Tapsell 1997).[3]

Samoan fine mats, *'ie tōga*, are clearly symbolic of a group (a family name or 'title') and never of an individual. Conversely, all of the other ceremonial goods, which are not in circulation for as long, or do not circulate at all (since they are only given once), do not bear the history of a group inscribed on them. These may include pigs, fish, certain tools, or domestic materials. Nowadays, these gifts may include very specific tinned foods, as well as paper money. But an old mat is a known and a renowned object. Even if it is held far from its place of origin, it retains the memory of the family that wove it and gave it away for the first time. It carries with it the genealogy of that family. Nothing of the sort may be said of a pig, a basket of fish or a banknote. Finally, a mat can be used to pay for anything and everything, including the ceremonial gifts required for a marriage (on the bride's side), a funeral, and other ceremonies. And it can also serve as the gift given to the carpenter for building a house, to the craftsman

---

[3] For a more extended discussion of the Samoan case as Marcel Mauss had outlined it in *The Gift*, see Tcherkézoff 1997b.

for making a boat. This is as true in Samoa today[4] as it was in the past. In Samoa, no other gift object is such a universal currency.

4. Ritual efficiency and rites of wrapping
Life-giving gift

As a fine mat carries the idea of the permanence and history of a whole social group, it is not surprising that such mats retain the power to give life. Here again we come back to Mauss who had stressed in *The Gift* that those specific objects of gift exchange were at the same time a 'property owned' by the givers' group and a general 'talisman', beneficial to everyone—and certainly to the recipient of the gift—because, being a symbol of a family group, they somehow possess a life-giving power.

Indeed, in Samoa, one can accomplish miracles with mats of this sort. According to the legends, such miracles can be acts of curing, bringing someone back to life, victory at war, and so on. One very tangible miracle can still be observed today: mats provide sanctuary. A person who has committed a murder or a serious insult (the culprit or the chief of the family group to whom the culprit belongs) can save his life by wrapping himself in a mat. To this ritual act are linked numerous legends about the first fine mat that saved the lives of Samoans held prisoner by Tongans (Tcherkézoff 2002). Until the 1950s, a mat or a length of *tapa* could be used to recover the soul, if a person had been lost at sea for example (or, before 1900, had fallen in battle and been beheaded), thus allowing funeral ceremonies to take place. In such cases, a fine mat or a *tapa* was spread out near the sea or at the place of battle. The first insect to crawl on it would be said to represent the will of the soul of the dead man to come to his resting place. Some of the legends also mention bones that, wrapped in *tapa* or mats, have come back to life. Rituals have the same effect (according to accounts from the 1960s). If descendants are bothered too often by the soul of a dead person, they dig up the bones, wash them, and wrap them up again in a *tapa* or a fine mat. In the neighbouring Tokelau culture, early observers found that an altar used to invoke a divinity took the form of an 'upright stone wrapped in fine mats' (Huntsman and Hooper 1996: 146). In Hawaii and Tahiti, *tapa* wrapped around images of the gods played much the same role (Valeri 1985; Babadzan 1993, 2003).

Fine mats and *tapa* were, and are, used in Polynesian ritual as *efficacious* objects, meaning that they may create or reveal—by wrapping-up—the presence of the sacred in a given place. Elsewhere this function may be fulfilled by an

---

[4] The ethnographic present that I use for Samoa, in this chapter and elsewhere in this book for contemporary Samoan facts, refers to my enquiries of the early 1980s (see Tcherkézoff 2003b). The years 1987-1995 were years of very rapid change in many contexts, due to a political decision to 'open' the country to the global economic system.

animal: pigs in Melanesia; sacred cows in East Africa and India; copper objects on the west coast of North America. In Polynesia it was and is cloth. A good summary of how this operated in Polynesian culture is provided by the custom of the Lau islands (far eastern Fiji) in relation to cloth:

> In the Lau islands, the symbolic function of cloth as a conduit between men and the gods is important and more visible than in other Oceanic archipelagos... the investiture of a chief, for example is conceived of as a funerary rite. The man dies to be reborn as a god. In order to achieve this he is symbolically set apart behind a screen of *tapa* for four days, the time it takes for the spirits [gods and ancestors] which inhabit the *tapa* to take possession of him and cause his rebirth as a chief. The cloth that serves to capture the spirits is called 'the cloth of the earth'... Thus in Fiji *tapa* is a path to be walked upon or a shelter held aloft by two rows of women with their arms raised; it protects the path of access to the status of becoming a chief. This path metaphorically served to convey the breath of the gods and the ancestors which came to meet the living: a roll of white *tapa*, placed in a temple (*bure kalou*) considered to be the spirit house, was the vessel or the receptacle of the spirits. The end of the cloth is left hanging. By taking hold of the end of the cloth, the priest whom visitors had come to consult could become possessed with a specific spirit (Bataille-Benguigui 1997: 181-4).[5]

Wrapping the Other

When Europeans appeared on the scene, they unknowingly entered this 'wrapping-up' system. In early cross-cultural encounters what Europeans call 'cloth' played a prominent and instant role in the interaction between Europeans and Polynesians. Guns and metal tools were also important, as we have already noted, and served to inflict both physical harm and cultural shock. Both sides perpetrated violent acts. When Polynesians attempted to appropriate these guns and tools, Europeans responded by avenging what they perceived to be acts of 'theft' and 'hostility'. Many fights would ensue until, in the 19th century, guns and tools became common in the islands and objects of trade. By contrast, and despite the considerable misunderstandings involved, cloth became instantly and pacifically an instrument of interaction. Coincidentally, covering the body in layers of cloth was a common sign of status. In the case of the Polynesians, these layers consisted of *tapa* and mats; in the case of the Europeans, the layers were the shirt, waistcoat, jacket and topcoat that distinguished the captain from the officers and the officers from the rest of the crew. This was a point of connection. The Polynesians recognised the captains, and the Europeans recognised the chiefs, whose bodies were sometimes entirely covered with mats

---

[5] Translated by Chloe Colchester.

and *tapa*, whereas their followers were only lightly dressed, and were often bare-chested as a sign of respect for their chief who was heavily dressed (we will discuss the logic behind this contrast below).

Of course, the Europeans did not realise that they had come to a civilisation where the established practice for initiating contact between strangers was to make a presentation of cloth to wrap around the body of the visitor. For instance, in past and contemporary Samoan practice, when a traveller arrives from another village, territory or island, he must offer his 'services' (*tautua*) and present food, or, today, food and money. He presents himself as someone who is ready to serve the local chief. In return he is presented with a fine mat (and money), or elsewhere (as in Tonga) with a gift of *tapa*. Such reciprocity works on two levels. For his part the host indicates that he considers the incoming stranger is 'superior' (*malo*) by presenting him with his most precious valuables. But the act of presenting cloth is also a means of *enveloping and thereby incorporating the stranger*. For, as a stranger, the new arrival must be incorporated, and whatever sacred powers he possesses must be domesticated and contained: the 'untouchable', *tapu*, must be made 'touchable', *noa*.

Obscurity and light, concealing and revealing

As other studies have indicated (Sahlins 1985a, 1985b; Valeri 1985; Babadzan 1993; Gell 1993: 125-40), Polynesian ritual played upon the duality of the exterior world (*Po*) that was wild, nocturnal, but vital, since it was the primordial world and as such the source of life; and the interior, domestic and diurnal world of light (*Ao*). Yet the existence of this diurnal world depended upon the degree to which one had domesticated the sources of light and life. It seems to me that the primary attribute of Polynesian cloth was precisely that it enabled people to capture, contain and release the sacred through procedures of re-covering and uncovering.

These actions served to obscure the source of life and at the same time they revealed its effects. One cannot stare at the sun—just as in the past one could not stare at a sacred chief—for fear of burning one's eyes. I have discussed the importance of the hierarchy of light and visibility in the Hawaiian case (chapter 9). But there had to be a means for this source of light to be made manifest on earth. This is why cloth was/is so often conceived of by Polynesians as being 'white' and 'luminous' (in Samoa, fine mats can be called ceremonially *mea sina* which literally means 'luminous-white things').

Thus, in Polynesia, cloth enabled the invisible bodies of the gods to be made manifest. In some other contexts, it revealed women's wombs, and it provided an analogue for skin. In different regions of the Pacific different permutations of this common symbolic system are accentuated. Bearing in mind that *tapa* is made from bark, we can recall how, in the Tahitian cosmogony, the appearance of the skin of the first Man—which is what gave shape to what was initially a formless blob—is determined by the various types of barks chosen by the Creator Ta'aroa.[6] This is why the simple act of wrapping cloth round a stone or an idol or a person transformed them into a manifestation of the gods, rendering them efficacious for ritual or status-oriented acts. This is also why cloth safeguarded life in Samoa: if a culprit was wrapped in fine mats he became untouchable, and if a person was lost at sea, fine mats could be used to bury him or her by proxy. The association between cloth and skin, and acts of dressing and undressing were features of a common symbolic complex.

Here I should emphasise that from the Polynesian point of view the skin covers and obscures the principle of vitality that is carried in the blood.[7] This principle of vitality is invisible by definition. Blood flowing in the body (the Samoan word is *toto*) can never be seen. For, when a wound or women's menstruation makes blood visible, it acquires a different name (*palapala*). Thus, the vital principle (in Samoa: *agaga, mauli*) is both invisible by definition and present by definition. Wrapped cloth as a cultural skin, covering the natural one, is itself evidence of this dual and contradictory concept. In some way the use of cloth as an envelope or covering demonstrates that within the body there is indeed, luminous although invisible, a life principle of sacred origin. The act of covering transforms this *ideational* potentiality into a *symbolic* social fact.[8] Once an object or a person is wrapped up in a cloth which is itself defined as a path for the gods (as we saw in the Fijian-Lauan case, see above Bataille-Benguigui), it now becomes certain that sacredness is held there, and it is quite logical that this sacredness remain unseen since it is covered.[9]

No doubt this is why, in Polynesia, these cloths were and are always presented either rolled up or wrapped around the body. The gift-givers arrive with the cloth wound around them, or with a mat rolled up under one arm. The cloth is

---

[6] 'O Shapeless nothing! ... Then Ta'aroa caused skins to grow on the child, to give him qualities, to make him a great god... the bark of the *hutu* to make the child hardy; the bark of the *atae* for a rough skin... the bark of the coconut tree for a porous skin for the child; the *parau* bark for a skin full of fissures... bark of the *maru* for a thick skin, the *apapae* for a thin skin, the *toi* bark for a shining skin... All these skins were placed on the child... (Henry 1928: 365-6, cited by Gell 1993: 127)

[7] The association between blood and the life-giving principle has been noted at a Polynesian comparative level by Gell (1993: *passim*) and is quite clear in the Samoan case (Tcherkézoff 2003b: 372 *ff*; see p. 376, for various comparative references for Tonga and Central and Eastern Polynesia).

[8] This transformation—which is indeed accomplished according to the logic that underpins the efficacy of all rituals—could be compared to the role of the secret in initiations. In most cases the content of the secret which is revealed to the initiates is meaningless. The main point is the consensus that 'there is a secret', which makes possible the subsequent transformation of the inititate from an uninitiated into an initiated person.

[9] This discussion can be enlarged on the linguistic level with the hypothesis that a proto-Polynesian word meaning 'to cover' is the etymological root of *toga/taonga/*etc., words denoting the sacred gift in the Samoan, Maori and similar contexts. From the same word would have come expressions denoting cooking in the earth oven (by covering the food placed in the earth oven): cooking food is also a cosmological transformation of *Po→Ao*.

spread out and displayed but, above all, the cloth is used to envelop the receiver in turn. The receiver is enveloped, or else the cloth is spread out at his feet or unfurled over the pile of other gifts such as food or tools. Cloth gifts of this kind still occur today throughout Western Polynesia, including the Lau islands in eastern Fiji (Douaire-Marsaudon 1997, Hooper 1982). In the past, the recipient of a gift might have been a god, materialised as a stick or a standing stone, or a chief, or indeed any visitor. The god, the foreign chief, the visitor would have been conceived of by the local people as occupying the dominant position. In rites of welcome, gifts of cloth serve to take into account this superiority and to establish a relationship that is not based on violence but on respect. In other words, these rites facilitate the transformation of an external form of sacredness that is dangerous to touch (*tapu, sa, ra'a, mo'a*), and render it 'touchable' (*noa*).

5. Some misunderstandings concerning nudity and Polynesian women's sexual appetites

The Polynesians' attempts to integrate new arrivals through such presentations of cloth gave rise to various misunderstandings. The Europeans saw these rites as an act of exposure, as a display of nudity and as an open invitation for sex. But, in Polynesian custom, the most respectful way to present cloth was to wind it around the body of a young girl/woman who had yet to bear a child. She would have been initially presented wrapped in a great length of *tapa* and/or mats, and to present the offering she would have divested herself of these wrappings until she stood 'naked'. Whether they responded with disapproval or delight, the European visitors were astounded.

In nearly all the accounts of first contact the use of this term 'naked' is highly ambiguous. Was the girl really stark naked? Would she not have kept on the waistband of *tapa*, her *maro*? Maximo Rodriguez, a Spanish voyager, visited Tahiti in 1774, soon after Cook's second visit. He provides an eyewitness account of the festival staged before the chiefs prior to a battle against another district:

> Some women decked in quantities of native cloth presented themselves before the Chiefs in order to strip themselves and make an offering of the cloth to the said Chiefs, being left with only a *maro* on to cover their nakedness. They call this festival a *taurua*, and after it they prepare for a *paraparau*, which is like a *tertulia* or well ordered conversazione of which the main topic is the wars these natives engage in against those of Morea (cited in Oliver 1974, III: 1237).

Here the 'naked' girl retained her *maro*. Certain passages from Bougainville also indicate that, in the European accounts, the expression 'quite naked' can in fact refer to a girl dressed in a 'waistband, *maro*':

> The inhabitants of Tahiti are often seen quite naked, having no other clothes than a sash, which covers their natural parts. However, the chief

people among them generally wrap themselves in a great piece of cloth, which hangs down to their knees. This is likewise the only dress of the women; and they know how to place it so artfully, as to make this simple dress susceptible of coquetry. (Bougainville 1772b: 250)

So we can see how a Polynesian dressed normally (i.e. wearing a *maro*) can turn into someone whose alleged complete nakedness indicates the first stirrings of sexual desire. In several other eyewitness accounts the observers do not even bother to specify whether the private parts are exposed or not. Descriptions of 'nakedness' therefore have to be treated with some caution. Europeans saw the *maro* as a form of underwear, and so in their view the person lacked clothing, was already undressed. Moreover, we know that European men regarded bare-chested women as being in effect naked, and sexually provocative.

Travellers who passed by Tahiti after 1767 (the date of initial contact) reinforced this view when they misunderstood the handling of the upper garment worn by the Tahitians. In that part of Polynesia the inhabitants frequently wore a kind of poncho or *tiputa*. It was made from a rectangular piece of *tapa*, with a hole made for the head, and it hung down to the hips. This piece of clothing did not have any ritual significance but simply provided protection from the cold, as many of the inhabitants were living in the mountainous interior at the time. But at ceremonies of welcome both men and women would remove the poncho as a gesture of respect. For the most part the European visitors had no understanding of the social meaning of this gesture, particularly when it came to the women. When they saw the women revealing their breasts in front of them they thought it was the prelude to a sexual encounter. Generally speaking, when Europeans saw dancers performing in a *maro* or a loincloth, they perceived them to be 'naked', and once they saw them as naked, they inevitably perceived them to be 'lascivious'.

The European male-centred view of the time reinforced this chain of cumulative misinterpretations. Bougainville wrote several commentaries on the 'nature of the fair sex', which, he suggested, was such as to lead all women on earth to 'desire mostly' the pleasures of sex, even if their education induced European women constantly to deny it (*les femmes paraissent ne pas vouloir ce qu'elles désirent le plus*). Hence the French admired a people—the Tahitians—who had apparently kept intact the original concordance between natural desire and collective behaviour, since 'they are not embarrassed to make love in public and frequently, while we hide ourselves to perform such natural actions' (*Nous nous cachons pour faire une oeuvre aussi naturelle: il la font en public et souvent*).[10]

---

[10] Such was the French interpretation after they had seen that a 'whole crowd' assisted at the sexual presentation of young girls to the Frenchmen. They misconstrued the presence of this assembly—composed of people who were chanting prayers and held a green bough as an offering—as a 'natural' Tahitian taste for watching love-making.

Bougainville's companion, the Prince of Nassau, noted in his journal that when the Tahitian girls undressed in front of the French, this was nothing to be suprised at. They were simply following a quite natural inclination to discard whatever was an obstacle to pleasure, namely clothes. Indeed, he called all female clothing 'a refined obstacle to pleasure' (*une parure importune pour le plaisir*).[11] These few examples show us that all the members of Bougainville's expedition perceived explicitly sexual connotations in the attitude of Tahitian females who disrobed in their presence.

6. On 'shaking the hips in a rotary motion': the dualism of the body

'Shaking the hips'

Furthermore, when the visitors saw these 'naked' bodies shake their hips while performing various dances, they believed the Tahitians to be possessed with irrepressible sexual desire. In fact, Polynesian dances are often composed of rapid, staccato movements of the hips. Such movements lifted the dancers' loincloths, adding to the visitors' impression that they were witnessing an act of exposure (these dancers, male and female, would have typically occupied the front row of the assembled dancers). They did not realise that the female dancers in the front row had to be virgins or at least girls who had never borne a child.[12] Sometimes the finale required these girls to strip off (with all the ambiguity that this implies: stark naked or still wearing a *maro*?) and present cloth offerings to their guests. To the European mind these various observations of 'nudity and shaking the hips' led to an inescapable conclusion: the dance's evocation of sexual activity was at best a fertility rite, or at worst intended to provoke both the spectators' and the dancers' lust, 'as it might be expected', wrote Hawkesworth, of a people whose customs glorified sexual activity (my words which summarise the stereotypical European account of Tahitian culture that developed after the visits of Wallis, Bougainville and Cook, 1767-69).[13]

The interpretation of Tahitian culture as one built on a generalised cult of sexuality was based upon the erroneous belief that 'unmarried women' were living a life of 'free love'. This belief was in turn based on impressions recorded by European voyagers on those few occasions when, in the very first moments of contact, chiefs had ordered a number of teenage girls to come forth 'naked',

---

[11] 'Journal de Fesche', in Taillemite ed. 1968: 15-16, note 2; 'Journal de Nassau', in *ibid.*: 51. See more extensive quotations in Taillemite (ed.) 1977, and further references in Tcherkézoff in press-1.

[12] Noted by Cook, Forster, Hamilton, etc. (see references in Tcherkézoff in press-1).

[13] 'It cannot be supposed that, among these people, chastity is held in much estimation. It might be expected that sisters and daughters would be offered to strangers' (Hawkesworth, 1773, II: 206-7). Hawkesworth was appointed by the Admiralty to write the official account of Cook's voyage; his rendering of both Cook's and Banks's notes reveals his tendency to make sexual allusions and condemn (what he thought were) Tahitian morals.

and had made clear signs to the newcomers that they expected them to have sex with the girls. After 1775 the idea of a Tahitian sex cult became widely established in salons throughout Europe, but the mass of documentary evidence attesting to this cannot be considered here. Let us simply say that Europeans justified their interpretation by claiming that all young Tahitians were educated in a cultural setting that was based on a cult of sexuality.

Blinkered by these preconceptions, Europeans could scarcely make anything other than a sexual interpretation of the way the girls moved their hips in the dance festivals. But this conclusion involved another error because it overlooked the fact that all Polynesian choreography was—and indeed remains—based upon a dualist conception of the body.

In their descriptions of Polynesian dances, all the 18th-century travellers noted the particular movement of the hips—a rapid oscillation from left to right—with wonder. J.R. Forster, the naturalist who accompanied Cook on his second voyage, tells us that, in the dances, 'they shake their hips in a rotatory motion, both when they are standing and when they are leaning prostrate on their knees and elbows, with a velocity which excited our astonishment' (cited in Oliver 1974, I: 332-3). The velocity 'excited our astonishment', since Europeans never shook this part of their body. For them, the hips were only meant to tremble during (lawful) intercourse. What other function could this part of the body have? What else could women shaking their hips possibly symbolise? Forster continues: 'The exercise of the common dramatic dances is very violent, the motion of the hands elegant, that of the feet not to be seen, that of the hips somewhat strange, and according to our notions indelicate' (*ibid.*). Forster's admission of cultural relativism—'according to our notions'—was highly unusual for the time. But his remark on the 'indelicate' motion underlines the fact that the movement of the hips was perceived by all European visitors as being not merely indelicate, but quite licentious and an overt invitation to wanton behaviour.[14]

The dual body

There could not have been any greater misunderstanding! For as it happens, a dualistic conception of the body is characteristic of Polynesian dance. While the upper part of the body tells the story, the lower part of the body only marks the beat to the accompaniment of the tambourine players, and other percussionists, and a small group of flute players and/or singers who supply the story's melody. All of this is consistent with the dual organisation of domestic and ceremonial space, with its implicit reference to a pre-Christian Sky/Earth cosmology, and indeed can be substantiated by any detailed observation of

---

[14] In order to imagine these early visitors' amazement and mistaken interpretations, it is worth recalling the introduction of the twist and the hula-hoop to Europe in the 1960s. Both dances just involved keeping the rhythm with frenetic hip movements. But the older generation were shocked: they could not help themselves reading more into it.

current dance practice, such as the performances at Pacific Art Festivals, for example. Two leading authorities on Polynesian art confirm this:

> Missionaries considered Polynesian dancing lascivious, when in fact the hip motions to which they objected so strongly were often little more than a time-keeping element ... In Polynesian dance ... small steps, and the hip movements that derive from them, keep the rhythm; it is the arms that give meaning to the performance. Polynesians considered the European form of dancing, in which bodies of men and women actually touched in public, as lascivious (Kaeppler 1997: 112).

And Sandra Silve, who teaches traditional Hawaiian hula in Paris, has recently remarked:

> Certain movements in Hawaiian dance are like the sign language used by people who are hearing-impaired. Each gesture corresponds to the expression of a word. The dancers' primary concern was to relate history and they concentrated on the movements of their arms and chest; the movement of the feet and of the lower part of the body, particularly the shaking of the hips, supplied the basic rhythm (Silve 1997:18).[15]

Thus we can see that the movement of the dancers' hips had nothing to do with sexual provocativeness. It had no figurative aspect whatsoever, it did not refer to anything.

As this discussion has revealed a dualistic conception of the body, it is important to consider whether the duality of the body played a role in acts of dressing and undressing. Indeed, there seem to have been quite different rules concerning the upper and the lower parts of the body.

7. Concerning the undressing of the upper part of the body in indigenous contexts

Polynesians attributed specific meaning to the undressing of the torso. Let us consider Tahiti between 1767 and 1789. We have already noted that the act of enveloping the other's body was a means of signalling the other's superiority that would be typically made to honour a visitor or a chief at formal occasions. Thus, if wrapping up the other was to acknowledge their superiority, we can expect that when an inferior presented himself before his superior, he could use the act of undressing as a sign of humility—at least for the upper part of the body. Cook, Banks and Parkinson noted something of the sort in 1773, though they never advanced a systematic explanation of this practice. Yet it is important to recognise that, during the period of contact, the registering of hierarchical relations in spatial terms was marked throughout Polynesia. For example, when

---

[15] Translated (from the interview in French) by Chloe Colchester.

Sacred cloth and sacred women.

Samoan fishermen passed in front of the house of a high chief they had to abase themselves, even if this involved lowering themselves from their canoe and swimming beside it. Even today, it is impossible to stand when one's superior is seated. So if one is obliged to leave a gathering one does so in a crouching position, while sustaining a deep bow. And if one carries a parasol for protection against the sun, it must either be lowered or closed when passing in front of a superior.[16]

Descriptions of these practices occur in the eyewitness accounts of the early contacts made between Europeans and Polynesians. During Cook's initial visit to Tahiti in 1769, Parkinson, the official draughtsman of the expedition, noted in his journal:

> Our tent was nearly filled with people; and soon after, Amoa, who is chief of several districts on the other side of the island, also came to us, and brought with him a hog. As soon as he appeared, the natives uncloathed themselves to the waist… On the 6th of July, in the evening, a young woman came to the entrance of the fort, whom we found to be a daughter of Oamo. The natives complimented her on her arrival, by uncovering their shoulders (Parkinson 1784: 32, 35).

This observation is confirmed by Cook (Beaglehole ed. 1955: I, 104). The rules of undressing were next noted by Forster in 1773. The case astonished him for it involved a father uncovering himself in front of his son. But the son had been installed in his father's place as paramount chief (cited by Oliver 1974, III: 1184). In September 1789, Morrison noted:

> On the 27th, having appointed that We should meet at Opparee, and make our presents to the Young King, We marchd in a body under Arms to Oparee, taking with us the Toobouai Images and several other presents of red Feathers, Friendly Island and Toobouai Cloth [*tapa*], Matting and

---

[16] This range of attitudes of humility among Samoan and other Pacific peoples has been raised in various discussions. Derek Freeman wanted to make of them a typical example of ethological determinism in human and primate social behaviour (see Tcherkézoff 2001a: 209-11). From an altogether different point of view—but one whose implications are no different, namely the expelling of the notion of culture—Alban Bensa (2000: 74) considers such attitudes as purely 'ephemeral', individual initiatives emerging from a '*situation d'interlocution*', at best a 'fashion' lasting rarely 'more than a generation', and rejects all attempt to detect in these attitudes anything 'cultural'. His example is the 'ethnological observation' that there is a Kanak obligation to sit down when a superior enters a house, contrasted with the European obligation of standing up (see the discussion in Tcherkézoff 2003b: 516-18). But as the Samoan examples make clear, these gestures of lowering were neither just the unconscious application of a universal phylogenetic code of dominance among living beings, nor an insignificant and ephemeral fashion, but were part of a specific *Polynesian cultural system* involving the conceptions of the cosmos and of the body. These cultural values are still prevalent. This has been noted throughout Polynesia and over centuries, up until the present. In addition to the facts for present-day Samoa mentioned here, we can look to the example of the Queen of Tonga, Sālote, at the parade for Queen Elizabeth's coronation in 1953. Queen Sālote rode in an open carriage in honour of Queen Elizabeth, even though it was raining (Adrienne Kaeppler, personal communication, January 2003).

> War Weapons Iron work &c.... when we March'd to his House in procession each attended by a friend to remove the Taheite Cloth [*tapa*] which we had on, all of Whom Stripd as they entered the Sacred Ground, the men to the Waist, and the Weomen uncovering their Shoulders and tucking their cloths up under their arm, and our Taheite Cloaths were removed (Morrison 1935: 77-8).

These accounts reveal that the act of unclothing the upper part of the body was an established gesture of respect. Conversely, it is logical that rank was made manifest by the number of layers of *tapa* that were wrapped around the body in ceremonial contexts. While noting that the way Tahitians wore *tapa* was varied, Parkinson detected a constant feature, namely that 'persons of distinction among them wrap a number of pieces of cloth about them' (Parkinson 1784: 338). Banks observed that

> The rich seem to shew their greatest pride in wearing a large quantity of cloth ... The poorer sort have only a small allowance of cloth ... It was not [an] uncommon thing for the richest of the men to come and see us with a large quantity of cloth rolled round their loins, ... sufficient to have clothed a dozen people (Journal of Banks, Beaglehole ed. 1962, I: 338).[17]

A corollary to this is the observation that the dancers were laden with *tapa*, far more than was strictly necessary either for reasons of modesty or for a festive occasion. During the same visit Banks noted this about the female dancers: 'On their hips rested a quantity of cloth pleated very full which reached almost up to their arms and fell down below into long peticoats [*sic*] reaching below their feet' (cited in Oliver 1974, I: 338). Another account by Max Radiguet, a young French officer writing in the Marquesas, relates that the mass of *tapa* wound around the young dancing girls in the clearing seemed to trap their bodies in a 'block of marble' (cited in Scemla, 1994: 838-46).[18] Parkinson's drawings from Cook's first voyage, together with Webber's drawings from the third, are eloquent: the mass of *tapa* enlarges the bodies of the dancers almost four or five times.[19]

8. Concerning the exposure of the lower body in indigenous contexts

Leaving to one side the occasions where priests stripped themselves naked before assuming different garb as they entered the interior of the temple, or the instances where young women disrobed to make a public gift of *tapa* cloth (which we

---
[17] Cited by Oliver (2002: 64).
[18] The whole narrative is in Tcherkézoff (in press-1).
[19] The drawings are reproduced in Oliver (1974, I: 333), Colchester (ed. 2003: 64-5) and in many other books describing European voyages in the Pacific (see also the iconographic pages in this volume).

shall return to), one might assume that the act of baring one's buttocks and private parts in an ostentatious manner was intended to be provocative. For we must recall Morrison's remarks (see note 2) regarding the care that people took to cover this part of their bodies in ordinary contexts, such as fishing in the lagoon (Morrison 1935: 225 cited in Oliver 1974, I: 153).

Contemporary observation from Samoa would appear to confirm this. Gestures of self-exposure are recognised, they have a specific name and, whether a man or a woman is involved, they are regarded as provocative. If somebody exposes themself in a non-ceremonial context it will cause a row. Only adult men or old women do it during festivities, making the crowd roar with laughter. It is a form of clowning that emerges when two teams are standing face to face. The local team of dancers may do it to provoke a response from the visiting team of dancers. Such rituals of clowning, of marking the inversion of respect, were also noted in 18th-century Tahiti, though in one particular case it was the representation of a god that was being dishonoured (Oliver 1974, III: 1307-8).

But again we should be wary of any quick assimilation to European conceptions of sexually offensive behaviour. The provocation was not intended to be gross since Polynesians did not equate sex and evil (in the sense of sin and filth).[20] If I may generalise from the more recent Samoan contexts, I would say that it was intended to convey an impression of domination, even physical force; in other words, it was an assertion of masculine authority, though in certain instances married women may convey this too.[21] This would also apply when the provocation was more scatological than sexual. Baring the buttocks is indeed a Samoan form of asserting domination. 'Eat shit!' was/is a popular insult in Samoa and could be interpreted in the light of Tikopian or Bellonan ritual formulas, where the priest attested to his humility and inferiority in front of the god by saying and repeating several times 'I eat your excrement' (Firth 1967: 210, 226; Monberg 1991: 268-70).

9. Concerning the undressing of the upper part of the body in early encounters and its subsequent adaptations

Let us go back to the quotation from Morrison,

> On the 27th, having appointed that We should meet at Opparee, and make our presents to the Young King, We marchd in a body under Arms to Oparee ... Having made known our business to Areepaeea—who told us that we must not approach the Young King as he was yet Sacred, unless we Strip'd the Clothing off from our Head & Shoulders, which

---

[20] There are certainly no pre-missionary indications of any such ideology.
[21] I am referring here to the fact that the evocation of the sexual act establishes a context of 'strong/weak, victorious/defeated' (*malo/vaivai*), a distinction which is explicitly associated with the context of war and (nowadays) sporting competition (Tcherkézoff 2003b: chap. 5, 7).

> we refused telling him that it was not Customary to remove any part of our Dress except our hats and if we were under arms it was not our Country manner to remove our hat even to the King. However that we might not seem to be deficient in point of Good Manners each was provided with a piece of Taheite Cloth to put over their Shoulders and take off in the Young Kings presence (Morrison 1935: 77-8).

Morrison refused to take off his shirt because he wanted to maintain respect for English manners, which prohibited one from removing one's shirt on formal occasions while prescribing the removal of the hat. Nevertheless, as he notes, English manners of the time decreed that one kept on one's hat if bearing arms. Therefore, since the English carried muskets, they could not take off their shirts and they could not even doff their hats in the king's presence. According to this code of conduct, it would have shown a lack of patriotism to do so in the Pacific. This presented a conundrum, but a compromise was soon reached, though Morrison does not tell us whether this was in response to a suggestion from the Tahitians or the Englishmen's own initiative. The crew would wear a length of *tapa* over their shirts and in this way they could show their respect to the new king by removing it in his presence while keeping on their shirts and hats—thus ingeniously satisfying both codes of dress:

> we March'd to his House in procession each attended by a friend to remove the Taheite Cloth which we had on, all of Whom Stripd as they entered the Sacred Ground, the men to the Waist, and the Weomen uncovering their Shoulders and tucking their cloths up under their arm, and our Taheite Cloaths were removed (*ibid.*).

Such ancient dress prescriptions and proscriptions have persisted, although they have been adapted in response to changing circumstances. For the missionary view was of course consistent with European notions of dress. To be dressed in a loincloth (*maro*) or a grass skirt made of leaves was to be regarded as naked, licentious, even evil. The missionaries begged men to be decently dressed in a shirt for church services just as they forced women to wear dresses which extended from the neck to the floor. For if European etiquette demanded that men remove their hats, torsos had to be covered in the presence of God. So how did Polynesians manage to reconcile this with their own code of dress?

In contemporary Samoa, after a church service there may be a gathering (*fono*) of the chiefs and village elders. When in the house men wear nothing but a *lavalava* (a Samoan sarong made from an island print), whereas to change for church, men put on a white shirt and sometimes a jacket and a sarong made of material in a single colour. When they go on to the *fono* they remove their shirt and jacket and sit bare-chested, out of respect to the founding ancestors whose names they bear, or else the lesser chiefs remove their shirts as a sign of respect while the paramount chief retains his.[22]

10. The whole body in early encounters: male gifts of cloth

Such demonstrations of respect were also made to Europeans. In their initial encounters, Polynesians wanted to achieve the cosmological incorporation of the new arrivals. Acts of unclothing were a prelude to the act of enveloping the new arrivals in cloth. Sources indicate that on various occasions Polynesian chiefs wrapped the ships' captains in *tapa* they had removed from their own bodies. The distinction between upper and lower part of the body was probably not pertinent here. The cloth, given in enormous quantities, enwrapped the whole body. A Tahitian chief gave, in succession, his upper and lower garment, his poncho (*tiputa*) and his sarong (*pareu*). The female dancers were literally covered with cloth before presenting it as we have seen in the remarks made by Banks and Radiguet: 'a great quantity rested on their hips', 'a block of marble'.

However another distinction seems to have been made: the gender of the donor was important. For though the chief divested himself of cloth, it appears he was not stripped naked. Unfortunately, the descriptions are vague, as it is evident that the European visitors were more interested in female nudity. Yet when women presented cloth, some accounts do specify that the lower half of the body was uncovered too. It thus seems that an additional dimension was operative when the giver was female, at least in some of those cases.

Let us first examine the case of the male donor. In 1768, the first Tahitian (it later emerged that his name was 'Aotourou' (probably Ahutoru) to climb aboard Bougainville's ship presented a plantain bough to the tallest officer he could see. Then, according to Vivès, the ship's surgeon,

> He wanted to swap his three ponchos [*tiputa*] or white cloths [i.e. *tapa*] that enveloped him [*ses trois ponches ou nappes blanches*] for a European shirt. Mr Lafontaine, one of our officers of about the same height, dressed him in a shirt, trousers, jacket and hat. He indicated his thanks and embraced him. He came back to Lafontaine, caressed him and embraced him and wrapped him in the loincloths [*pagnes*] he had been wearing. In return Mr Lafontaine gave him a shirt, trousers and a jacket which we had much difficulty to put on him, so large were his shoulders.[23]

---

[22] Those who are tattooed remove their shirt; the others sometimes keep their shirt on to hide their shame at not being tattooed. In that case they show respect by undoing the buttons of their shirt and exposing their chest (the tattooing runs from the base of the back to the thighs). A chief is ashamed not to have a tattoo. Although for some time tattooing has been a personal and individual choice, men who want to become the chief (*matai*) of their family still frequently choose to be tattooed.

[23] 'Journal de Vivès', in Taillemite, ed. 1977: 237; translated by Chloe Colchester.

In 1841, the first captain to stay on the atoll of Fakaofo (part of the Tokelau archipelago next to Samoa), whose inhabitants had already experienced violent encounters with Europeans at sea and gunfire on their shores, was enveloped by a chief who seemed overcome by fear: 'The King ... pointed at the sun, howled, hugged me again, and again, moaned, howled, pointed to the sun, put a mat around my waist, and secured it with a cord of human hair' (Huntsman and Hooper 1996:143,146).

11. Female gifts of cloth in early encounters

In 1789 some of the crew of the *Bounty*, commanded by Captain Bligh, mutinied after their stay in Tahiti (1788-1789). The ship was on its way back to England when the mutineers forced it to return to Tahiti. Thus it was that Morrison returned to Tahiti and lived there for more than a year, and compiled his famous journal. Once Bligh had returned to England, a punitive exhibition was mounted under the command of Captain Edwards (see Part One). Hamilton, the ship's surgeon, relates the story of their arrival in Tahiti:

> The king, the two queens and retinue, came on board to pay us a formal visit, preceded by a band of music. The ladies each had about sixty or seventy yards of Otaheitee cloth wrapt round them and were so bulky and unwieldy with it, they were obliged to be hoisted on board like horn cattle (Thompson ed. 1915: 107).

If the narrator was not exaggerating about the 'sixty or seventy yards' of 'Otaheitee cloth' (i.e. *tapa*), it is not surprising to read that the women had to be heaved aboard with ropes like bales from one of the wharves on the Thames. The followers brought with them food of many different kinds 'as a present for the captain'. Hamilton continues: 'As soon as they were on board, the Captain debarassoit [*sic*, i.e. relieved] the ladies, by rolling their linen round his middle; an indispensable ceremony here in receiving a present of cloth' (*ibid*.).

Previous visitors had also remarked upon this important ceremony. The following episode is described in Cook's Journal, as well as that of the naturalist Joseph Banks. It is a well-known episode as it has often—but erroneously—been listed among the instances of sexually provocative Tahitian female gestures. But a third source, most important as it gives us the key element for understanding the scene, is never quoted: the narrative of the draughtsman, Sydney Parkinson.

Let us summarise the data from the three journals to see the way in which the ceremony actually began. It was 12 May 1769. That morning a double-hulled canoe approached the small fortified encampment that Cook had ordered to be built on the beach. Once again Banks was aboard the longboat anchored near the shore, busy 'bartering with the Indians'. The Tahitians with whom he was conducting the exchange indicated that he should go to meet the group of people who had just arrived. Banks disembarked from the longboat. The group had

Sacred cloth and sacred women.

already disembarked and was ten yards away. These people formed a line, having halted their approach, and signalled to Banks to do likewise. One man stepped out from the group and passed along the line formed by it, carrying branches. He approached Banks with a small bunch of parakeet feathers and two boughs, one of which was a young plantain ('with some plantain and malape-leaves', says Parkinson). Tupaia, a Tahitian who had become an assistant for the English, 'acted as my representative', Banks noted: he received the boughs and placed them in Banks's longboat. He repeated this action six times. With each gift, the gift-giver said a few words 'that we could not understand'.

According to Cook and Banks, when this was finished another man approached, holding a great bundle of cloth (*tapa*) in his arms. He unfurled it and started to spread three pieces upon the ground. A woman from the group (Cook speaks of a 'young woman') stood at the fore:

> [Banks: The woman] stepd upon [the cloths] and quickly unveiling all her charms gave me a most convenient opportunity of admiring them, by turning herself gradually round (Beaglehole 1962: 275).

> [Cook: The young woman] Step'd upon the Cloth and with as much Innocency as one could possibly conceve, expose'd herself entirely naked from the waist downwards, in this manner she turn'd her Self once or twice round, I am not certain which, then step'd of [*sic*] the Cloth and drop'd down her clothes (Beaglehole 1955: 93).

Both Banks and Cook indicate that this was repeated for each set of pieces of *tapa* of which there were nine in all. The woman 'once more displayed her naked beauties'. Banks adds that, after she had stepped upon the final lot of *tapa*, she 'immediately approached me', and the man following behind her gathered up the pieces of *tapa* and she 'immediately gave me to understand that this present was destined for me'. Cook indicates that the woman embraced Banks. In this case it does seem that the female giver was 'entirely naked from the waist downwards', thus without even a *maro*. Parkinson provides confirmation, saying that she 'exposed herself quite naked'.

But Parkinson also adds a crucial observation: the whole thing started with the pieces of *tapa* that *the young woman was wearing*:

> A woman passed along the next [after the man who had presented the feathers, the bough and the leaves], having a great many clothes upon her, which she took off, and, spreading them upon the ground, turned round, and exposed herself quite naked; more garments being handed to her, by the company, she spread them also upon the ground and then exposed herself as before; then the people gathered up all her clothes, took leave, and retired (Parkinson 1984 [1784]: 27).

The woman stepped forward having first wound *tapa* around herself ('upon her'), then she disrobed completely; next other lengths of *tapa* were given to her that she spread on the ground.

Apparently, Banks had not described the very beginning of this episode because he was still in the longboat, whereas Parkinson was already at the front row of the space where the performance was being enacted. The spreading of the lengths of *tapa* over the ground, even if, once this had happened a second time, the *tapa* had not been wound around the woman, was only the continuation of the first act. As such we might suppose that this first part of the ritual performance in which the woman arrives wrapped in pieces of *tapa*, then spreads them out and gives them to the man whom she wants to honour and incorporate, was the model for what followed and which was the only part of the performance that had been observed by Banks.

We should also bear in mind that the opening of the ceremony consisted of a gift of *maro ura* (as we know from Banks: 'a small bunch of parakeet feathers') and of 'plantain' boughs, as was the case during the sexual presentation of young girls to the French the previous year (according to the most detailed journal, that of Fesche).[24] We should take note that, in this ceremony of gifts of cloth to Cook and to Banks, and in the ceremony of the gifts of cloth later offered to the portrait of Cook (see chapter 9 and below), the *tapa* that were presented were those that enveloped the bodies of the female dancers and/or were those over which they and the other male dancers had danced. But the dance floor was the seat of the gods (as shown by many ethnographic examples from Western Polynesia). In all of this, we should also perceive the concept of wrapping-up-in ('wrapping-in' if we were to follow Gell's [1993] terminology). It was applied to the Europeans who were the images of the gods and who, as such, had to be wrapped up in cloth.

Parkinson's precision could also explain what may seem strange in Cook's formulation: naked 'from the waist downwards' and 'dropped down her clothes' after stepping and turning on the pieces of cloth spread on the ground. One

---

[24] We might also ask whether there is a relationship between this type of gift and the demonstration that was made, *in the same place, one or two days later*, when the Tahitian woman whom the English called 'Queen Obarea' apparently wanted to get two young people to have intercourse in front of the English. This scene ('Point Venus scene') became famous throughout Europe through the intermediary of Hawkesworth, and then of Voltaire (Rennie 1998). Voltaire elaborated at length about what had been described, very briefly, by Cook, and contributed to persuading Europeans of the predilection for 'lovemaking-in-public' among the Tahitians (Tcherkézoff in press-1). In fact, the girl gave the impression that she was 'following instructions'. Moreover, according to another witness, the two young people were so terrified that they were unable to perform the sexual act that the Tahitian dignitaries seemed to expect of them—and which they apparently wished to be demonstrated to the English, perhaps to give them a better understanding of what they had to do when young girls were presented to them (see the discussion of these hypotheses in *ibid.*). The possible correlation between the two events reinforces the conclusion I suggest below, namely that there was certainly a general relationship between the gift of cloth and the presentation of a young girl—to the gods, to the chiefs and to the first Europeans.

might think that the young woman lifted up her poncho and then dropped it again at the end, which would then raise the question of a deliberate stripping of only the lower part of the body. But, more probably, Cook (whose style of writing, in his notes, is always very hesitant), wanted to remark that *even* the part usually not shown ('from the waist downwards') was 'entirely naked'; and the 'dropping of clothes' would refer to the various stages when the woman took off the *tapa* wound around her and/or dropped (that is: spread on the floor) the additional pieces of *tapa* that were handed to her by her company.

A little later, Bligh's ship, the *Bounty*, returned to Tahiti, albeit in the hands of the mutineers. In 1790 Morrison witnessed a ceremonial dance (*heiva*) performed before Captain Cook's portrait (which had been painted by Webber and presented to the Tahitians in 1777). I have already mentioned this event in the previous chapter in order to illustrate the ritual power of 'images'. But Morrison also gives us some details about acts of undressing:

> On the 1st of February [1790] our attention was drawn from our Work by a Heiva ... Evry thing being ready Captain Cooks picture was brought (by an Old Man who has the Charge of it) and placed in front, and the Cloth with which it was covered being removed, evry person present paid the Homage of striping off their Upper Garments, the Men bareing their bodys to the Waist, Poeno not excepted, and the Weomen uncovering their Shoulders. The Master of the Ceremonies then made the Oodoo (or usual offering) making a long speech to the Picture, acknowledging Captain Cook to be Chief of Maatavye and placing a Young Plantain tree with a sucking pig tyed to it before the Picture ...
>
> After which they proceeded to perform their dance, which was done by two young weomen Neatly and elegantly dressd in fine Cloth, and two Men, the whole was conducted with much regularity and exactness, beating drums & playing flutes to which they kept true time for near four Hours.
>
> On a signal being given the Weomen Slip'd off their Dresses and retired, and the whole of the Cloth and Matting which was spread to perform on, was rolld up to the Picture and the old man took posession of it for the use of Captain Cook (Morrison 1935: 85-6).

Morrison's narrative is interesting because he distinguishes the moment when, as the Image-of-Cook became visible, all the assistants uncovered only their shoulders and chest as a gesture of respect in front of a superior, from the moment when the women finished their dance and removed '[all] their dresses' to present it to the Image-of-Cook.

It is important to realise that the presentation of offerings of cloth by naked female dancers was not a recent innovation that had just emerged during the period of contact. One cannot assume that it was occasioned by European demand. There is nothing to suggest that the new arrivals requested *tapa*, for they did not know what to do with it. During the very first encounter, in 1767, Wallis did not even want to take the *tapa* that the Tahitians had left for him on the beach (the initial encounter took place at a distance). Banks quickly rid himself of these unending gifts. In any case there are enough sources, such as Rodriguez and, later, Wilson, which indicate that the practice was already well-established between Polynesians. I have already drawn attention to the observation made by Rodriguez soon after Cook's second visit: 'Some women decked in quantities of native cloth presented themselves before the Chiefs in order to strip themselves and make an offering of the cloth to the said Chiefs' (cited in Oliver 1974, III: 1237). Twenty years later, this practice is still observable. Wilson, the captain of the first ship of missionaries to arrive at Tahiti (1797), mentioned the *heiva* dances:

> Any number of women may perform at once; but as the dress is very expensive, seldom more than two or four dance; and when this is done before the chief, the dresses are presented to him after the *heiva* is finished; and these contain thirty or forty yards of cloth, from one to four yards wide (Wilson 1799, cited in Oliver 1974, I: 338).

Wilson conveys how the young girls could be laden with *tapa* during the dance. Thirty yards is equivalent to some twenty-seven metres of a cloth that could be more than three metres wide. Hamilton therefore scarcely exaggerated—or not at all—when he mentioned, six years before, the fifty metres worn by these women who had to be hoisted on board like packages. Between the two decades, Bligh's account (1788) provides additional confirmation of this (Oliver 1974: 956). For the same period Morrison insists on the fact that, at the feasts organised at each 'visit' between local groups (a very common practice, he says), the gifts of food (pigs, tubers) had always to be accompanied by gifts of cloth (Oliver 1974: 345).

It is equally interesting to note with Morrison that the presence of the local chief, or 'Poeno' (probably Poino), can be enough to create the point of intersection for the circulation of the gifts of cloth. The chief was therefore an attractor of gifts in the same way as the Image-of-Cook—which is a further confirmation of what I have suggested in the previous chapter about the gods, the chiefs and the Europeans. Morrison relates:

> Several Baskets of Provisions Consisting of Fish, Plantains, Bread-fruit, Tarro & Cocoa Nuts were brought and presented to us, and at Poenos request we fired the Musquettoon which we Charged with Slugs & firing into a large Apple tree brought down several of the Fruit at which they expressd much wonder and departed well pleased.

On the 2nd Came another Heiva, which Poeno brought to the Square; this was Conducted in the same manner, and attended by the Inhabitants as before, but Captain Cooks picture was not present, Poeno receiving the Cloth and Matting which he devided amongst us, the Whole Amounting to near one Hundred Fathoms....

On the 6th we received a Vist from Eddea [Itia] who was come down to visit her Son the Young King at Oparre. She brought presents of Cloth for each as did also her Sister Teano (wife to Vayheeadoa [Vehiatua], Chief of Tyarrabboo [Taiarapu]) who accompanied her - She Staid at the Square some days, and the Vacant space near the Square was made use of for Dancing Wrestling and throwing the Javlin; and the young Men & Weomen frequented this place for their amusement afterwards when the weather permitted, so that we were entertaind with a dance almost evry evening while we remaind here without going from home to see it (Morrison 1935: 86-7).

12. Conclusion

It seems that this method of making an offering was peculiar to young women or rather to young girls. Cook specifically mentions 'young girls' in his notes on dances. Such offerings were made at the end of a dance and, according to both the sources relating to Cook's voyages as well as missionary sources on Samoa, the females in the front row were 'virgins' (Tcherkézoff 2003b: 384) or 'without any connection with men' (Tcherkézoff in press-1).

It is possible that the young women offering cloth remained clothed in a *maro*, which means that they were only 'naked' from the European point of view. In that case, all these accounts simply document the respectful presentation of cloth before a superior (chief or European guest), as a means of enveloping and incorporating this superior. Then again, it is possible that these accounts describe how the young girls' or women's bodies were deliberately stripped naked, and if so we should regard these cases as being linked to the more specifically sexual displays which are recorded as having occurred in the first instances of contact. We are then left with the same three interpretations that I advanced for the similar scene reported by the ex-surgeon Stevens who narrated to Williams his landing in Samoa: 'the females gathered around him in great numbers, and some took their mats off before him, exposing their persons as much as possible to his view' (see above chapter 6, section 8).

These interpretations are centred around the main hypothesis about the sacredness of unmarried females, and their role in Polynesian fertility rites and the capturing of the life-giving powers of external forces (the gods) through the containment—that is the wrapping-up—of their 'images' (chiefs, first Europeans). In this vein, one additional fact should be mentioned for the Tahitian case.

The episode is told by Forster senior. A chief from Raiatea often came to visit Cook's ship. One day when he was there he saw two of his sisters coming towards the ship in a canoe. He asked Forster to turn to the younger one and say 'Veheina-poowa' (*vahine* + ?).[25] As soon as Forster had uttered this word, the elder sister

> immediately lifted up the garments of the younger, showing that she had the marks of puberty. When she had done this two or three times, she refused to go through the same ceremony again.

Forster then relates that after asking some questions about what had taken place, he grasped that there had been some teasing involved. A very common form of criticism would be to tell a girl that she is not yet pubescent. He also indicates in the following lines that, as soon as the signs of 'puberty' were visible (without being more precise), the girl was tattooed.

> The young women are obliged to undergo a very painful operation, viz., to have *large arched stripes punctured on their buttock*; these curious marks are reputed honourable, and it is thought a mark of pre-eminence to be capable of bearing children.

And he added that, if a man tries to criticise a pubescent girl for not yet being so, then the girl will not hesitate to show by such explicit means that this is not the case.[26]

It is clearly regrettable that, in their accounts about dancing and the giving of *tapa*, observers like Cook and Banks did not concern themselves with the question of tattooing, which they treated separately in the summaries they made about customs. However, Banks and, later, Morrison make it quite clear that tattooing of the girls did take place. Banks: 'This morning I saw the operation of *Tattowing* the buttocks performed upon a girl of about 12 years old'.[27] Morrison suggests that it was the general rule, and that as long as the tattooing remained unfinished (which could take months, with long intervals in between because of the intense pain) the girl remained a child: 'till which time they never Conceive themselves Company for Weoman—being only Counted as Children till they have their Tattowing done'.[28]

We therefore have a significant piece of evidence to add to the argument: *for a girl*, the fact of revealing the lower part of the body can be entirely linked to the symbolism of childbearing and have nothing to do with the expression of

---

[25] *Pua* as a metaphor for a young girl who is 'coming into bloom', flowering (a state of maturity that is still only at the flowering stage)?
[26] Forster's text is cited by Oliver (1974: 607-8) in relation to the markers relative to life stages, and is taken up again by Gell (1993: 138).
[27] Taken from Banks's journal edited by J.C. Beaglehole, cited by Oliver (1974: 432).
[28] Morrison's Journal cited by Oliver, *ibid*.

desire.[29] This episode should be kept in mind when one reads the various accounts of the presentation of 'disrobed' young Polynesian girls during first contacts. This information from Forster, Banks and Morrison is in keeping with the general hypotheses developed in chapter 3: the presentation of young girls to the Europeans was linked to the value placed on the ability to bear a child.

Relying on Morrison and on other sources such as Teuira Henry, Oliver attempts a generalisation in relation to these presentations of cloth:

> Particular interest attaches to Morrison's statement concerning the necessity to accompany food ('which Nature produces') with gifts of objects ('procured by the Assistance of labour or the Art of Man'). Of all these products of 'the Art of Man' bark cloth was perhaps the most usual one given to visitors, and it was presented either in single pieces or a long roll. The most ceremonious method of presentation was that whereby a long roll was presented wound round one of the donor's people (usually a young woman): after placing the free end in the guest's hands the bark-cloth-laden agent of the donor then turned round and round until the strip was completely unrolled, leaving her completely nude. It may be imagined how charmed were the European visitors —at least the nonclerical ones— by this display of liberality and finesse (Oliver 1974: 348).

But, in this last sentence, Oliver infers the presence of an element of sexual attraction which is undoubtedly misplaced and which occurs to him under the influence of the Western myth about Polynesian sexuality.[30] Indeed, we should not think that the idea was only to charm the recipient and to arouse his sexual desire. In my interpretation, the fact of choosing young women for this type of gift was not determined by attributing sexual desire to men with an appetite for young women, but was a reference to the possibility of procreation. The

---

[29] Gell (1993: 139-40) has also noted Forster's remark, but, although he is careful to avoid revisiting our Western myth, still misinterprets its significance by focusing only on tattooing. He refers to this scene to provide an explanation of the episode of 12 May 1769, namely the ceremonial presentation of cloth in which a young woman stepped upon the lengths of *tapa* and undressed. The young woman would, he suggests, have undressed herself to show Banks the marks of puberty (even though the journals are silent on the subject). In doing so, she would have removed the taboo from her gift of cloth and rendered it acceptable by Banks as an opening for a secular bartering of goods relationship, a relation between 'exchange partners', the partners being in this case Banks (and the other Englishmen) and the woman (and her party). But, as the whole of my discussion here illustrates, the link between the stripping of females and the gift of cloth related to a wider sociological and cosmological scheme and could by no means be limited to the encounters with the Europeans. And it cannot be reduced to a display of the marks of puberty (which has never been mentioned in these contexts of gift-giving). Besides, Gell's hypothesis of desacralising the gift, for the scene in question, wrongly assumes that the tattooing of the buttocks to mark the appearance of puberty signified the desacralising of the *tapu* state of any girl. It seems to me, following Morrison, that it was only the beginning of the process of transition from *tapu* to *noa*, a process that—for girls—came to an end *only with marriage-and-the-first-child*.

[30] See my discussion of Oliver's analysis of sexuality in ancient Tahiti in Tcherkézoff (in press-1).

'young woman' was there as a pubescent girl, but one who had not yet borne a child.

These female displays were not evidence of any 'sexual hospitality' offered to male voyagers in search of rest and pleasure, but rather, evidence of the attempt to capture through impregnation, real or metaphorical, apparently super-human powers. To capture these powers is to incorporate these new arrivals. In Polynesian civilisation, to incorporate was and, in some cases, still is to envelop. My hypothesis is that it was intended that *both cloth and the young girls'/women's bodies be used to envelop the new arrivals.*

This incorporation was achieved through wrapping up the body of the new arrival in the sacred cloth, in order to domesticate his dangerous sacredness, but also through wrapping up the body of the new arrival with the body of a young girl (through a sexual act intended to bring procreation). Sexual attraction, if there were any such dimension, was only meant to arouse the desire of the visiting male so that he could perform what was expected of him, and not to defer to any cult of sexual pleasure and to please the male visitor by offering him sexual hospitality. Both the cloth and the young girls were a very specific kind of 'wrapping' material which contained a super-human principle of life. Both were a channel for godly forces and signs of life. Gods could follow 'the path of the cloth' to come down on earth, as in the Lau Islands, or they could follow the channel of the young female's body and come down on earth in the guise of a child. And that is why children were considered a priori to be *tapu*; at birth, they still belonged to the godly world. Conferring on them a state of *noa* ('touchable', a state of humanity) involved a long process of desacralisation rites; for a female, the last step was marriage, and marriage meant the production of a child who would himself be *tapu*.

Perhaps the hypothesis already made for the Samoan case should indeed be generalised: young girls/women were the most effective means of incorporating what came from afar. As such they became the main 'tool' of the chiefs' policy when the *Papālagi-Popa'a* appeared on Polynesian shores.

Chapter 11

The Papālagi ('Europeans') and the Sky. Etymology and divinity, linguistic and anthropological dialogue

1. The antiquity of the expression 'Papalagi'[1]

Europeans have been labelled 'Papālangi' in Western Polynesia (written *Papālangi* in Tongan, *Papālagi* in Samoan), apparently since the early contacts. The word is already mentioned in Cook's narrative. When James Cook was in Tonga in 1777, he noted that this word was used to refer to his expedition as well as to the coming of European boats long before him (this could only have been the Dutch expeditions of the 17th century, the last being Tasman's expedition more than a century before, in 1643). The Tongans said: (Cook's transcription) *ko e vaka no papalangi* 'the boats of/from the *papalangi*' (we shall return to the discussion of the translation). In the Samoan context, the earliest published recording of the word seems to date from a book written in 1837 by the first missionary to Samoa, John Williams. In that text Williams recalled that he heard the word when he arrived for the first time in Samoa in 1830. Before arriving in Samoa, Williams had met in Tonga a Samoan man named Fauea. This man, who had been away from Samoa for some years, was happy to board Williams's ship. When the party landed in Samoa (Savai'i Island), Fauea addressed his fellows with a speech mentioning the great powers of the 'papalangis' (Williams 1841: 282, who adds in a note: 'Foreigners'). In some cases, Europeans are still dubbed *Papālagi* in contemporary Pacific languages. Certainly in Samoan this is an absolutely common, everyday word, not in any way a metaphoric ceremonial expression used in special circumstances, nor is it used with either laudatory or derogatory intent.

The word thus predates Cook's arrival and must have been coined when the inhabitants of the region saw Europeans for the first time: at least when they saw Tasman in 1643 and, perhaps, at the arrival of LeMaire's expedition in 1616. The latter was the first recorded European encounter, the first experience that Polynesians had of being shot by European muskets and the first occasion when European goods were acquired in the northern islands of the Tongan

---

[1] The sections on the 'sky-burster' hypothesis have been published in the *Journal of the Polynesian Society*, vol. 108, n°4, 1999 ('Who said that the 17th-18th centuries Papālagi ('Europeans') were 'sky-bursters'? A Eurocentric projection onto Polynesia') and are reproduced here (with minor changes) with kind permission of the Society.

archipelago—islands that were places of regular passage for Tongans and Samoans. If another word had been coined in 1616, why would it have been replaced in 1643? LeMaire's actions had, even more than Tasman's, all the ingredients that dramatically forced the Polynesians to attribute a non-human nature to Europeans.

2. The invention of the notion of 'bursting through'

Let us consider again an example already mentioned in chapter 9: the Mangaia song about Cook's arrival, recorded by the missionary Gill: '*No Tangaroa te vaka*: *kua tere i te aka i te rangi ē ...*'. I noted there how we should translate those words: 'It is the boat belonging to/originating from Tangaroa, it has sailed on/from the sky; they are very frightening *akua*'. The first line says only: 'it is the boat of Tangaroa', with the genitive form indicating that the possessor is the origin of the possession (*no* instead of *na*). The second line says that this boat *tere* on the sky (more precisely, that the boat *tere* 'on the root (*aka*) of the sky'?). *Tere* is given in the *Cook Islands Maori Dictionary* (Buse *et al*. 1995) as 'be under way (as ship), sail along, ... travel ... run its course'. The line thus says only that 'this boat has sailed on/from the sky'. These new creatures had travelled in the sky, as 'frightening *akua*' (which probably meant only 'partial manifestations of the gods', as we can conclude from the discussion in chapter 9) and they were on a boat 'of/from Tangaroa'.

But Gill has given a different translation: 'Tangaroa has sent a ship / Which has burst through the solid blue-vault' (Gill 1880: 183). It was Gill who, on his own initiative, added that they had 'burst through' the sky. Invention can be seen plainly in this case, since there is nothing in the apparent etymologies of the Mangaian words reproduced here which could have given Gill the idea of 'bursting'.

Was this Gill's invention or, more plausibly, an already established tradition among missionaries? It is interesting to note that the idea that Europeans came as 'sky-bursters' was used by London Missionary Society (LMS) missionaries in the Cook Islands as their own interpretation of local expressions. For it is the same missionary society which arrived in Samoa after having landed in the Cooks, and it was the missionary George Turner, established in Samoa from 1843 and founder of a theological college in 1844, who asserted in his ethnological notes—which would become *the* authoritative work on 'early Samoa'—that the Samoan word *Papālagi* must be understood as 'sky-bursters':

> The God of the 'men who had burst through the heavens' began to be feared. Of old the Samoans thought the heavens ended at the horizon, and hence the name which they give, to this day, to the white men, viz., *pāpālangi*, or heaven-bursters (Turner 1986 [1861]: 9).

The Papālagi ('Europeans') and the Sky. Etymology and divinity, linguistic and anthropological dialogue

Turner's book of 1861, in which the author gathers together papers he published in the local missionary magazine during the late 1840s and 1850s, would be widely read by all missionaries and many others—and W. W. Gill was certainly no exception. We are uncertain whether the LMS missionaries arrived in Samoa bringing with them this tradition that they had invented in the Cooks or, more probably, if the LMS group invented it once they were established in Samoa—because they thought there was a linguistic argument (*pā* 'to burst', *lagi* 'sky') to support it—and spread the idea through Turner's writings. But, in any case, the meaning of 'bursting through' is most certainly a missionary invention, which rapidly became a full-blown European tradition. I suspect it is because of that tradition of interpreting the word *Papāla(n)gi* that, a century later, Beaglehole added to his edition of Cook's journals a note of his own, when mentioning the Tongan expression noted by Cook (*ko e vaka no papalangi* 'the boats of/from the *papalangi*'): 'ships burst from the sky' (Beaglehole 1955-67, III: 178, note 1), while Cook himself had given a different translation (see below).

What is quite revealing in Turner's passage is that the idea seemed logical to him *because of his view of the Polynesian cosmos,* namely, the heavens as a closed hemisphere that rested on the earth: 'Of old the Samoans thought the heavens ended at the horizon, and hence the name'. Thus, he found it logical that, for the Polynesians, anything extraordinary must have been understood as coming from *beyond that heavenly limit*. The fact that, in the Europeans' interpretations, cosmological representations more than linguistic arguments had been the main reason behind the invention of this tradition is confirmed by Gill's passage where he forcefully applied the idea to a word (*tere*) in which there is no etymological stem that could mean 'to burst'.

3. The Samoan contemporary interpretation

Today, when Samoans happen to offer an etymological explanation of the word in response to foreigners' queries (which is of course rare and limited to teachers and the like), they give the same explanation as Turner, presenting it as self-evident. I offer the hypothesis that this sense of linguistic certainty comes from the fact that the English expression 'sky-bursters' has itself, in a way, been frozen in Samoa since the early mission days when English was taught in Samoan mission schools. It seems evident to me that the Samoans who offer this etymology using the traditional (1840s) English expression of 'sky-bursters' do not really mean that their ancestors thought that Europeans came from the other side of the sky. More generally, as we have seen in chapter 9, Europeans were said to travel in the sky, to come from the sky/the sun, but not from another world, from another *lalolagi* in Samoan terms.

4. The cosmological contradiction

Herein lies the problem. 'Bursting through' the sky implies an other-side of the sky, thus another world. Such a representation could not have been a pre-contact Polynesian view; nor do we find it during the early contacts. It seems to me that this was the view that *Europeans had* in their *projective* reasoning when interpreting Polynesian cosmology. They knew that, in nearly every Polynesian culture they had encountered, cosmogonic myths told of a world where Earth and Sky were joined together until the civilising hero succeeded in separating them, thus creating a space for the Light and hence for human life. Since those beginnings, the Sky was a vault that joined with the Earth only at the horizon, at the edge of the world, which no one could reach. In the European vision of this 'Polynesian' universe, the image of the sky vault resting on the earth is 'the Polynesian universe', hence only a part of the great universe (as seen by Europeans). What European missionaries neglected in their interpretation is that for the Polynesians the Sky was an absolute limit, the limit of the very universe, and they did not realise that their translation was in fact saying something about their own view of the European arrival through Polynesian images: 'we (Europeans) came, as they (Polynesians) thought, from another world beyond their sky-vault'. They did not realise that this translation led to the idea of another side of the sky, an idea that is totally absurd for Polynesian pre-contact cosmology.[2]

As we know, the Polynesian Sky was so utterly conceived as an absolute limit in cosmogonic descriptions that the sun and the light were conceived as filling the space *between* Sky and Earth. The sun, the moon and the stars are created *within* the space organised by the ten heavenly levels. In the Tahitian cosmogony recorded in Teuira Henry (1928), once the Sky is propped up, the sun, the moon and the stars appear but are moving around in disorder. Ra'i-tupua leaves the tenth level of the Sky, goes down all of the nine levels and, standing on the first one, only then contemplates the disorder. The text adds that 'the moon had been created within, the sun had been created within, the stars had been created within' ('...le soleil fut créé à l'intérieur...', Babadzan ed. 1993: 80). This is also why the Sky was thought of as an entity layered in different levels, with the great creator Tangaroa seated at the last level. The limit—precisely because it is the very last conceivable entity—can be dense and filled with many subdivisions. But this does not mean that there is something beyond the limit. On the contrary, if there were something beyond the Sky, the limit would not have been conceived as dense space, subdivided into levels (and in 'ten' levels

---

[2] I mentioned in chapter 9 that, in the Samoan case, this 'absolute limit' was of course quite flexible and could at any time include new 'islands' as the horizon was broadened through voyaging or knowledge gained from stories told by neighbouring peoples. Still, there was not any idea of two 'worlds'. There can be only one *lalolagi*, one '[world]-under-the-sky' (see also Tcherkézoff 2000c).

as told in the Samoan or Tahitian cosmology, which amounts symbolically to an 'infinity' of levels).

5. No 'bursting' at all: linguistic arguments

Thus, I am highly sceptical that the first part of the word *Papālagi* comes from the verb *pā* 'to burst', as is so often said in Samoa and about Samoa. Let us note that, at least today, the plural of *pā* is *pāpā* and not *papā*. It seems to have been no different in the 19th century since, in his ethnological work, Turner spells the word *'pāpālangi'* when implying that the first part of this word is from the stem *pā*. But Pratt's dictionary (the first version of which was compiled in the same period and to which Turner contributed) spells the entry translated as 'a foreigner' as '*PAPĀLAGI*', with only the second 'a' being a long vowel. (It is true that, in the first two editions of Pratt's dictionary, there had been inconsistencies. However, 'foreigner' is the translation given for *Papālagi* in the last edition (1911) which is generally accurate, and it is also noted thus in Milner's 1966 dictionary.)

The word *pā* is applied today to such sounds as the bursting of a tyre, and also to the same things mentioned for the 19th century in Pratt's dictionary: 'to explode as a gun, thunder; to burst as an abcess; to break forth into lamentation ...'. (The same applies to the Tongan '*pā*'.) The only usage that I found where *pā* is related to the sky applies indeed to the thunder: '*Ua pā (mai) le fāititili*', 'the thunder has just crashed'. Of course, the sound of cannon and muskets may have been compared by Polynesians to the sound of thunder. The word '*pā*' spoken in its reduplicated form describes the repetition of the action, but then it is always *pāpā*. If one wants to explain to a child where the thunder comes from: '*Ua pāpā (mai) le fāititili mai le lagi*, 'the thunders always crash from the sky'; the particle *mai*, 'from', before the word 'sky' (*le lagi*) could not have been dropped to compose a word **pāpālagi*. Also, is it linguistically admissible that this improbable form **pāpālagi* would have evolved into *papālagi* with the first 'a' becoming a short vowel, so short, in fact, that the word is actually pronounced in Samoa as [p:ālagi]?[3]

Interestingly, John B. Stair (missionary in Samoa, 1838-1845), writing his memoirs in 1897, followed the LMS tradition about 'sky-bursters', but apparently expressed some doubts because he raised the possibility of a linguistic link between the word in question and European guns:

> These marvellous visitors they called *pāpālangi* [he spells it like Turner] (sky-bursters), for, said they, these people have either burst through the

---

[3] One actually gets the impression that the word is [p:ālagi] and becomes *papālagi* only in formal discourse (and in written Samoan).

clouds with their ship; or else, lifting them up, they have passed beneath, and come to visit us. It is possible the name *pāpālangi* may have been given to commemorate the noise of ships' guns, as they first heard the dread sound [Stair adds a note here:] After recently perusing this MS., my friend, the Rev. Samuel Ella, says 'This is also my idea' (Stair 1897: 24).

Stair is more accurate than others in his imaginative notion of bursting through, since he supposes it was through the 'clouds', which does not contradict the cosmological aspect of the Sky as the limit. Perhaps, he refers to some discussions he had with the Samoans on this point ('...said they...'). The problem, however, is that *lagi* is not 'clouds' but 'sky/Sky'. The other problem is that Stair and Turner spell our word correctly for an interpretation based on the plural form of *pā*, bursting, but incorrectly if we are to judge from contemporary pronunciation and dictionaries, and even from dictionaries of their own time. Thus the hypothesis of a reference to the burst of guns is unacceptable.

6. Another hypothesis[4]

More promising is the Samoan example of *papā-vao* [*papa-a-vao*] 'edge of forest or bush'; similarly, **papa-a-lagi* could have been coined as 'edge of the sky'. There is also *papātua* 'back (of man, animal)', equivalent to *tua*, the tough side of a thing as opposed to the smooth side, hence also 'back' in numerous contexts.

But this word, with a composition recorded in contemporary Samoan (Milner 1966) only with *vao* 'bush' or *tua*, might be the polysemic Samoan (and pan-Polynesian) *papa* that can mean a 'board, plank' (such as used for scraping bark-cloth), and (flat) 'rock' (the big and flat black volcanic rocks), and 'make level, flatten' (as in preparing the lawn in front of the house that is ceremonial and honorific); or perhaps, if it is the same word, a type of 'coarse floor mat'. For Tongan, presented in this way by Churchward's dictionary (1959), we find: papa[1]: 'planks'; papa[2]: 'floor mat'; papa[3]: 'flat hard sandstone forming a layer or bed of the coast'; papa[4]: 'flat and smooth and hard' (track, sides of a hole). This semantic field may seem heterogeneous but there is unity if one refers it to the

---

[4] The whole of the following discussion assumes that, whatever the origin of the first part of our word may be, the second part refers to the sky. This assumption, i.e., that the Samoan word *Papālagi* is to be decomposed as *Papā+lagi*, obvious as it might seem, is only a hypothesis. The grounds for the hypothesis are the constant utterances made by Polynesians in first contacts that Europeans had to do with the sky. Also, in the list of Proto-Polynesian morphemic stems (see POLLEX [Biggs and Clark 1999]), there is no other possibility, as no stem such as **palagi* is proposed (except one, **palagi*, with reflexes recorded throughout Polynesia, but which is semantically totally unrelated to our topic because it designates the 'surgeon fish' [*Acanthurus sp.*]). It implies that any other option than considering the composition of the word as deriving in part from 'sky' (*lagi*) would involve a theory of borrowing from a non-Polynesian language —an option which must always be left open, if we consider, for example, the recent demonstrations that various Polynesian words are in fact borrowings from the Dutch through early contacts with the Dutch expeditions (Geraghty and Tent 1997a, 1997b).

cosmogony. The world began with flat surfaces, which are (in the Samoan myths): *papa'ele* 'earth' (cf. *'ele'ele* 'earth, soil'), *papaone* 'sandy', *papatā* 'solid rock'. The unity of the category is revealed (preserved?) in Central-Eastern languages where *papa* is also all kinds of 'layer', 'base', 'stratum', which can then apply also to the status system, to 'genealogies' and to ideal levels of the cosmos.

Can this word, with this idea of 'cosmogonic surface / level', apply to the sky? It does not seem that the Samoan cosmogonic myths make use of a *'papa(a)lagi'* in this way. I do not know about Tonga.[5] But the idea and the word are recorded elsewhere:

> The Pukapukan idea of the cosmos, complementing the ideology of the soul, is that the cosmos consists of three major levels, indefinitely extensive flat surfaces. The level of this world of humans comprises *te papa wenua* and *te papa moana*, the level of the land and of sea. Above is *te papa langi*, the level of the sky. The sky meets land or sea at the horizon, which is thought of as the side of the sky, *te tawa o te langi*. Below the level of this world is the Po, the Underworld, itself made up of three further indefinitely extensive levels, *te kapi lunga, te kapi lalo*, and *te po likuliku* (Beaglehole and Beaglehole 1938: 326).[6]

Thus we might propose that the word *papālagi* meant only '(beings) of the sky/belonging to the level of the sky', as opposed to '(beings) belonging to the level of the earth/sea'. Note also, in 19th-century Samoan (Pratt's dictionary), that *papatā*, 'standing rock', can be applied metaphorically to persons: 'a courageous man, a hard-working man'. It is possible, then, that the idea of the 'level of the sky' became similarly applied to Europeans.

This hypothesis is reinforced by a remark again made by Cook about his talk with the Tongans. First he mentioned that they remembered the earlier coming of European ships (Tasman's expedition): 'they informed us that their ancestors had told them that two ships, ('Towacka no papalangie') like ours had once been at the island'. He then added the following remark: 'For what reason I know not, but they call our Ships *Towacka no papalangie* and us *Tangata no papalangie*; that is cloth ships and cloth men' (Beaglehole 1955-67, III: 178). On the same page, in addition to note 1 where Beaglehole proposes the translation 'ships burst from the sky', Beaglehole added another note saying that, probably, 'the Tongans also transferred the word *papalangi* to the things the foreigners brought' (p. 178, note 3). We shall see in the last part of this chapter that the transformation could have been just the other way, from things to people.

---

[5] In a personal communication (February 2003), Fergus Clunie has drawn my attention to the Tongan word 'PAPAAELANGI' 'horizon' found in Baker's 1897 dictionary (Baker 1897).
[6] Ross Clark notes (personal communication, 1999) that *'paparangi* as a cosmic location is also mentioned for the Tuamotus, by Langdon who cites Stimson, Emory and Montiton as sources' (Langdon 1975).

Irrespective of the reason that caused Cook to understand that *papalangi* referred to 'cloth', what is significant for the present discussion is the expression *tangata no papalangi*. Literally it may be glossed 'people of the *papalangi*'. Thus, the word *papalangi* designated a location, a place from which those 'people' (*tangata*) originate; the gloss would be 'the (cosmic) place/level (of the) sky'. Moreover, again the genitive form used is *no*, as in Gill's quotation from Mangaia: the *papalangi* is thus the origin of the relationship of possession. The expression noted by Cook then meant 'people [*tagata*] originating from [*no*] the cosmic level Sky [*papalangi*]'. In the same manner, the expression *vaka no papalangi* could just have meant 'the boats from the cosmic place *papalangi*'.

The rather general meaning of 'people of the (level of the) sky' fits well with the fact that, when they first encountered Europeans, there were *more questions* raised for Polynesians *than certainties*, as we have seen in chapter 9. Europeans were certainly perceived as a kind of 'celestial' creature. In Eastern Polynesia, we know that Hawaiians thought that those creatures whose skin reddened when exposed to the sun, and who were constantly looking towards the sun with their optical devices, were somehow related to that part of the universe (see John Ledyard's comment). But no Polynesian knew for sure if these celestial creatures were images of gods or spirits —but what kind of spirits? ('spirits, *tupua*, but not [as] our spirits', said the Maori). In his observations, Gill noted the '*Solo*' (the chorus) of the song commemorating Cook's passage: '*E pai kua aa teia* ? Of what sort are they?' (1880: 185). This note confirms yet again that all the Polynesian interpretations of the nature of the *Papālagi* were followed by a question mark.

The configuration of the Polynesian vision of the first Europeans—the certainty of them being 'not-simply-earthly-hence-celestial-creatures' and indeterminacy as to the sort of celestial creatures that they might be—favours an etymology where the first part of our word *Papā-lagi* is not too precise, and definitely does not mean that Europeans were sky-'bursters'. The implausibility of an etymological 'sky-bursters' origin holds whatever might be other findings or propositions about the meaning of *papā-*. The 'sky-bursters' idea is another product of the already very long list of Eurocentric projections arising from various attempts to interpret Polynesian concepts.

For the rest, there are still uncertainties. The first possibility is that the word *papālangi* was indeed coined in Western Polynesia: (i) in the Tongan-Samoan-Futuna-Alofi islands, when the northern inhabitants had the misfortune of an encounter with LeMaire's expedition (given that Niuatoputapu and Tafahi were just as much 'Tongan' as 'Samoan'), or when Tasman's expedition landed in the main part of the Tongan archipelago; or (ii) at the latest, in the Samoan islands in 1722 when Roggeveen passed by. In all of those cases, I do not see a better candidate than the cosmogonic concept *papa*.

But there is the possibility that the word had been coined in the Tuamotus, an archipelago that was visited by LeMaire's same expedition of 1616 before it reached Western Polynesia, and even ten years earlier by Quiros (1606). Contacts between West and East are indeed plausible, so it is not impossible that a word coined in the Tuamotus (Paumotu language) was brought into Western Polynesia. In that case, the Tahitian *Popa'ā* / *Papa'ā* could also derive from that Paumotuan source. Davies's dictionary of the mid-19th century has: 'Papaa, *s.* a foreigner, formerly applied to the inhabitants of the *Paumotu* islands before europeans [*sic*] visited them, but since to all foreigners; in some islands it is *papalangy* [*sic*]'. This last remark is crucial for the hypothesis of a Tuamotuan origin, dating possibly from the encounters with the Dutch in 1616 or with the Spaniards in 1606, especially as the Tuamotuan worldview had a 'Paparangi' concept of a cosmic location comparable to the Cook Island *papalangi* cosmic location.

7. European gifts and the unwarranted encounter between the etymology of papālagi and the apotheosis of Captain Cook[7]

Since the publication in 1999 of the analysis presented in the previous sections, Paul Geraghty and Jan Tent have published an extensive study of the etymology of *papālagi*, with new and promising data. I have mentioned their publications on words used in contemporary Polynesian languages which are borrowings from the Dutch. This has prompted me to leave open the possibility that *papāla(n)gi* itself could have originated from a foreign language. Now Geraghty and Tent (2001) put forward the hypothesis that indeed our word *papāla(n)gi* originates from a non-Polynesian language: it could have been borrowed from Malay. But they conclude that, beyond the linguistic discussion, anyone raising the hypothesis of one of the word's components being 'sky' is falling into the type of 'Western-inspired myth' which made 'Beaglehole, Malo, Badger, Scarr and Sahlins' suppose that Captain Cook had been considered by the Hawaiians as 'an incarnation of Lono'. This myth is based on the 'European presumption of superiority' which made and still makes Europeans think that, in early encounters, they had been 'considered 'gods' or 'spirits' by the Polynesians' (*ibid.*:185-186, 202-3). I find it surprising that linguists could, even *en passant*, fall into the trap of the Obeyesekere-type of discourse, if I may coin this expression—a discourse that is a Western-inspired misconception of the pre-Christian Polynesian cosmology, as well as a misreading of Sahlins's analysis.

---

[7] This section was written in January 2003 and published as a 'shorter communication' in the *Journal of the Polynesian Society* (vol. 112, n°1, 2003, pp. 65-73); it is reprinted here with minor modifications, with kind permission of the Society.

More on the etymology of 'papāla(n)gi'

The origin would be the Malay word *barang*, 'thing, object, goods, article, commodity, luggage', adopted by Tongans who would have heard it from Tasman's crew in 1643 (Geraghty and Tent 2001). The word is well attested to in 17th century Malay. There were, most probably, Malay-speaking crew members on Tasman's ships. In those years the Dutch sailors themselves had adopted a number of local Malay words in their everyday language. Thus it is highly probable that, in 1643, the Tongans heard from the Dutch that the gifts handed over to them (cloth, beads, iron tools, etc.) were *'barang'*. The phonological transformation to **pala(n)gi, vala(n)gi* in the West-Polynesia-and-Fiji region is regular (*ibid.* : 190-9). One unsolved problem rests with the reduplication of *pa-*, but there are several possible explanations (*ibid.* : 199-200). One may also raise the question: did the story of our word *papāla(n)gi* begin with Tasman and not with LeMaire (or even the Spaniards in the Tuamotus, since we cannot exclude the possibility that the word was coined by Polynesians themselves)? While it is correct that the Tongans whom Cook met seemed to have mentioned only Tasman's passage, it is reasonable to assume that the impacts of events at sea during LeMaire's pasage (the killings and the handing over of various 'trinkets') would have induced the inhabitants to coin a word for the creatures they encountered. Could the *'barang* hypothesis' be applied retrospectively to the 1616 events?

Irrespective of the Tasman/LeMaire question, the strongest argument for the *'barang* hypothesis' is the existence of several passages, in early and late European journals and in early word-lists, that indicate without a doubt that our word *papāla(n)gi* was used locally to refer to a variety of European goods (*ibid.*: 192-4):

—'European cloth' (explicitly distinguished from local cloth) : Tonga (four recordings by Cook's companions in 1773 for **pālāngho, palangee, babba'langa, papalangee*, one by Malaspina in 1793 for **papaa-langui*, one by Labillardière, 1793, for **papalangui*) and Samoa (19th-century missionaries' dictionary for *āpāpālagi, āpapalagi*); there is also this rather odd translation offered by Cook in 1777: 'that two ships, ('Towacka no papalangie') like ours had once been at the island. For what reason I know not, but they call our Ships *Towacka no papalangie* and us *Tangata no papalangie*; that is cloth ships and cloth men' (Beaglehole 1955-67, III: 178). Whether Cook was right or wrong in his translation of *that* phrase (see below), it is clear that he knew of a Tongan word **papalangie* referring to 'cloth'. It is possible that the Fijian word *vāvālagi* should also be included as an example for the gloss of 'European cloth' (the case rests on an interpretation of a poetic text related to an event of 1800) (Geraghty and Tent 2001: 195-7).

—'European manufactures, goods' (including cloth): Tonga (Mariner, Dumont d'Urville): *papalagi, papa langui*.

—'broken glass': Tuvalu; 'beads': Rotuma, for (respectively) *pāpalagi* and *papalagi* (from dictionaries).

—'iron': Marquesas: three references, from 1773 to 1840 for **papa'annëë, pappa ane, papa-ani*; metal: Nukuoro/Kapingamarangi and Mokil for (respectively) *baalanga* and *pahrang* (ibid.: 193-4). From the Marquesan case, the authors are able to suggest that this word spread in Eastern Polynesia in a truncated form and resulted in all the *papā, papa'a, papa'ā* and *popa'ā* forms that are used to designate the 'Europeans' (ibid.: 200).

By the early nineteenth century everywhere in Western Polynesia and Fiji *papāla(n)gi* is recorded as referring also or only to Europeans as persons and to the place of origin of Europeans (ibid.: 171-5). It is not difficult to agree with the authors that, by that time, the meaning of the word had expanded from 'European goods (given in first contacts)' to Europeans themselves and to their world. It is important to note, however, that this extension had already taken place by the time of Cook's voyages. The translation given by Cook as 'cloth ships' and 'cloth men' is not accurate. Although it is presented by Geraghty and Tent in the opening of their analysis, certainly to attract the reader's attention to an etymology based on 'cloth' (ibid.: 172), it cannot account for what Cook heard as **Towacka no papalangie* and **Tangata no papalangie*. As I have said, the presence of '*no*' obliges us to understand that the Tongans were talking of the boats and the people 'originating from the Papalangie'. Whatever they imagined this Papalangie to be, it could not have been just 'cloth'. They could not have meant 'the people originating from the cloth'. Rather, the meaning had to be something like the 'boats of the people of the place of these [wonderful] goods' and, in the second case, 'the people of the place of these goods'. Considering this argument, it is remarkable that Mariner tells us that in Tonga the word *papalagi*, as he heard it in the years 1806 to 1808, meant 'White people, Europeans' (and, in one occurrence, the 'place of origin of the Europeans') *as well as* 'European manufactures such as cloth, linen, etc.'); the same remark is made by Dumont d'Urville in 1827 (Geraghty and Tent 2001: 171, 173, 193).

The importance of the gifts in first contacts

The discussion based on linguistics must rest at this point. The '*barang* etymology hypothesis' is very appealing, not only for the linguistic reasons that the authors presented in detail and that I have summarised here, but also for anthropological reasons.

All the previous chapters which analysed the scene of first contacts in Polynesia have shown us the extent to which, on each side of the encounter, the interpretation of the nature of the Other rested on the interpretation of the *gifts* offered by this Other. The interpretation of the nature of the objects given and the interpretation of the reasons and the manner of giving them were critical to any conclusion or understanding that was reached regarding the people involved. The three main categories of European objects that produced a rich variety of Polynesian interpretations during the first encounters were of course cloth, glass beads and iron tools—i.e. the three specific (early or evolved) meanings of our word *papāla(n)gi* noted by Geraghty and Tent. That the whole linguistic story may have begun around the gifts of cloth on Tongan shores is indeed a particularly welcome example of what we have seen in the previous chapter on the role of cloth in first contacts in Polynesia.

Still, the '*barang* etymology' is only a hypothesis. The only certitude is that (i) if the origin is a Polynesian one, it is *papa+lagi* with a reference to the 'sky', and (ii) if the origin is foreign, the '*barang* hypothesis' is a very appealing possibility.

More generally, Geraghty and Tent's analysis is another strong illustration of the benefits of the multidisciplinary method that is required for all ethnohistorical Polynesian studies (Kirch and Green 2001),[8] at least when the anthropological discussion takes into account the two sides of the encounter, just as the linguistic approach must do. But, at some point, our two analysts of the etymology of *papāla(n)gi* have forgotten this imperative.

On Europeans as 'gods': the unwarranted link

Geraghty and Tent's data as well as data provided in dictionaries show that, if indeed the origin is the word *barang*, the early meaning of 'European cloth or goods' had been *forgotten* by Polynesian speakers of the early 19th century, perhaps even as early as the late 18th century or even earlier. The Samoan and other occurrences of *papālagi* in documents of the early (and later) 19th century never refer to meanings such as 'cloth' or 'goods', and we know that in Samoa other words were used to refer to European goods and to European and indigenous cloth ('*oloa, 'ie, 'ie toga*, etc.).[9] We cannot know if the double meaning of both 'European people' and 'European goods', noted for Tongan usage by

---

[8] Kirch and Green call for a 'triangular' method (anthropology, archeology, linguistics). When archeology cannot help, as in the case of the 'first contacts', at least anthropology and linguistics must always be side by side in Polynesian studies.

[9] See the special issue of the *Journal of the Polynesian Society* on Samoan mats, vol. 108, n°2, 2000, which includes studies on the Tongan (A. Kaeppler, P. Herda) and Samoan cases (P. Schoeffel); and Tcherkézoff 1997b, 2002. The case of the Samoan word *āpāpālagi* as 'foreign cloth' (in the Samoan → English part of the dictionary) and 'foreign cloth' as '*āpapalagi*' (in the English → Samoan part) is mysterious. Lists were compiled in the 1840s. Although these two entries stayed on during the various revisions of the LMS dictionary (from 1878 to 1911—these revisions added many words but rarely deleted entries from former printings), the word is not indicated in Krämer's descriptions. In any event, its form (with the initial *a-*) and the fact that it did not designate the Europeans as people (who were *papālagi*) both indicate that, when noted by the missionaries in the 1840s, it was already a different word, in the Samoan linguistic consciousness, than *papālagi* (see Pratt 1862-1911).

Mariner and Dumont d'Urville, was still explicit and transparent for Tongan speakers or whether the two European observers had simply noted two meanings for what they heard as the same phonological unit. It is clear, however, that by 1840 in Samoa the double meaning for a single word of this sort did not exist (Turner who wrote many pages on gifts of cloth and who commented on the 'sky-bursters' would have noted this strange coincidence). This implies that by that time, a word *papālagi*, 'Europeans', was used without any known etymology (if the origin were the 17th-century *barang*, there was no memory of it) and there was room, therefore, for an *indigenous* folk etymology of the word *papālagi* as 'the people [or the side, or the people of the side] of the sky', based on *papa+lagi*.

Geraghty and Tent do not raise the issue in this way. After having noted the very early meanings of 'cloth, goods' and the later meaning of 'Europeans', and after commenting that such a semantic extension is easily understandable, they remark that in European writings from the 1790s (e.g., George Vason in Tonga) onwards up until the present, it was first proposed and then assumed (by early voyagers and residents, later by missionaries and scholars, some of them linguists) that the etymology of *papāla(n)gi* is something like 'people of the sky'; or in adjective form 'pertaining to people of the sky'. Indeed, all these writers proposed etymologies of this kind. In the Samoan case, it was 'sky-bursters'. The idea of 'bursting' proved to be entirely Eurocentric. Geraghty and Tent now assume that the notion of 'sky' is also a purely European invention and what is more, that it *can only be so*. They suggest that the first such invention could have been made by Vason in 1797 in Tonga (Geraghty and Tent 2001: 173).

Given this assumption, they then question why Europeans invented such 'spurious etymologies implying that the Polynesians and Fijians viewed Europeans as gods'. Leaving to 'historians' to find out why such etymologies have become 'so overwhelmingly popular in the literature of the past two centuries' (*ibid.*: 203), they still attempt an answer to why the etymology was proposed in the first place. They claim that the obvious reason is 'the European presumption of superiority' (which made Europeans think that the indigenous population had seen them as gods) and add that 'a case in point is Captain James Cook'. Suddenly departing the linguistic ground, Geraghty and Tent raise the Sahlins-Obeyesekere debate, refer to the claim that 'Cook being an incarnation of Lono is a Western inspired-myth' and open a discussion on the prevailing 'misunderstanding' which makes numerous scholars, among them 'Beaglehole, Malo... and Sahlins', assume that 'early European visitors were deified' (*ibid.*: 185-9).

In developing this argument, the authors commit two errors. First, they repeat the very same misinterpretation of Marshall Sahlins's position that was made by Obeyesekere and others. We know now from chapter 9 the biases and ambiguities that have accumulated around this idea of 'deification' and the mistranslations of *atua*. It is regrettable that Geraghty and Tent found the need to refer to the critiques of Sahlins by Obeyesekere (1992) and Bergendorff (*et al.* 1988) in order to dismiss any discussion of etymologies of *papālagi* as people of 'the sky'. It is all the more curious that they themselves offer the same critique I made with regard to the word *atua*, when they discuss the example of the Fijian word *kalou* (Geraghty and Tent 2001: 186). Europeans of the time as well as some contemporary scholars did indeed misunderstand the meaning of *atua*, *kalou*, etc. This does not mean that one should disregard the fact that indigenous people did apply these terms to Europeans or that one should not try to understand what they meant by doing so.

The second error Geraghty and Tent commit is that by ascribing the 'sky' etymologies to a Western-inspired myth of first contacts with Polynesians, they dispossess the Polynesians of their own (possible) interpretation of the word *papālagi*, once the first meaning had been forgotten or obscured through the process of semantic expansion (from 'European goods' to 'Europeans'). It may very well be that Vason was the first to see the morpheme *lagi* with the meaning 'sky' in the word, or it may not. It is certainly true that the idea of 'bursting through (the sky)' was invented by LMS missionaries. But would that invention have been adopted by Samoans so easily if the Samoans themselves had not heard in the component *lagi* the meaning 'sky'? Geraghty and Tent are neglecting the Polynesian and Fijian ideas that were expressed repeatedly during first contacts, namely that the Europeans, whatever their nature, travelled by 'boats of/originating from Tagaroa' and that they had passed 'near the sun'.[10] When residents such as Vason or Mariner, who were linguistically well integrated into the local population, assumed the presence of a reference to the 'sky' in the word *papālagi* when used by indigenous speakers, as the missionaries did in Samoa (even if the latter added the mistaken meaning of 'bursting through'), it is highly probable that they had discussed this point with their local friends. This, in turn, implies that their interlocutors did not contradict them on this point.

I think we can maintain the hypothesis that an indigenous (and not only European) folk etymology of the word *papāla(n)gi* as somehow referring to the 'sky' may have been operating since the early 19th century and probably earlier. We can leave open the discussion as to how much this indigenous interpretation appeared within a dialogue held locally with the first European visitors and residents, and later the first missionaries, all of whom had indeed, as Christians, a 'sky'-oriented cosmology and who, from the late 19th century onwards, became prone, erroneously, to attribute to the inhabitants a view of the 'divinity' of the first Europeans. The critical point is, however, that *the two sides of this dialogue*

---

[10] Although Geraghty and Tent (2001: 174) do mention the Fijian example of 1808 about 'peppa langa tooranga martinasinger' [*papalagi turaga matanisiga*] which means 'the Papalagi are chiefs from the sun' (see above chapter 9).

did not mean the same thing at all when talking of 'lagi' *and* 'Sky' *and of* 'atua' *and* 'God'. Not only their views of the cosmos, but their entire conception of time and space were very different (Tcherkézoff 1998b).

In sum, the discussion of the ethno-historical-linguistic uses of *papālagi* should not be linked to the biased Bergendorff-Obeyesekere discussion of the 'divinity of Captain Cook'. In the same way that the Polynesians applied the word *atua* to Europeans they *may* very well have reinterpreted *papālagi* on the basis of the component *–lagi*, with or without the influence of external teachers; or they *may* have coined the word from the start, using the two morphemes *papa+lagi* (since the '*barang* hypothesis', attractive as it is, is still only a hypothesis). Raising the possibility that they could have done so *by no means* amounts to adopting the position which Obeyesekere sees as 'the Western myth of the Europeans' "divinity"' (and one where Sahlins never happened to stand).

Conclusion: Ethnohistory-in-the-field

This study of the 18th-century encounters between Samoans and Europeans which was the subject of Part One of this book, together with the comparative analysis of other Polynesian cases in Part Two, makes a further contribution to an historical anthropology or ethnohistory which has only recently begun to be written. The subject of this relatively new field is the cross-cultural encounters between the Polynesians and the Europeans (*Papālagi-Popa'a-Pakeha-Haole*) from the 16th century. It embraces the earliest encounters as they occurred throughout the Pacific, and their subsequent development.

By applying the same critical reading that has been attempted here for Samoa to the literature available for each Polynesian Islands group (including Fiji and the Outliers), including among our sources the very first texts, whether in Spanish or in Dutch, we would be in a position to reconstruct a history of the first contacts in Polynesia. No longer, then, would Ulafala Aiavao (whom I quoted at the beginning of this study) need to remind us that we tend to forget the dualism and the asymmetry of the scene, that there were two sides who came together in the 'discoveries' just as there are still two sides who meet in contemporary encounters.

Meanwhile, some comparative hypotheses have been advanced about (i) the Polynesian interpretation of the nature of the *Papālagi*; (ii) the irrelevance of any analysis in terms of the crude barter of goods; and (iii) the irrelevance, equally, of any analysis in terms of sexual hospitality, least of all in respect of those cultures completely misread by Westerners as valuing sexual freedom in adolescence.

On the first point, the comparison has been broad enough to enable us to put forward a conclusive generalisation. The Samoan examples from the western area of the Polynesian region and a number of instances from the central and eastern areas all point to the same configuration, namely that Europeans have in the past been considered as *atua, aitu, tupua, kalou*. However they were not deemed to be 'gods' but, rather, they were considered as 'images' of the super-human forces. They were envoys from elsewhere, *perhaps* from the gods. But these ideas were questions in the minds of the inhabitants, not definitive statements. Whatever their nature, these '*atua*' sailed 'on the boats of [the god] Tangaroa', they came 'from the [far away cosmic place called] Papalangie...'. They were nothing more nor less than that. The idea that the Polynesians conceived of the Europeans as a Christian-type of 'divinity' is a Western projection. However, the critique of Eurocentric analysis should not prevent us from considering why the Polynesians called the Europeans '*atua*'. Closing the case by saying simply that the inhabitants 'could not have taken men for gods' only serves to replace ethnohistory with ethnocentrism.

On the question of the 'bartering' of goods and the corresponding 'thefts', the whole range of Samoan-European early encounters and the early gifts of cloth in the Tahitian-European case also provide sufficient evidence, from both sides of the Polynesian region, to undertake a complete reconsideration of these views.

As to the question of sexual hospitality and assumptions about a cultural value supposedly ascribed to sexual freedom in Polynesia, the Samoan case leaves us in no doubt about the inaccuracies and misinterpretations of long-established European views. To validate this last conclusion definitively at a pan-Polynesian level would ideally require a sequential reconsideration of all cases of first contacts in Polynesia. Yet the ethnographic and historical evidence from Samoa is sufficient to call into question current models of explanation in terms of cultural beliefs and practices that promote free sex, and to urge us to reconsider the sexual nature of these first contacts. Furthermore, the analysis of the Western misconceptions about Polynesian 'nudity', through the analysis of the Tahitian gifts of cloth, adds weight to the Samoan case and has confirmed that we must depart from any explanation in terms of sexual freedom. If we take into account the fact that a similar study made of the journals of the French first contact in Tahiti (concerning the sexual presentations enacted by Tahitian girls [Tcherkezoff, in press-1]) affirms the need to revise earlier theories, we then have a strong case, based on studies from both sides of Polynesia, to assert a broadly based and unqualified conclusion, namely, that the story of sexual freedom practised on a wide scale during adolescence in Polynesia is indeed a Western myth and nothing more than that.

These conclusions have been reached by using an ethnohistorical method where the prefix 'ethno-' strongly implies that the results from field-based ethnography should be added to the historical study of archives and published texts. That is why a 'deconstructive' strategy—such as that followed by Obeyesekere (1992, 1998, 2003), and described in those terms by Sahlins (2003:1)—which is based solely on a reading of past European narratives cannot help us and, in fact, only obscures the matter by creating artificial controversies.

I do not deny that there is some place for a deconstructive methodology. There is no doubt that it is useful in revealing the regime of power on whose behalf European narratives have been constructed: one underpinned by 'discovery', missionary and colonising goals, models and practices. It prevents us from accepting uncritically the interpretations and explanations that the authors of those narratives have made. This is exactly the kind of sceptical attitude that I have adopted here in my analysis of the conclusions reached by Lapérouse or Dumont d'Urville about 'Samoan girls' and which have been naïvely accepted by James Côté and other uncritical champions of Mead's *Coming of Age in Samoa*.

But once we have strong grounds for supposing that such conclusions are biased, all the ethnohistorical work of reconstructing what happened is still in front of us. 'Reconstructing *what happened*?' Some would question even the possibility of such a reconstruction.

A first objection concerns the relationship between culture and socio-cultural change. To claim that we have reconstructed what occurred implies thinking that, during the event of first contact (the arrival of the Europeans)—let us say that it happened at the point in time t—the islanders attempted an interpretation of this event. We therefore reconstruct this interpretation; that was the aim of each chapter of this book. In doing so we suppose that, at the point in time $t-1$, the islanders had some kind of conceptual framework and, more generally, a 'culture'—can I risk using that term? It was composed of various elements that we treat, when we reconstruct the various interpretations, as if they were all interrelated, parts of a single whole, at the risk of reifying everything of the historical period $t-1$ as a 'culture', as if a coherent cultural identity had been in place from immemorial times up until this period $t-1$. In fact, if it were possible for us to work on the period $t-1$, we would of course try to find that dynamic movement that always characterises social facts and we would go back to $t-2$ (where the problem would begin again). But of course we are unable to go back that far. The problem of ethnohistorical work on 'first contacts' is that, at a given point, it comes up against a complete absence of sources.

What is 'that dynamic movement that always characterises social facts'? The interpretative work effected at the point in time t by the islanders according to their $t-1$ conceptual framework obviously involved a modification of their $t-1$ categories. From the moment that the Europeans were taken for ancestors of a new kind, the ancestors of the Polynesians could never be quite the same again. There came into being a vision of the world that grew broader and broader, little by little breaking down the existing sociocentrism to make the notion of 'man' (*ta(n)gata*) something much greater than it had previously been. From the moment that 'divine' fecundation was seen as being able to combine the sacred vital principle and the mechanical act of impregnation in the body of a European man, then every European was suitable to be taken as a son-in-law. Now a new Polynesian social class had access to a formerly strict form of hypergamy where 'divine' son-in-laws had been limited to high chiefs. It is therefore clear that every interpretation becomes history and that no society has a 'culture' that is exactly the same before and after a given event, whether exogenous or endogenous.

If this observation about the dynamics of the historical process is quite obvious, it is still necessary to avoid falling into the trap of the facile response which would be to say (as certain post-modernists do)¹ that, as a result, the notions of 'culture' and of sociocultural 'identity' are meaningless. Dispensing with these notions would leave us with no basis on which to analyse and understand the indigenous interpretive mechanisms by virtue of which indigenous people made their decisions and constructed their future, all of which we analyse later as their 'history', making our analysis of it a study in 'ethnohistory'. At every point in time t, change is occurring. But to understand how this change is occurring, it is necessary to assume a minimal coherence of identity at the point in time $t-1$ which has allowed people to interpret an event, whatever it may be.

The list of such critical events resulting from 'contacts' is a long one. It extends from the disruption imposed from outside (the most catastrophic being an invasion that brings death to the majority or even the whole of the population: atolls depopulated by Peruvian slavers, the genocide of the Tasmanians, and so on), to the cases where an event that one believed to be of little consequence, to have been integrated and assimilated, produces—sometimes much later on—a secondary effect. This secondary effect then affects the core values of a people and triggers an upheaval, but the process leading up to it has gone on unnoticed, sometimes remaining so until it is too late.²

A second objection to 'reconstructing what happened' is raised by some historians and anthropologists. Let us again take the Hawaiian case. Although such researchers criticise the 'polemical and political' background of Obeyesekere's question as to 'whether Hawaiians were foolish enough to take Cook for Lono', they still interest themselves in a 'more radical epistemological query' raised by Obeyesekere, namely 'how someone who makes interpretations while situated in the twentieth century could know what were the thoughts of the Hawaiians of the eighteenth century' (Merle and Naepels 2003: 23). Any 'anthropological information [on first contacts] constituted during the 19th and 20th centuries from ethnographical enquiries and from the record of oral literature' requires, they say, that we understand how 'an event such as the encounter with Cook or Wallis has become a narrative within the indigenous society that later came to be recorded by a European ethnographer'. The authors urge that what is needed is 'the deconstruction of the fabrication of this anthropological knowledge' (*ibid.*). They add that the same analysis should of course also be applied to the fabrication of the European voyagers' narratives within the European society (*ibid.*: 22).

---

[1] See the discussion in Tcherkézoff (2003b:Postface).
[2] See Tcherkézoff (1997a) concerning certain forms of land tenure and of private ownership of houses or domestic goods. That is why, for the collection in which this article appears (Tcherkézoff and Marsaudon 1997), we chose the subtitle 'Identities and cultural transformations' (*Identités et transformations culturelles*) to qualify the main title *The South Pacific Today* (*Le Pacifique-Sud aujourd'hui*). The concept of (ethnohistorical) 'transformations' has no value without that of sociocultural 'identity'.

I entirely agree with this call for a close scrutiny of how (i) the published European narratives and (ii) the indigenous narratives recorded by ethnographers were constructed. My analysis of Dumont d'Urville's narrative of his stay in Samoa affords a clear example. Such a critical examination reveals the role played by the local beachcomber Frazior in the fabrication of the narrative. And certainly, although I have not considered it here, the famous Maori narrative about Cook's arrival and their conception of the European voyagers as 'the spirits which are not like our spirits' requires exactly the same examination. Yet I would still maintain that it is possible to understand *some* aspects of the way of seeing of the 18th-century Polynesians when they met the first Europeans, through comparing the accounts of early encounters in different parts of Polynesia and cautiously drawing on later or even recent *field-based ethnography*. Thus our data are not limited to 'narratives' (whether these be European or indigenous narratives).

Obeyesekere and his followers would go further yet. Not merely the conclusions proffered, but every phrase of the European narratives must be read as an expression of the regime of power under whose auspices the author conducted his voyage and produced his narrative. This position provides a cheap *solution de facilité*, an easy way out: it dispenses with the difficulty of scrutinising any European voyage narrative for information, since it allows us to conclude from the start that there cannot be any fact, any trace of ethnographic truth, contained in those narratives.

As Sahlins warns us, we should not indulge in this 'post-modernist' strategy of 'creating doubts about apparent "truths" by arguing that their status as truths is derived [only] from the regime of power on whose behalf they have been constructed' (Sahlins 2003: 1). Sahlins further cautions us that for any pre-contact or early contact practice (as for instance in the case of 'cannibalism' evoked by Sahlins in this recent article) this deconstructive attitude only obscures the historical practices, without delivering any alternative conclusion:

the allegation that good descriptions of Fijian cannibalism are really bad prejudices of European imperialists has submerged its historical practice in a thick layer of epistemic murk. The deconstructive strategy [followed by Obeyesekere] is not to deny the existence of cannibalism altogether ... rather to establish doubt about it. Not that there was no cannibalism, then, only that the European reports of it are fabrications (Obeyesekere 1998). Even so, not all such reports need be questioned. It is enough to create sufficient uncertainty about a few of them so as to cast suspicion on all the rest, and thus dismiss the whole historical record by implication (*ibid.*: 64-65). Literary criticism of one or two European texts, reducing them to some fictional genre such as sailors' yarns, serves the purpose of obscuring the factuality of scores of cannibal events, which then remain unmentioned and unexamined (Sahlins 2003: 1).

We know that for some topics or some periods we have only European reports as a source. Should one, therefore, claim that a doubt must be cast on the entire field and upon the whole period? The very notion of the 'factuality' of some 'events' would be an illusion. Everything then becomes subject to radical doubt, anything a possible 'fabrication'. If, adopting the postmodernist perspective, we were to return to our main topic—the role of sexuality in early encounters—each of the two following statements would be quite plausible, and neither of them could be verified or finally disproved: (i) Samoans offered sexual hospitality to the French of Lapérouse; or (ii) they did not offer such hospitality but, rather, they organised a sacred marriage ceremony in which the French were unaware of the role assigned to them. Perhaps Lapérouse's conclusions were an instance of wild European myth-making, but then again perhaps not. In such a slippery epistemological regime, one could argue that, a hundred and fifty years later, Mead's conclusions about Samoan sexual freedom in adolescence in the late 1920s could have been as 'right' as they were 'wrong'. In this radically sceptical paradigm we could never know anything as there is no such thing as reliable truth to be extracted from ethnography... But this dismissal of any search for historical truth in fact opens the door to all kinds of disturbing and condescending Eurocentric fantasies about the 'natives'. Whatever the imagination of European travellers of the past or of the present might produce could, in this mind-set, always be wrong or... right!

As the analyses that I have presented in this book make clear, we can deal only with facts, not fantasies. There are the facts to be revealed from an internal textual analysis. This kind of close analysis was able to reveal, for example, that Lapérouse's assertions about the sexual hospitality offered by the Samoans were in fact his own interpretations and conclusions, whereas the scene in which we are given a description of the marriage display came from what he, or one of his lieutenants, had actually observed. There are also facts of a strictly ethnographic type: this same scene is described by early 19th-century observers in Samoa such as Williams and Pritchard who explicitly state that they have been told by the Samoans that they are witnessing a 'marriage'.

Even recent ethnography can assist in ethnohistorical study. It should be clear by now that the reconsideration proposed here in Part One of all the early European visits to Samoa, and even the reconsideration in Part Two of some of the 18th-century events that happened outside Samoa, in Central and Eastern Polynesia, would not have been possible had I not been guided by hypotheses that emerged from the field enquiries that I conducted during the 1980s and 1990s in Samoa. I strongly advocate the potential—and the application of the method that I have employed in order to do so—of *extrapolating backwards* from more recent ethnographic accounts, as well as from those from the 19th century (at least in those cases where the 19th-century ethnographer had worked in the local language). This approach constitutes a kind of *ethnohistory-in-the-field*. It is quite different from a purely textual ethnohistory and is, of course, at the opposite end of the methodological spectrum from those deconstructive strategies which reduce all ethnography to the status of a mere tool of imperialism.

Narratives of 19th-century Samoan marriages and field observations from the 1980s about Samoan houses have given us important clues in reinterpreting Lapérouse's account of the apparently sexual welcome offered by Samoans in 1787. Other recent observations in Samoa about the social nature of the 'chiefs' have helped us to raise questions about the meaning of the '*atua*' nature of the Europeans in the eyes of the 18th-century Hawaiians, Tahitians, Cook Islanders, and other Polynesians. This insight into indigenous perceptions has suggested comparative hypotheses about Eastern Polynesian first contacts which, in turn, helped us to revisit the Samoan case and to reinterpret Lapérouse's account of the so-called 'thefts' carried out by the Samoans on the French boats of de Langle's party. Finally, ethnohistory-in-the-field has enabled us to re-analyse the whole account of the so-called 'massacre' that ensued from these 'thefts' on that fateful day of 11 December 1787.

Ethnohistorical research advances dialectically from the field to the archives and back again. At the same time, it proceeds from a hypothetical generalisation built on one case to a verification of that hypothesis by reference to other cases that can then confirm, contradict, or enrich the initial hypothesis. This, in essence, defines the ethnohistorical method that I have employed in this book, whose aim has been to propose to present-day generations of Polynesians certain hypotheses about how their forefathers discovered the *Papālagi*.

Illustrations

SAMOA
Early European views…

1. J. F. G. de Lapérouse
2.
3.
4.

In relation to the encounters with Samoans, no drawing was made (or survived) from the Bougainville expedition or from the Lapérouse expedition. For the official and posthumous publication of the Lapérouse expedition narrative (1797), only the 'Massacre' was drawn and engraved by Parisian artists (in a style which departed from the 1770-1790s' 'noble' representations of Tahitians; see pictures in the section on Tahiti). This view went right through into the German colonial period: the 1797 French engraving was reproduced or redrawn many times, as in this case (pl. 2) for a German account of Samoa. The author, formerly Supreme Judge of 'German Samoa', has compared on two adjacent pages what he called in his captions the 'Samoan raid on the French' (pl. 2) and the 'Hawaiian murder of Captain Cook' (pl. 4).

'First Contacts' in Polynesia

... and colonial times

5.

In 1883, the French had elevated on the site a monument stating that their marines gave their life 'for science and for their country'. It is in another German colonial book of 1902 that the picture of this French statement found a place (pl. 3).

The same German literature gives us an example of the dominating European male gaze at Samoan girls (pl. 5)--captionned just: *'Stilleben'* ('Quiet Life')!

Illustrations

From the Dumont d'Urville expedition, we have only sketches of houses and of Apia, with a few drawings of Samoan faces so conventional that they have no historical value, and one magnificent drawing of the inside of a house *fale tele:*

6. 'Huts of the Natives in Apia'

7. 'Central square of Apia'

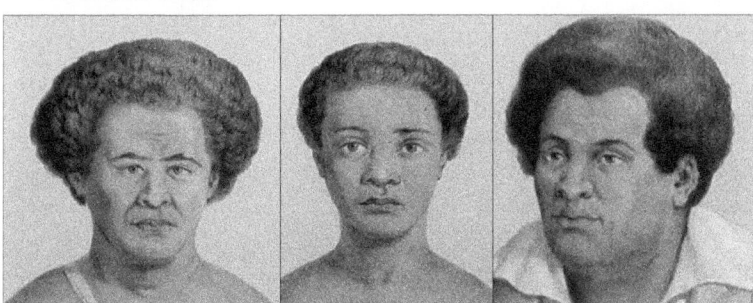

8. 'Chief Apia'   'young girl of Apia'   'Peha, Chief of the district of Opoulou'

213

'First Contacts' in Polynesia

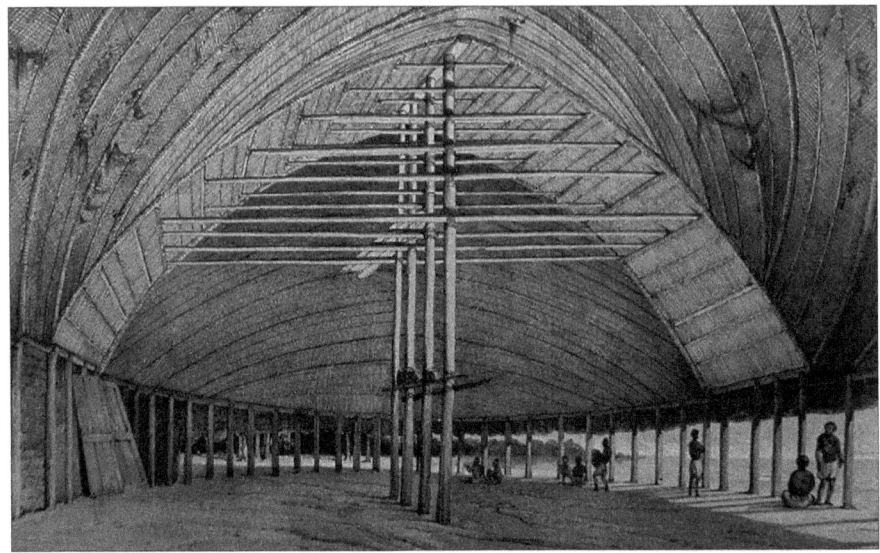
9. 'View of the inside of the meeting house of Apia'

Then photographs replaced engravings, while Samoan houses remained the same

10.

11.

Early Europeans misinterpreted...

...in terms of 'lascivious gestures' the ceremonial role of young girls who, as *'taupou'*, had to stand in front, in the centre: for dances...

12.

13.

...and in Kava offerings:

14.

'First Contacts' in Polynesia

'Taupou' and Manaia or Chiefs, all wrapped in *siapo* and fine mats, represented the dignity *mamalu* of the Samoan way *aganuu FaaSamoa*

15.   16.

17.   18.   19.

Illustrations

TAHITI: the view from the literary salons in London and Paris

20.

21.

22.

23.

24.

20. Louis-Antoine de Bougainville

21. James Cook

22. 'Amusements of the Otahi-tians and the British', as viewed by a French artist for a compi-lation of voyage narratives published in France in 1788: nude Tahitian women are eager to meet the new male voyagers

23. 'Captn Wallis on arrival at O'Taheite [Tahiti] in conversation with Queen Oberea while her attendants are performing a favourite Dance called the Timorodee', *imagined for a com-pilation of voyage narratives (London, 1780)*

24. 'A view of the inside of a house in the Island of Ulietea [Raiatea, Eastern Polynesia], with the representation of a dance to the music of the country', *imagined for the official publication of the voyages of Byron, Carteret, Wallis and Cook (London, 1773)*

'First Contacts' in Polynesia

TAHITI: a more realistic view

25.

25. The first Tahitians who came on board (Cook's 2nd voyage).

George Forster's narrative, published in 1777, tells that the man presented his two sisters and his wife. The two sisters followed an officer who led them into the cabins. One of the sisters was ready to 'grant her favours' to one officer when the boat touched the reef and everyone jumped back on deck. This engraving, made for a compilation of voyage narratives (London, 1780), is faithful to the account.

Webber, draftsman on Cook's 3rd voyage, and Sydney Parkinson, draftsman on Cook's 1st voyage, had both noted how Tahitian girls were laden with barkcloth during the dances:

26.

27.

28.

Sources of Illustrations

Scans of the originals were received from the Macmillan Brown Library (MBL); scans or photographs of originals or published reproductions of engravings or published photographs were framed and made by the author (ST), from books located in ANU libraries and, in the Dumont d'Urville case, in the National Library of Australia (NLA).

SAMOA:

1. Portrait of Lapérouse: from a set of portraits in vol. 1 of J.S.C. Dumont D'Urville, *Voyage pittoresque autour du monde: résumé général des voyages de découvertes de Magellan, Tasman, Dampier..., publié sous la direction de M. Dumont d'Urville*, Paris, Tenré, 1834-35, vol. 1 (scan Macmillan Brown Library-MBL).

2.&4. 'Überfall der Samoaner auf die Expedition Laperouses in Tutuila, 1787. Nach einem alten Stich' and 'Cooks Ermorbung in Hawaii, 1779. Nach einem alten Stich': Erich Schultz-Ewerth, *Errinerungen an Samoa*, A. Ocherl, Berlin, 1926, pp. 40-41 (scan Serge Tcherkézoff-ST). The original was drawn by N. Ozanne and engraved by N.B. Déquevauviller in *Voyage de La Pérouse autour du monde*, Paris, Imprimerie Nationale, 1797: Atlas, plate no. 66.

3. 'Denkmal in der Massacre-Bay (Tutuila)': F. Reinecke, *Samoa*, Berlin, W. Süsserott, 1902, p. 29 (scan ST)

4. 'Stillleben': Reinecke, *op. cit.*, p. 217 (scan ST).

6. 'Cases de naturels à Apia, Ile Opoulou': drawn by Goupil, lithograph by P. Blanchard, in J.S.C. Dumont d'Urville, *Voyage au Pôle sud et dans l'Océanie*, Paris, Gide, 1846: vol 'Atlas pittoresque': pl. 72 (photograph ST with NLA permission, call number: Pict. Section, NL shelves 593, P593, PIC S11207).

7. 'Grande place d'Apia, Ile Opoulou': drawn by Lebreton, lithograph by E. Ciceri, in *ibid.*, pl. 81 (ph. *Idem*, PIC S11216).

8. 'Chef d'Apia, Ile Opoulou', 'Jeune fille d'Apia, Ile Opoulou': drawn by Goupil, lithograph by Bayot, in *ibid.*, pl. 84 (ph. *idem*, PIC S11219); 'Peha, chef du district d'Opoulou', in *ibid.* (ph. *idem*).

9. 'Intérieur de la maison publique d'Apia, Ile Opoulou': drawn by Goupil, lithograph by P. Blanchard, in *ibid.*, pl. 71 (ph. *idem*, PIC S11206).

10. 'Huttennbau': Erich Scheurmann, *Samoa: ein Bilderwerk Herausgegeben und Eingeleited von*, Konstanz, Erschienen im See Vlg., 1927, pl. 46 (scan ST).

11. 'Hütteninneres': Scheurmann, *op. cit.*, pl. 45 (scan ST).

12. 'Tanz einer Dorfjungfrau mit Gefolge': Scheurmann, *op. cit.*, pl. 97 (scan ST).

13. 'Stehtanz einer Dorfjungfrau, von sitzenden Männern begleitet': Augustin Krämer, *Die Samoa Inseln*, Stuttgart, 1902-03, vol. 2, p. 235 (scan ST).

14. 'Junge Häuptlingstochter (taupou) bei der Kawa': Krämer, *op. cit.*, vol. 1, p. 19 (scan ST).

15. 'Dorfjungfrauen': Scheurmann, *op. cit.*, pl. 94 (scan ST).

16. 'Samoanerin mit schlitzförmigen Augen im Kopfschmuck (tuiga) mit doppeltem Stirnband aus *Nautilus*-Schalen (fuiono), Halsschmuck aus Pottwalzähnen ('ulalei) und Bruskette aus *Pandanus*-Bohnen und *Cananga*-Blüten': Krämer, *op. cit.*, vol. 2, p. 276 (scan ST).

17. 'Der Sprecherhäuptling Moefa'auō von Lufilufi': Krämer, *op. cit.*, vol. 1, p. 273 (scan ST).

18. 'Samoanischer Krieger': Scheurmann, *op. cit.*, pl. 84 (scan ST).

19. 'Häuptlinge in Tapamatten': Scheurmann, *op. cit.*, pl. 48 (scan ST).

TAHITI:

20. & 21. Extracted from a set of portraits in vol. 1 of Dumont D'Urville, *Voyage pittoresque...* (scan MBL).

22. 'Amusements of the Otahitians and the Bristish': engraved for the frontispiece of vol. 8 of Jean Pierre Bérenger, *Collections de tous les voyages faits autour du monde par les différentes nations de l'Europe*, Lausanne, Heubach, 1788-89 (scan NLA).

23. 'Captn Wallis ... in conversation with Queen Oberea ... a favourite Dance called the Timorodee': engraved for John Hamilton Moore, *A new and complete collection of voyages and travels, containing all that have been remarkable from the earliest period to the present time, comprehending an extensive system of geography, describing, in the most accurate manner, every place worthy of notice, in Europe, Asia, Africa, and America*, Londres, Alexander Hogg (n.d., probably 1780), vol. 2, facing p. 158 (scan MBL). (This name 'timorodee' was mentioned in the Cook Voyages accounts and came to represent the Tahitian supposed-to-be inclination to 'lascivious' dancing; see Tcherkézoff in press-1).

24. '... in the Island of Ulietea, with the representation of a dance...': engraved for the official narrative (arranged by J. Hawkesworth) of the voyages of Byron, Carteret, Wallis and Cook (1st voyage), London, 1773, p. 265 (scan MBL).

25. 'O-Tai, his wife and sisters visiting Capt. Cook on board the *Resolution Sloop* at O-Taheitee': engraved for Moore, *op. cit.*, vol. 2, facing p. 1129 (scan MBL).

26. 'A young woman of Otaheite, bringing a present': drawing by John Webber (1777); from the reproduction in Rüdiger Joppien and Bernard Smith, *The Art of Captain Cook's Voyages* (4 vols), Melbourne, Oxford University Press, 1987, vol. 1 p. 59 (scan ST).

27. Drawing (no caption) of Sydney Parkinson (1ˢᵗ Cook Voyage, 1769); from D. Oliver, *Ancient Tahitian Society*, Canberra, ANU Press, 1974, pp. 333-4 (scan ST).

28. 'A dance at Otaheite': following faithfully a drawing by John Webber (3ʳᵈ Cook Voyage, 1777), engraved for Moore, *op. cit.*, vol. 1 (scan MBL).

Bibliography

AIAVAO, Ulafala

1994—'Strange ways of the European race', *Islands Business Pacific* (November issue), 74.

AIONO, Fanaafi Le Tagaloa

1986—'Western Samoa: the sacred covenant', pp. 103-10 in *Land Rights of Pacific Women* [collective, no eds]. Suva, University of the South Pacific (Institute of Pacific Studies).

1992—'The Samoan culture and government', pp. 117-38 in R. Crocombe, U. Neemia, A. Ravuvu and W. Von Busch (eds), *Culture and Democracy in the South Pacific*. Suva, University of the South Pacific (Institute of Pacific Studies).

ANAE, Melani, Nite Fuamatu, Ieti Lima, Kirk Mariner, Julie Park and Tamasailau Suaali'i-Sauni

2000—*Tiute ma Matafaioi a nisi Tane Samoa i le Faiga o Aiga. The Roles and Responsibilities of Some Samoan Men in Reproduction*. Auckland, The University of Auckland Pacific Health Research Centre, Department of Maori and Pacific Health.

BABADZAN, Alain

1982—*Naissance d'une tradition. Changement culturel et syncrétisme religieux aux Iles Australes (Polynésie française)*. Paris, Ed. IRD (ex-Orstom).

1993—*Les dépouilles des dieux. Essai sur la religion tahitienne à l'époque de la découverte*. Paris, Press of the 'Maison des Sciences de l'Homme'.

2003—'The gods stripped bare', in C. Colchester (ed.), *Clothing the Pacific*. Oxford, Berg, pp. 25-50.

BABADZAN, Alain (ed.)

1993—*Mythes tahitiens, réunis par Teuira Henry*. Paris, Gallimard ('L'aube des peuples').

BAKER, Shirley

1897—*An English and Tongan Vocabulary, also a Tongan and English Vocabulary with a list of idiomatic phrases; and a Tongan Grammar*. Auckland [no publ.].

BARÉ, Jean-François

1981—*Les temps et les pouvoirs*, 2 vols. Paris, IRD (ex-Orstom) Publ.

1985—*Le malentendu pacifique. Des premières rencontres entre Polynésiens et Anglais et de ce qui s'ensuivit avec les Français jusqu'à nos jours*. Paris,

Hachette ('Histoire des gens') [since then republished, same title, Paris, Archives Contemporaines, 2000].

BATAILLE-BENGUIGUI, Marie-Claire

1997—'Le tapa, vêtement des hommes, symbole de statut et véhicule du divin', in Annick Notter (ed.), *La découverte du paradis. Océanie: curieux, navigateurs et savants*. Paris, Somogy Editions d'art / Association des conservateurs des musées du Nord-Pas-de-Calais.

BEAGLEHOLE, J C, ed.

1955-1974—*The Journals of James Cook*. The Hakluyt Society, Cambridge, University Press.

1962—*The Endeavour Journal of Joseph Banks 1768-1771*. Sydney, Angus and Robertson.

BEAGLEHOLE, Ernest, and Pearl BEAGLEHOLE

1938— *Ethnology of Pukapuka*. Honolulu, Bernice P. Bishop Museum ('Bulletin', 150).

[BEHRENS, Carl Friedrich] 'Monsieur de B***'

1739—*Histoire de l'expedition de trois vaisseaux envoyés par la Compagnie des Indes Occidentales des Provinces-Unies, aux Terres Australes en MDCCXXI*. La Haye [den Haag], Aux Depens de la Compagnie [At the expense of the Cy] (French translation, under the name of the author's initial letter only, of the original in German: *Reise durch die Südlander und um die Welt*, Frankfurt and Leipzig, 1737).

BERGENDORFF, Steen, Ulla HASAGER and Peter HENRIQUES

1988—'Mythopraxis and history: on the interpretation of the Makahiki', *Journal of the Polynesian Society,* 97: 391-408.

BLANCKAERT, Claude

1998—'La 'naturalisation' de l'Homme de Linné à Darwin. Archéologie du débat Nature / Culture', in Albert Ducros, Jacqueline Ducros et Fredéric Joulian (eds), *La culture est-elle naturelle? Histoire, épistémologie et applications récentes du concept de culture*. Paris, Editions Errance, pp. 15-24.

BOROFSKY Robert

1997—'Cook, Lono, Obeyesekere and Sahlins', *Current Anthropology,* 38: 255-65.

BOUGAINVILLE, Louis Antoine (Comte de)

1771—*Voyage autour du monde par la frégate La Boudeuse et la flûte L'Etoile… 1766, 1767, 1768, 1769*. Paris, Saillant and Nyon (1 vol.).

1772a— *Voyage autour du monde par la frégate du Roi La Boudeuse et la flûte L'Etoile, en 1766, 1767, 1768 & 1769. Seconde édition augmentée*. Paris, Saillant and Nyon (3 vols)[the third volume has a different title: *Supplément au Voyage de M. de Bougainville ou Journal d'un voyage autour du monde fait par MM. Banks & Solander, Anglois, en 1768, 1769, 1770, 1771, traduit de l'Anglois par M. de Fréville*; it is the French translation of an anonymous publication which appeared in London in 1771 and which is the first account of Cook's first voyage].

1772b—*A Voyage Round the World, Performed by Order of His Most Christian Majesty, in the Years 1766, 1767, 1768 and 1769*, translated by J.R Forster. London, J. Nourse and T. Davies. *A Voyage round the world..., by Lewis de Bougainville, translated from the French by John Reinhold Forster*. London, J. Nourse and T. Davies.

1968—*Voyage autour du monde*. Paris, Payot (reprint of the 1771 ed.).

BROSSES, Charles de

1756—*Histoire des navigations aux Terres Australes: contenant ce que l'on scait des moeurs et des productions des Contrées découvertes jusqu'à ce jour et où il est traité de l'utilité d'y faire de plus amples découvertes et des moyens d'y former un établissement*. Paris, Durand, 1756.

BUSE, Jasper with Raututi Taringa (Bruce Biggs & Rangi Moeka'a eds)

1995—*Cook Islands Maori Dictionary*. Rarotonga, Ministry of Education / London, SOAS / Suva, USP, IPS / Auckland, CPS / Canberra, ANU, RSPAS.

CAMPBELL, Ian C.

1998—*'Gone Native' in Polynesia: captivity narratives and experiences from the South Pacific*. Westport (Connecticut), Greenwood Press ('Contributions to the Study of World History', 63).

CHURCHWARD, C. Maxwell

1959, *Tongan Dictionary (Tongan-English and English-Tongan)*. Nukualofa, Government Printing.

CLARK, Joseph G.

1848—*Lights and Shadows of Sailor Life, as exemplified in fifteen years' experience, including the more thrilling events of the U.S. Exploring Expedition...* Boston, Benjamin Mussey and C°.

COLCHESTER, Chloe (ed.)

2003—*Clothing the Pacific*. Oxford, Berg.

COLVOCORESSES, Geo M.

1852—*Four Years in a Government Exploring Expedition, to the Islands of......* New York, Cornish, Lamport and C°.

COPPET, Daniel de

1973—'Premier troc, double illusion', *L'Homme*, 13 (1-2): 10-22.

CÔTÉ, James E.

1994—*Adolescent Storm and Stress. An evaluation of the Mead-Freeman controversy.* Hillsdale (N.J.), Lawrence Erlbaum ('Research Monographs in Adolescence', 1).

1997—'A social history of youth in Samoa: religion, capitalism and cultural disenfranchisement', *International Journal of Comparative Sociology*, 38(4): 217-28.

DANIELSSON, Bengt

1956—*Love in the South Seas.* New York, Reynal (trans. from Swedish; orig. ed. 1954).

1981—*Tahiti autrefois.* Papeete, Hibiscus Editions.

[DAVIES, John]

1851—*A Tahitian and English Dictionary.* Tahiti, LMS Press (reprint, New York, AMS Press, 1978).

DENING, Greg

1966—'Ethnohistory in Polynesia: the value of ethnohistorical evidence', *Journal of Pacific History*, 1(1): 23-42.

1974—*The Marquesan Journal of Edward Robarts, 1797-1824.* Canberra, ANU.

1980—*Islands and Beaches. Discourse on a silent land: Marquesas 1774-1880.* Carlton, Melbourne University Press (reprint 1988, Chicago, Dorsey Press).

1984—*The Death of Captain Cook.* Sydney, Library Society (State Library of NSW).

1988—*History's Anthropology: the death of William Gooch.* Washington, University Press of America (ASAO Special Publications, 2) (revised ed. 1995 *The death of William Gooch: a history's anthropology.* Honolulu, University of Hawaii Press).

1992—*Mr Bligh's Bad Language: passion, power and theatre on the* Bounty. Cambridge, Cambridge University Press.

1996—*Performances.* Chicago, Chicago University Press.

1998—*Readings / Writings.* Carlton, Melbourne University Press.

2004—*Beach Crossings: voyaging across times, cultures and the self*. Melbourne, the Miegunyah Press.

DOUAIRE-MARSAUDON, Françoise,

1993—'Les premiers fruits. Parenté, identité sexuelle et pouvoirs en Polynésie occidentale (Tonga, Wallis et Futuna', Doctorat. Paris, EHESS (reference sous 'Marsaudon, Françoise').

1997—'Nourritures et richesses: les objets cérémoniels du don comme signe d'identité à Tonga et à Wallis', in S. Tcherkézoff et F. Douaire-Marsaudon (eds), *Le Pacifique-sud aujourd'hui: identités et transformations culturelles*. Paris, Ed. du CNRS, coll. Ethnologie.

1998)—*Les premiers fruits. Parenté, identité sexuelle et pouvoirs en Polynésie occidentale (Tonga, Wallis et Futuna)*. Paris, CNRS Editions / Editions de la Maison des Sciences de l'Homme (Chemins de l'ethnologie).

DOUGLAS, Bronwen

1999a—'Art as ethno-historical text: science, representation and indigenous presence in eighteenth and nineteenth century Oceanic voyage literature', in Nicholas Thomas and Diane Losche (eds), *Double Vision: art histories and colonial histories in the Pacific*. Cambridge, Cambridge University Press, 65-99.

1999b—'Science and the art of representing 'Savages': reading 'race' in text and image in South Seas voyage literature', *History and Anthropology*, 1999, vol. 11, n°2-3, pp. 157-201.

n.d., 'Inventing "Race": The "Science of Man" and the Pacific Connection', in B. Douglas and C. Ballard (eds), 'Foreign Bodies: Oceania and Racial Science 1750-1940' (symposium of 18-19 October 2001, Division of Pacific and Asian History, RSPAS, ANU).

DUMONT D'URVILLE, Jules Sébastien César

1842—*Voyage au Pôle sud et dans l'Océanie, sur les corvettes l'Astrolabe et la Zélée, sous le commandement de M. J. Dumont-d'Urville. Histoire du voyage (tome quatrième)*. Paris, Gide [the publication in Paris of the more than twenty volumes of the voyage, including treaties by naturalists etc., took some fifteen years; 1842 is the date of vol. 4 which contains the narrative of the call at Samoa].

DUNMORE, John

1985—*Pacific Explorer: the life of Jean-François de La Pérouse, 1741-1788*. Palmerston North, The Dunmore Press / Sydney, Hedley Australia.

DUNMORE, John (ed.)

1994-1995—*The Journal of Jean-François de Galaup de Lapérouse, 1785-1788* (2 vols). London, Hakluyt Society (2nd ser., n° 179-180) (translation of John Dunmore and Maurice de Brossard (eds), 1985).

2002—*The Pacific Journal of Louis-Antoine de Bougainville*. London, for the Hakluyt Society, printed by the Cambridge University Press, 2002.

DUNMORE, John & Maurice de BROSSARD (eds)

1985—*Le voyage de Lapérouse, 1785-1788: récit et documents originaux*. Paris, Imprimerie Nationale.

ERSKINE, John Elphinstone

1853—*Journal of a Cruise Among the Islands of the Western Pacific, including the Feejees and Others Inhabited by the Polynesian Negro Races, in HMS Havannah*.London, John Murray [facsimile by Southern Reprints, Papakura, New Zealand, 1987].

FERDON, Edwin N.

1987—*Early Tonga, As the Explorers Saw It, 1616-1810*. Tucson, The University of Arizona Press.

FIRTH, Raymond

1936—*We The Tikopia. A sociological study of kinship in primitive Polynesia*. London, Allen & Unwin, 1936.

1967—*The Work of the Gods in Tikopia*. (London School of Economics, Monographs on Social Anthropology, 1-2), London, The Athlone Press.

FREEMAN, J. Derek

1983—*Margaret Mead and Samoa. The making and unmaking of an anthropological myth*. Cambridge (Mass.), Harvard University Press.

1999—*The Fateful Hoaxing of Margaret Mead. A historical analysis of her Samoan research*. Boulder (Col.), Westview Press.

GALLIOT, Sebastien

2001—'Le tatouage aux Samoas. Un essai d'ethnologie VERIF', MA thesis (Aix-Marseille, Université de Provence, Department of anthropology and CREDO).

GELL, Alfred

1993—*Wrapping in Images. Tattooing in Polynesia*. Oxford, Clarendon Press.

GERAGHTY, Paul and Jan TENT

1997a—'Early Dutch loanwords in Polynesia', *Journal of the Polynesian Society*, 106(2): 131-60.

1997b—'More early Dutch loanwords in Polynesia', *Journal of the Polynesian Society*, 106(4): 395-408.

2001—'Exploding sky or exploded myth. The origin of papālagi', *Journal of the Polynesian Society,* 110 (2): 171-214.

GILL, Wyatt

1880—*Historical Sketches of Savage Life in Polynesia.* Wellington, Government Printer.

GILSON, Richard P.

1970—*Samoa, 1830-1900: the politics of a multi-cultural community.* Melbourne, Oxford University Press.

GIRARD, Charles (ed.)

1999—*Lettres reçues d'Océanie par l'administration générale des pères maristes pendant le généralat de Jean-Claude Colin* (4 vols). Rome, Centre d'études maristes (private publication of only 25 copies; one copy has been given to the Library of the CREDO).

GRIJP, Paul van der

1994—'A history of misunderstandings: early European encounters with Tongans', chap. 3 in Toon van Meijl and Paul van der Grijp (eds), *European imagery and colonial history in the Pacific.* Saarbrucken, Vlg für Entwicklungspolitik Breitenbach GmbH (Nijmegen Studies in Development and Cultural Change, vol. 19).

n.d.—'The ritual of the Turmeric in Futuna', in the 2nd symposium of the Western Polynesia (including Fiji) Workshop: 'Cosmology and Society' (S. Tcherkézoff and S. Hooper eds, CREDO, Marseille, 25-28 May 2001).

GUILLON, Jacques (Amiral)

1986—*Dumont d'Urville, 1790-1842.* Paris, Editions France-Empire.

HANSON, Allan F.

1970—'Théorie rapaienne de la conception', *Bulletin de la Société des études océaniennes,*vol.14, n° 170:281-4.

HAU'OFA, Epeli, Vijay NAIDU, and Eric WADDELL (eds)

1993—*A new Oceania: rediscovering our sea of islands.* Suva, University of the South Pacific Press (School of Social and Economic Development).

HAWKESWORTH, John

1773—*An Account of the Voyages Undertaken by Order of Her Present Majesty for Making Discoveries in the Southern Hemisphere and Successively Performed* by Commodore Byron, Captain Wallis, Captain Carteret and Captain Cook, in the Dolphin, drawn up from the Journals.* London, W. Stratham.

HENRY, Teuira

1928—*Ancient Tahiti*. Honolulu, Bernice P. Bishop Museum ('Bulletin', 48).

HOLMES, Lowell D.

1987—*Quest for the real Samoa: the Mead / Freeman controversy and beyond*. South Hadley (Mass.), Bergin & Garvey.

HOME, [?] [Captain]

1850—'Notes among the Islands of the Pacific. Extracts from the remarks of HMS *North Star*, Capt. Sir E. Home', *Nautical Magazine*, vol.'1850':218-24.

HOOPER, Steven

1982—'A study of valuables in the chiefdom of Lau, Fiji', PhD thesis, Department of Anthropology, Cambridge University.

HUNTSMAN, Judith and Anthony HOOPER

1996—*Tokelau: A Historical Ethnography*. Auckland University Press.

[JACKSON, John]

1853—'Appendix' [containing 'the narrative of an Englishman, John Jackson...'], in Erskine 1853: 411-77.

JOLLY, Margaret

1992—'Ill-natured comparisons': racism and relativism in European representations of ni-Vanuata from Cook's second voyage', *History and Anthropology*, 5 (3-4): 331-64.

1997a—'From Point Venus to Bali Ha'i: eroticism and exoticism in representations of the Pacific', in Lenore Manderson and Margaret Jolly (eds), *Sites of Desire, Economies of Pleasure: sexualities in Asia and the Pacific*, Chicago, The University of Chicago Press, 99-122.

1997b—'White shadows in the darkness: representations of Polynesian women in early cinema', in M. Quanchi (ed.), *Imaging, Representation: photography and film in the Pacific. Pacific Studies* (Special Issue), 20(4): 125-50.

n.d.—'Women of the East, women of the West: representations of Pacific women on Cook's voyages', chap. 2 in M. Jolly, *An Ocean of Difference: colonialisms, maternalisms, feminisms in the Pacific*. Durham, Duke University Press.

KAEPPLER, Adrienne L.

1978—'Exchange patterns in goods and spouses: Fiji, Tonga and Samoa', *Mankind*, 11: 246-52.

1997— 'Polynesia and Micronesia', in Adrienne L. Kaeppler, Christian Kaufmann, Douglas Newton (eds), *Oceanic Art*, New York, Harry N. Abrams [original: *L'art océanien*, Paris, Editions Citadelles & Mazenod 1993].

1999—'Kie Hingoa: mats of power, rank, prestige and history', *Journal of the Polynesian Society*, 108(2): 168-232.

n.d.—'The Tu'i Tonga: creator of rank and prestige goods', in the 2nd symposium of the Western Polynesia (including Fiji) Workshop: 'Cosmology and Society' (S. Tcherkézoff and S. Hooper eds, CREDO, Marseille, 25-28 May 2001).

KIRCH, Patrick V. and Roger GREEN

2001—*Hawaiki: ancestral Polynesia, an essay in historical anthropology*. Cambridge, Cambridge University Press.

KOTZEBUE, Otto von

1830— *A New Voyage Round the World in the Years 1823, 1824, 1825 and 1826* (2 vols). London, H. Colburn and R. Bentley (reprint: Amsterdam, N. Israel / New York, Da Capo, 1967).

KRÄMER, Augustin

1994-95—*The Samoan Islands* (2 vols). Auckland, Polynesian Press / Honolulu, University of Hawai'i Press (translation of *Die Samoa-Inseln*, 2 vols, Stuttgart, 1902-1903).

KÜCHLER, Suzanne,

2003—'The poncho and the quilt: material Christianity in the Cook islands', in C. Colchester ed., *Clothing the Pacific*. Oxford, Berg, pp. 97-116.

LAFOND DE LURCY, Gabriel

1845—'Quelques semaines dans les archipels de Samoa et Viti', *Bulletin de la Société de Géographie* ('3ème série, n°3, Première section'): 5-30.

LAMB, Jonathan, Vanessa SMITH and Nicholas THOMAS

2000—*Exploration and Exchange: a South Seas anthology, 1680-1900*. Chicago, University of Chicago Press.

LANGDON, Robert

1975—*The Lost Caravel*. Sydney, Pacific Publications.

LEACOCK, Eleanor

1987—'Postface' to Holmes's 1987 book.

LEGGE, Christopher

1966—'William Diaper: a biographical sketch', *Journal of Pacific History*, 1: 79-90.

LINNEKIN, Jocelyn

1991—'Ignoble savages and other European visions: the La Pérouse affair in Samoan history', *Journal of Pacific History,* 26 (1): 3-26.

MAGEO, Jeannette Marie

1994—'Hairdos and don'ts: hair symbolism and sexual history in Samoa', *Man*, 29: 407-32.

1996—'Continuity and shape shifting: Samoan spirits in culture history', in J.M.Mageo and A. Howard (eds), *Spirits in Culture, History, and Mind*. London, Routledge, pp. 29-54.

1998—*Theorizing Self in Samoa: emotions, genders and sexualities*. Ann Arbor, The University of Michigan Press.

2001—'The third meaning in cultural memory: history, identity, and spirit possession in Samoa', in J.M.Mageo (ed.), *Cultural Memory: reconfiguring history and identity in the postcolonial Pacific*. Honolulu, University of Hawai'i Press, pp. 58-80.

MA'IA'I, Fanaafi

1960—*Stories of Old Samoa*. Christchurch, Whitcombe & Tombs [author's name later became Aiono Dr. Fanaafi Le Tagaloa].

MAUSS, Marcel

1925—*Essai sur le don. Forme et raison de l'échange dans les sociétés archaïques*. Paris, L'Année sociologique ('Nouvelle série').

MEAD, Margaret

1928—*Coming of Age in Samoa*. New York, Morrow.

MERLE, Isabelle and Michel NAEPELS

2003—'Introduction', in I. Merle and M. Naepels (eds), *Les rivages du temps: histoire et anthropologie du Pacifique*. Paris, L'Harmattan ('Cahiers du Pacifique Sud contemporain', 3).

MILNER, George B.

1966—*Samoan Dictionary: Samoan-English, English-Samoan*. London, Oxford University Press.

MONBERG, Torben

1991—*Bellona Islands: beliefs and rituals*, Pacific Islands Monographs Series, 9. Honolulu, University of Hawaii Press.

MONFAT, Antoine

1890—*Les Samoa ou archipel des navigateurs. Étude historique et religieuse*. Lyon, E. Vitte.

MORRISON, James

1935—*The Journal of James Morrison, Boatswain's Mate of the Bounty, Describing the Mutiny and Subsequent Misfortunes of the Mutineers together with an Account of the Island of Tahiti,* Owen Rutter (ed.). London, The Golden Cockerel Press.

1989—*Journal de James Morrison, second maître à bord de la 'Bounty', traduit de l'anglais par Bertrand Jaunez*. Papeete, Société des Etudes Océaniennes, 3rd edition [1st ed. 1981].

MOYLE, Richard (ed.)

1984—*The Samoan Journals of John Williams, 1830 and 1832*. Canberra, Australian National University Press.

MOYLE, Richard

1988— *Traditional Samoan Music*. Auckland, Auckland University Press.

NERO, Karen and Nicholas THOMAS

2002—*An Account of the Pelew Islands: George Keate*. London, Leicester University Press.

OBEYESEKERE, Gananath

1992—*The Apotheosis of Captain Cook: European mythmaking in the Pacific*. Princeton University Press.

1998—'Cannibal feasts in nineteenth-century Fiji: seamen's yarns and the ethnographic imagination', in F. Barker (ed.), *Cannibalism and the Colonial World*. Cambridge U.P., pp. 63-86.

2003—'Cannibal talk: dialogical misunderstandings in the South Seas', Huxley Memorial Lecture (Manchester University, 15 July, during the Decennial Conference of the Association of Social Anthropologists).

OLIVER, Douglas

1974—*Ancient Tahitian Society*. Honolulu / Canberra, University of Hawaii Press / Australian National University Press.

2002—*Polynesia in Early Historic Times*. Honolulu, The Bess Press.

PARKINSON, Sydney

1984— *A Journal of a Voyage to the South Seas*. London, Caliban Books [facsimile of the 1784 ed.; 1st ed: 1773].

PAWLEY, Andrew K.

1982—'The etymology of Samoan t upōu', in R. Carle, M. Heinschke, P. W. Pink, C. Rost, K. Stadtlander, *GAVA' Studies in Austronesian languages and cultures, dedicated to Hans Kähler*. Berlin, Dietrich Reimer (Veröffentlichungen des Seminars für Indonesiche und Südseesprachen der Universität Hamburg, Band 17), pp. 263-72.

POLLEX (Polynesian Lexicon)

1999—unpublished electronic file of proto-Polynesian words (compiled by Bruce Biggs and Ross Clark, Auckland University, Maori Studies et Department of anthropology).

PRATT, George (Rev.)

1862—*Dictionary of the Samoan language*. Apia, Malua.

1878— *A Grammar and Dictionary of the Samoan Language, with English and Samoan Vocabulary*, edited by S.J.Whitmee. London, Trubner (republished '3rd revised edition' in 1893, London, The Religious Tract Society).

1911— *Pratt's Grammar and Dictionary of the Samoan Language*. Apia, Malua Printing Press (4th edition, posthumous, compiled and introduced by J.E. Newell; republished in 1960, 1977).

PRITCHARD, William T.

1864—'Notes on certain anthropological matters respecting the South Seas Islanders'. London, *Memoirs of the Anthropological Society*, vol.1, pp.325-6 (ref. in B. Danielsson, 1956, p.116).

1866— *Polynesian Reminiscences, or Life in the South Pacific Islands*. London, Dawsons.

RALSTON, Caroline

1977—*Grass Huts and Warehouses: Pacific beach communities of the 19th century*. Canberra, Australian National University Press.

RENNIE, Neil

1998— 'The Point Venus 'scene', in Margarette Lincoln (ed.), *Science and Eexploration in the Pacific: European voyages to the southern oceans in the eighteenth century*. Woodbridge (Suffolk), The Boydell Press & National Maritime Museum, pp. 135-46.

RICHARDS, Rhys

1992—*Samoa's Forgotten Whaling Heritage: American whaling in Samoan waters, 1824-1878: a chronological selection of extracts from primary sources, mainly whaling logbooks, journals and contemporary news items.*

Wellington, Lithographic Services (for the Western Samoa Historical and Cultural Trust).

ROSENMAN, Helen

1992—*Two Voyages to the South Seas: Australia, New Zealand, Oceania 1826-1829, Straits of Magellan, Chile, Oceania… 1837-1840 in the corvettes…, Translated from the French and retold by.* Honolulu, University of Hawaii Press [short summary with some excerpts of the French publications of 1830-1835 and 1841-1854].

RYAN, Tom

2002— '"Le President des Terres Australes": Charles de Brosses and the French Enlightenment Beginnings of Oceanic Anthropology', *Journal of Pacific History*, 37(2):157-86.

SAHLINS, Marshall

1979—'L'apothéose du capitaine Cook', in M. Izard and P. Smith (eds), *La fonction symbolique*. Paris, Gallimard, pp. 307-39 (English translation 1982, 'The apotheosis of Captain Cook', in M. Izard and P. Smith (eds), *Between Belief and Transgression: structuralist essays in religion, history and myth*. Chicago, University of Chicago Press, pp.73-102).

1981— *Historical Metaphors and Mythical Realities. Structure in the early history of the Sandwich Islands Kingdom*. Ann Arbor, The University of Michigan Press ('Association for Social Anthropology in Oceania, Special Publications', n°1).

1985a—*Islands of History*. The University of Chicago Press.

1985b—'Hierarchy and humanity in Polynesia', in J.Huntsman and A. Hooper (eds), *Transformations of Polynesian Culture*. Auckland, The Polynesian Society, pp. 195-217.

1989—'Captain Cook at Hawaii', *Journal of the Polynesian Society*, 98 (4): 371-423.

1991—'The *Makahiki* at O'ahu, 1788', *Journal of the Polynesian Society*, 100(3): 299-301.

1994—'The discovery of the true savage', in Donna Merwick (ed.), *Essays in Honour of Greg Dening*. Parkville, The University of Melbourne (History Department), pp. 41-94.

1995—'*How 'Natives' Think': about Captain Cook for example*. Chicago, The University of Chicago Press

2003, 'Artificially maintained controversies: global warming and Fijian cannibalism', *Anthropology Today*, 19(3): 1-5.

SALMOND, Anne

1991—*Two Worlds: first meetings between Maori and Europeans 1642-1772*. Honolulu, University of Hawaii Press.

1997—*In Between Worlds: early exchanges between Maori and Europeans, 1773-1815*. Auckland, Viking.

SAURA, Bruno

1990—*Les bûchers de Faaite: paganisme ancestral ou dérapage chrétien en Polynésie française*. Papeete, Cobalt/ Editions de l'Après-Midi.

1993—*Politique et religion à Tahiti*. Papeete, Polymages-Scoop.

1998—*Des Tahitiens, des Français: leurs représentations réciproques aujourd'hui*. Papeete, Ch. Gleizal (Les Essais).

SCEMLA, Jean-Jo

1994—*Le voyage en Polynésie: anthologie des voyageurs occidentaux de Cook à Segalen*. Paris, Laffont ('Bouquins').

SCHOEFFEL, Penelope

1978—'Gender, status and power in Samoa'. *Canberra Anthropology*, 1(2): 69-81.

1979—'Daughters of Sina: a study of gender, status and power in Samoa', PhD thesis, Canberra, Australian National University.

1995—'The Samoan concept of *feagaiga* and its transformation', in J. Huntsman (ed.), *Tonga and Samoa: images of gender and polity*. Christchurch, University of Canterbury Press (Macmillan Brown Centre for Pacific Studies), pp. 85-106.

SCHOUTEN, Guill. [Willem]

1619—*Journal ou relation exacte du voyage de Guill. Schouten dans les Indes, par un nouveau destroit et par les grandes mers australes qu'il a descouvert, vers le pole antarctique. Ensemble des nouvelles terres auparavant incognues...*. Paris, 'chez M. Gobert'.

SCHULTZ[-EWERTH], Erich [Bernhard Theodor]

1911—'The most important principles of Samoan family law and the laws of inheritance', *Journal of the Polynesian Society*, vol. 20:43-53 [translation of *Die wichtigsten Grundsätze des samoanischen Familien- und Erbrechts*. Apia, Lübke, 1905; an enlarged version of 43 pages was published the same year in German: *Samoanisches Falilien-, Immobiliar- und Erbrecht*. Apia, Lübke, 1911].

SHANKMAN, Paul

1996—'The history of Samoan sexual conduct and the Mead-Freeman controversy', *American Anthropologist*, 98: 555-67.

2001—'Interethnic unions and the regulation of sex in colonial Samoa, 1839-1945', *Journal of the Polynesian Society*, 110 (2): 119-48.

n.d.—'Between the lines: rereading original sources in the Mead-Freeman controversy', paper circulated at the ASAO meeting (February 2001, Miami).

SHARP, Andrew (ed.)

1970—*The Journal of Jacob Roggeveen*. Oxford, Clarendon Press (translation from the original published in Dutch in 1838).

SILVE, Sandra

1997—Interview, *Le Monde*, 2-3 November 1997, p. 18.

STAIR, John B. (Rev.)

1897—*Old Samoa, or Flotsam and Jetsam from the Pacific Ocean*. London, The Religious Tract Society.

SUAALI'I-SAUNI, Tamasailau

2001—'Samoans and gender: some reflections on male, female and fa'afafine gender identities', in C. Macpherson, P. Spoonley, M. Anae (eds), *Tangata O Te Moana Nui: the evolving identities of Pacific peoples in Aotearoa/ New Zealand*. Palmerston North, Dunmore Press.

TAILLEMITE, Etienne (ed.),

1968—'Hommage à Bougainville', *Journal de la Société des Océanistes*, vol. 24, n° 24

1977—*Bougainville et ses compagnons autour du monde 1766-1769, journaux de navigation établis et commentés par*. Paris, Imprimerie Nationale, 2 vols.

TAPSELL, Paul

1997— 'The flight of pareraututu: an investigation of taonga from a tribal perspective', *Journal of the Polynesian Society*, 106 (4): 323-74.

TCHERKÉZOFF, Serge

1987—*Dual Classification Reconsidered*. Cambridge, Cambridge University Press.

1993—'The illusion of dualism in Samoa: "brothers-and-sisters" are not "men-and-women", in T. del Valle (ed.), *Gendered Anthropology*. London, Routledge and Kegan Paul, pp. 54-87.

1994a—'L'inclusion du contraire (L. Dumont), la hiérarchie enchevêtrée (J.P. Dupuy) et le rapport sacré/ pouvoir. Relectures et révision des modèles à propos de l'Inde. Ière Partie: un modèle asymétrique' er IIème Partie: 'statut et pouvoir en Inde: la logique concrète de l'inclusion du contraire'. *Culture*, 14(2): 113-34 and 15(1): 33-48.

1994b—'Hierarchical reversal, ten years on (Africa, India, Polynesia). Ist Part: the hierarchical structure' and 'IInd Part: Rodney Needham's counterpoints', *Journal of Anthropological Society of Oxford JASO*, 25(2): 133-67 and 25(3): 229-53.

1995a—'L'autocar à Samoa ou la hiérarchie au quotidien', *Gradhiva*, 18: 47-56.

1995b—'La totalité durkheimienne (E. Durkheim et R. Hertz): un modèle holiste du rapport sacré/ profane', *L'Ethnographie*, 91(1): 53-69.

1997a—'Culture, nation, société: changements secondaires et bouleversements possibles au Samoa Occidental. Vers un modèle pour l'étude des dynamiques culturelles', in S. Tcherkézoff et F. Douaire-Marsaudon (eds), *Le Pacifique-sud aujourd'hui: identités et transformations culturelles*. Paris, Ed. du CNRS, ('Ethnologie'), pp. 309-73.

1997b—'Le *mana*, le fait "total" et "l'esprit" dans la chose donnée. Marcel Mauss, les "cadeaux à Samoa" et la méthode comparative en Polynésie', *Anthropologie et Sociétés*, 21 (2-3): 193-223.

1998a—'Is aristocracy good for democracy? A contemporary debate in Western Samoa', in Jürg Wassmann (ed.), *Pacific Answers to Western Hegemony: cultural practices of identity construction*. Oxford, Berg ('Explorations in Anthropology Series'), pp.417-34.

1998b—'*Mua / Muri*: ordre, espace et temps en Polynésie. Le cas samoan comparé au tahitien et le rapport à l'Occident', *Bulletin de la Société des Etudes Océaniennes*, 276: 27-51.

1999—'Qu'est-ce qu'un acte sexuel au Samoa Occidental', in P. Descola, J. Hamel and P. Lemonnier (eds), *La production du social: autour de Maurice Godelier*. Paris, Fayard, 369-87.

2000a—'Are the Samoan chiefs *matai* "out of time"? Tradition *and* democracy: contemporary ambiguities and historical transformations of the concept of chief', in Elise Huffer and Asofou So'o (eds), *Governance in Samoa*. Canberra / Suva, Australian National University (National Centre for Development Studies, 'Asia-Pacific' Series) / University of the South Pacific (Institute of Pacific Studies), pp. 113-33.

2000b—'The Samoan category *matai* ("chief"): a singularity in Polynesia? Historical and etymological comparative queries', *Journal of the Polynesian Society*, 109(2): 151-90.

2000c—'Multiculturalism and construction of a national Identity: the historical case of Samoan / European relations', *The New Pacific Review* (special issue 'Pacific Identities'): 1 (1): 168-86.

2001a—*Le mythe occidental de la sexualité polynésienne (1928-1999): Margaret Mead, Derek Freeman et Samoa*. Paris, Presses Universitaires de France ('Ethnologies').

2001b—'Is anthropology about individual agency or culture? Or why "Old Derek" is doubly wrong', *Journal of the Polynesian Society,* 110 (1): 59-78.

2001c—'Samoa again: on "Durkheimian bees", Freemanian passions and Fa'amu's "confession"', *Journal of the Polynesian Society,* 110 (4): 431-36.

2002—'Subjects and objects in Samoa: ceremonial mats have a "soul"', chap. 1 in Bernard Juillerat et Monique Jeudy-Ballini (eds), *People and Things: social mediations in Oceania*. Durham, Carolina Academic Press: 27-51.

2003a—'A long and unfortunate voyage toward the invention of the Melanesia / Polynesia opposition (1595-1832)', *Journal of Pacific History* (special issue: 'Dumont d'Urville's Oceanic provinces: fundamental precincts or arbitrary constructs', Geoffrey Clark, ed.), 38 (2): 175-96.

2003b—*FaaSamoa, une identité polynésienne (économie, politique, sexualité): l'anthropologie comme dialogue culturel*. Paris, L'Harmattan ('Connaissance des Hommes').

In press-1—*Tahiti, 1768: la face cachée des premiers contacts et la naissance du mythe occidental*. Pape'ete, Au Vent des Îles (published in 2004).

In press-2—'"Soeur ou épouse, il faut choisir". L'énigme de l'exogamie villageoise à Samoa', in F. Héritier et E. Copet-Rougier (eds), *Frère/soeur: la relation essentielle de parenté*. Paris, Ed. des Archives Contemporaines (coll. 'Ordres Sociaux')/ Odile Jacob.

n.d.— *Inventing the Polynesia/ Melanesia distinction (1595-1985). The French male-and-racial gaze in Oceanic encounters*. (French version published *Polynésie/Mélanésie: l'invention française des 'races' et des régions de l'Océanie*, Papeete, Au Vent des Iles, 2008.)

TCHERKEZOFF, Serge and DOUAIRE-MARSAUDON, Françoise (eds)

1997—*Le Pacifique-sud aujourd'hui: identités et transformations culturelles*. Paris, Ed. du CNRS ('Ethnologie').

TE RANGI HIROA (P. H. Buck)

1930— *Samoan Material Culture*. Honolulu, B.P. Bishop Museum Publications (Bulletin, 75).

THOMAS, Nicholas

1990— *Marquesan Societies: inequality and political transformation in eastern Polynesia*. Oxford, Clarendon Press.

1997— *In Oceania: visions, artifacts, histories.* Durham (NC), Duke University Press.

THOMAS, Nicholas, Harriet GUEST and Michael DETTELBACH (eds)

1996— *Observations made During a Voyage Round the World, Johann Reinhold Forster.* Honolulu, University of Hawai'i Press.

THOMAS, Nicholas and Diane LOSCHE

1999—*Double Vision: art histories and colonial histories in the Pacific.* Cambridge, Cambridge University Press.

THOMPSON, Basil (ed.)

1915—*Voyage of H.M.S. 'Pandora', despatched to arrest the mutineers of the 'Bounty' in the South Seas, 1790-1791, being the narratives of Captain Edward Edwards, R.N., The Commander, and George Hamilton, the Surgeon, with introduction and notes by Basil Thompson.* London, Francis Edwards.

TIFFANY, Sharon W.

2001—'Imagining the South Seas: thoughts on the Sexual Politics of Paradise in Samoa', *Pacific Studies,* 24 (3-4): 19-47.

TURNER, George

1986—*Samoa: nineteen years in Polynesia.* Apia, Western Samoa Historical and Cultural Trust, Commercial Printers [reprint of the Samoan chapters of *Nineteen Years in Polynesia: missionary life, travel and researches in the islands of the Pacific,* London, 1861].

VALERI, Valerio

1985—*Kingship and Sacrifice: ritual and society in ancient Hawaii.* The University of Chicago Press.

WACHTEL, Nathan

1977—*The Vision of the Vanquished: the Spanish conquest of Peru through Indian eyes, 1530-1570.* Hassocks, Harvester Press [1st ed.: 1971, *La vision des vaincus, Les Indiens du Pérou devant la Conquête espagnole.* Paris, Gallimard].

WALPOLE, Fred (Lieutenant)

1849—*Four Years in the Pacific in HMS 'Collingwood' from 1844 to 1848.* London, Richard Bentley, 2 vols. [for Samoa, see vol. 2].

WHITE, J.

1989— *Ancient History of the Maori.* Wellington.

WILLIAMS, H.W.

1971—*Dictionary of the Maori language*. Wellington, Government Printing.

WILLIAMS, John

1841—*A Narrative of Missionary Enterprises in the South Sea Islands*. London, John Snow.

WILLIAMSON, Robert W.

1924—*The Social and Political Systems of Central Polynesia* (3 vols). Cambridge, Cambridge University Press.

1933—*Religious and Cosmic Beliefs of Central Polynesia* (2 vols). Cambridge, Cambridge University Press.

1939—*Essays in Polynesian Ethnology, edited by Ralph Piddington*. Cambridge, Cambridge University Press (Part I: Chs 1-5 [manuscripts left by Williamson after his death in 1932]).

WORTH, [?] [Captain]

1852—'Voyage of HMS "Calypso", Captain Worth, to the Pacific', *Nautical Magazine*.

ZIMMERMANN, Francis

1998—'Sahlins, Obeyesekere et la mort du capitaine Cook', *L'Homme,* 146: 191-205.

www.ingramcontent.com/pod-product-compliance
Lightning Source LLC
Chambersburg PA
CBHW060930180426
43192CB00045B/2872